I0762854

THERAPY NATION

ALSO BY JONATHAN ALPERT

Be Fearless: Change Your Life in 28 Days

THERAPY NATION

How America Got Hooked on Therapy and Why It's Left Us More Anxious and Divided

JONATHAN ALPERT

HANOVER
SQUARE
PRESS

ISBN-13: 978-1-335-00065-1

Therapy Nation

Hanover Square Press
22 Adelaide St. West, 41st Floor
Toronto, Ontario M5H 4E3, Canada
HanoverSqPress.com

HarperCollins Publishers
Macken House, 39/40 Mayor Street Upper,
Dublin 1, D01 C9W8, Ireland
www.HarperCollins.com

Printed in U.S.A.
26 27 28 29 30 LBC 5 4 3 2 1

For my parents, always.

CONTENTS

INTRODUCTION 1

Chapter One: Is Therapy Making Us Sicker? 13
Chapter Two: Social Media and Cultural Decay 23
Chapter Three: When Politics Became Our Identity 41
Chapter Four: COVID and the Isolation Trap 73
Chapter Five: The Rise of Therapy Nation 91
Chapter Six: How Therapy Turned Into a Social Justice Crusade 111
Chapter Seven: Munchausen's by Google 135
Chapter Eight: The Cult of Trauma 155
Chapter Nine: A Nation of Emotional Lightweights 175
Chapter Ten: The Problem with Validation Culture 189
Chapter Eleven: The Weaponization of Psychology 207
Chapter Twelve: The Elements of Bad Therapy 225
Chapter Thirteen: What's the Point of Therapy? 251
Chapter Fourteen: The Cult of Therapy 267
Chapter Fifteen: Back to Sanity 279

ACKNOWLEDGMENTS 285
ENDNOTES 287

INTRODUCTION

More Americans are in therapy today than ever before.

You'd think this would make us a nation of the mentally strong.

The rise of therapy was supposed to be a good thing—an enlightened step forward in a society once too proud to talk about mental health. But instead of producing a healthier, more resilient population, modern therapy has become something else entirely.

Millions of Americans are stuck in endless sessions, revisiting the same childhood stories, the same traumas, the same feelings, with no end in sight, and no measurable progress. In fact, data only shows things getting worse. In 2023, the number of Americans diagnosed with depression hit a record high of 29%—up nearly 10 points from 2015.[1] A recent global survey revealed that America had fallen out of the ranks of the top twenty happiest nations for the first time in the survey's history.[2]

Therapy has never been more ubiquitous, yet we're anxious, fragile, lost, and more divided than ever.

I've been a practicing psychotherapist for more than two decades. I've seen therapy at its best—transformative, energizing, and empowering in the truest sense of the word. But I've also seen it at its worst: passive, indulgent, and emotionally crippling. In these moments, therapy encourages dependence instead of growth.

It fosters weakness instead of strength. It confuses feeling better in the moment with getting better in the long run.

This book is about what happens when therapy goes wrong—and how that failure isn't just a private struggle but a public crisis. It examines a mental health profession that, too often, doesn't heal but instead reinforces dysfunction, self-absorption, and the quiet decline of resilience across American life.

One woman in her thirties, Amy, came to my office feeling perplexed. She had spent most of her life in and out of therapy, starting as a teenager. Yet despite all these years of "doing the work," she remained depressed, anxious, and stuck in the same patterns. Her previous therapist had spent session after session rehashing old dramas and childhood wounds, but Amy saw little progress.

Notably, all of Amy's friends were also in therapy. Comparing notes from their visits had become a common topic of conversation. Therapy-speak terms like *toxic* and *narcissist* and *trauma*—became parts of their everyday lexicon. They had unintentionally created an echo chamber where every other sentence seemed to begin with "my therapist says . . ." It was the ultimate "safe space"—the only problem was that they were all stuck in it. Amy realized it wasn't working for her anymore.

She and her friends had fallen into some of the most common traps of modern therapy. They entered with the best of intentions: to better understand themselves and engage more fully with the world. But unending reflection left them paralyzed. They grew dependent on their therapists for validation and became mired in a cycle without concrete tools to build resilient, genuinely empowered lives beyond therapy's bubble.

We live in a therapy-obsessed culture where it's no longer simply a treatment option, but an expected—even mandatory—part of self-care. The belief that therapy should be a permanent fixture in one's life has fueled a cycle of dependency, trapping people in a loop that breeds fragility instead of building strength.

Sadly, these issues are not new. I've spent my career pushing back against them in my practice by focusing on tangible results and helping patients build resilience. I've spoken out publicly—though doing so hasn't always won me favor with colleagues. After more than a decade in the profession, I laid out my growing concerns in an op-ed for *The New York Times*, titled "In Therapy Forever? Enough Already," published in 2012. In it, I distilled what I was seeing firsthand:

"Popular misconceptions reinforce the belief that therapy is about resting on a couch and talking about one's problems. So that's what patients often do. And just as often, this leads to codependence. The therapist, of course, depends on the patient for money, and the patient depends on the therapist for emotional support. And, for many therapy patients, it is satisfying to have someone listen, and they leave sessions feeling better. But there's a difference between feeling good and changing your life."[3]

Then, as now, my goal wasn't to write myself out of a job—it was to push both patients and practitioners to do some serious soul-searching. I urged therapists who kept patients coming back for endless sessions to ask a crucial question: *Are my patients actually improving? And if not, why?* At the same time, I wanted people to step back and consider whether therapy was truly helping—or if they were just treading water.

To my surprise, the op-ed didn't just resonate—it landed like a bomb. For weeks, it remained one of *The New York Times's* most-read articles. *The Today Show* picked it up as a "hot topic," and the *Times* was flooded with letters to the editor and phone calls. The message was clear: The conversation wasn't just needed—it was long overdue.

I knew that publishing the op-ed in not only a national paper of record but also in the "hometown paper" of the most therapized city in America—and perhaps the world—New York City, would ruffle some feathers among my colleagues. What I didn't anticipate, however, was the intensity of the backlash.

Therapists from across the country flooded my inbox with hostile emails. Colleagues in my own building—people I'd once greeted warmly in the hallway—held an emergency meeting to decide, quite literally, "what to do about Jonathan." Some even filed a petition with the New York State licensing board to revoke my license. When that failed, they turned to the press. To their credit, *The New York Times* stood by me and the piece. But the backlash didn't stop there. I was booted from a graduate school alumni networking group. And to top it all off, I was personally attacked from the podium—by the commencement speaker—at NYU's psychology graduation that year.

Of course, no one likes criticism or public ridicule. I valued getting along with my office neighbors and colleagues, too. I could have backed down, issued an apology, or softened my stance. But that would have contradicted the very advice I give clients grappling with the sting of criticism: Engage thoughtfully, stand firm in your beliefs, quiet the negative self-talk, and accept that you can't please everyone. If I couldn't live by those principles in that moment, what kind of example would I be setting?

Once the initial backlash subsided, I began to see the full impact of the article—and the change it sparked. Despite the wave of criticism, I received just as many supportive emails, both immediately and for years after. People who had been in therapy for years—sometimes decades—wrote to share their frustration. Many said the piece captured exactly what they had been experiencing in their sessions. Some were angry, realizing they'd spent tens of thousands of dollars with little to show for it. They felt misled, even betrayed.

One of the most revealing conversations I had was with a fellow therapist whose office was just down the hall from mine. We had been friendly—until the op-ed hit. After it was published, she abruptly stopped speaking to me. A year of silence passed before she finally worked up the courage to approach me. "The reason I haven't talked to you," she confessed, "is because of your op-ed."

That wasn't exactly a shock. But what came next was: Several of her patients had shown up to their sessions holding a copy of my article, demanding answers as to why they weren't improving.

Her response was telling—and it spoke volumes about the therapy industry. Instead of engaging with the real questions I raised—why so many therapists trap patients in endless, unproductive therapy—she, like many others, reflexively defended a system that thrives on keeping people stuck. This knee-jerk reaction exposed the deeply ingrained issue at the heart of therapy: an institutional resistance to change. The fact that so many therapists refuse to even entertain the idea that the therapy industry might need to evolve speaks to how powerfully entrenched the system is—and how desperately it clings to its outdated practices.

It's time to rethink how the public approaches therapy—and how therapists approach the public. The truth is, most people aren't meant to stay in therapy forever. Bad therapy doesn't just waste time; it keeps people mired in self-pity and dependence, when what they need most is therapy that empowers them to grow, get better, and move on.

I also believe some therapists are exploiting societal division—and even profiting from it. In doing so, they enable fragility and dysfunction. What happens in the therapy room, for better or worse, spills over into society. When therapists fail their patients, the consequences extend beyond the individual—to families, communities, and the wider society.

To consider these ideas is to confront the deep flaws in our industry—flaws that many of my colleagues, from therapists to psychiatrists, would rather ignore. They avoid discussing them among themselves and even more so with the public.

My colleagues would rather I not say this, but I will: As access to mental health care has expanded, so have rates of mental illness. And this isn't simply a matter of greater awareness leading to more diagnoses. The more therapy people get, the more fragile, anxious, and dysfunctional they seem to become. This isn't just an individual crisis—it's a societal one. Which raises an uncomfortable but urgent question: Is modern therapy not only failing patients, but making them—and the culture at large—sicker?

I've wrestled with this question for a long time—indeed, for most of my career. When I finished graduate school in my mid-twenties, I was eager to join the ranks of the helpers, to make a real difference. But soon after I began practicing, the cracks in my idealistic vision became too obvious to ignore.

I watched senior colleagues treat the same patients month after month, year after year, with little to no progress. When I asked about their approach, I discovered that for many, therapy had become little more than passive listening. They saw themselves as sounding boards—nothing more. Open-ended questions and a detached demeanor were the norm. There was no actionable guidance, no clear solution. Astonishingly, they were proud of this. They insisted patients had to arrive at their own conclusions. But I couldn't shake the question: How many actually did?

Instead, I saw an endless cycle of venting, complaining, and blaming. Session after session, patients unloaded their frustrations—sometimes turning forty-five minutes into a full-blown rant. Maybe they felt fleeting relief, but how long did it last? As they returned week after week, it became painfully clear: Those emotional releases weren't driving real change. The reprieve faded within days, sometimes hours, leaving them right where they started—mired in the same patterns.

From these early experiences, I learned a fundamental truth: This passive form of therapy doesn't free patients—it traps them. Stuck in repetitive cycles of venting and stagnation, they mistake temporary relief for genuine progress, never breaking free to make lasting, meaningful change.

Now, after more than two decades in practice, I've had the privilege of working with clients from all walks of life—from the corridors of power in Washington, D.C., and the high-stakes world of Wall Street to the quiet, anxiety-ridden suburbs and everywhere in between. Sadly, the issues I first noticed as a therapist-in-training haven't just persisted—they've only gotten worse. When new clients reach out to me, I often hear some version of the same troubling refrain:

> *"I've been in therapy for years, decades even."*
>
> *"My therapist just sat, listened, and nodded her head, offering nothing more than vague utterances of reassurance."*
>
> *"My therapist just kept asking, 'And how does that make you feel?' over and over."*
>
> *"My therapist told me I need to keep seeing him, or else I will fall apart."*

I developed an approach that is direct and results driven—I challenge my patients' limiting beliefs, dig deep to uncover the root of their struggles, and focus on real, actionable solutions. I don't believe in perpetual self-exploration or simply validating feelings. Instead, I push my patients to confront hard truths and take meaningful action. I know I'm not the only therapist who works this way, but I've seen enough evidence to convince me that "sounding board" therapy—trapping patients in the same feedback loops that lead nowhere—is still, unfortunately, the norm.

There are some encouraging signs, though, that this is shifting.

Other professionals have joined my fight. In 2023, David Burns, MD, author of the mega-bestseller *Feeling Good*, examined why therapy sometimes fails, including when therapists choose being "nice" over holding patients accountable.[4] Many others—psychologists, psychiatrists, and mental health counselors—have also penned opinion pieces that focus on the many problems with endless therapy.[5, 6, 7] In 2022, *Wired* magazine dared to publish an exposé titled "Why Therapy Is Broken," exploring the many flaws in my profession.[8] The following year, *Time* magazine declared,

"America Has Reached Peak Therapy? Why Is Our Mental Health Getting Worse?"[9] In 2024, *Vox* published, "Teletherapy Can Really Help, and Really Hurt."[10]

On social media, video after video mock therapists who continually ask, "And how does this make you feel?" rather than offering real, concrete advice. These videos lampoon what I call the Cult of Therapy—shedding light on how therapy has turned some people into chronic complainers, blaming everyone and everything for their problems while avoiding personal responsibility. Even podcaster Joe Rogan has pointed this out, observing in a June 2024 episode of his show that several of his friends have been in therapy for years but are no better off than before. He questioned especially the wisdom of "going to a therapist and talking about yourself constantly."[11]

I've written this book to show what's at stake—and how we can all be part of the solution. My goal is to offer an insider's perspective on what's wrong with the therapy industry and, more importantly, how everyone—whether directly involved or not—can help make it better. This isn't just an issue for those in therapy or for therapists themselves, or even for the friends and loved ones of frustrated patients. This is a pervasive American crisis, and it's only getting worse.

Most people know the grim litany by now: Depression rates have jumped.[12] Drug addiction and overdoses are on the rise.[13] Nearly 22% of Americans say they haven't made a new friend in more than five years.[14] One in three people struggle with loneliness.[15] Suicide rates are rising, too.[16]

The mental health strain is showing up all across our society. Our political divides have grown into dangerous chasms, with 36% of Republicans and 27% of Democrats viewing members of the opposing political party as a "threat to the nation's well-being."[17, 18] Increasingly, people are carefully curating every aspect of their lives to avoid confronting differing opinions. They choose restaurants, news outlets, television shows, movies, clothing stores, roommates, friends, and even romantic partners based on whether they align with their preexisting worldview.

One of my patients is a die-hard foodie who loves exploring new restaurants. His wife, however, insists on dining only at female- or minority-owned establishments. While she has the right to make her personal choice, her rigid stance has created tension—particularly when she imposes these views on her husband and others. Though he shares some of her social convictions, at times, a meal is just a meal.

I encounter similar tensions with patients who feel compelled to sever ties with friends—not due to personal grievances, but simply because of differing opinions on world issues, sometimes even the most obscure ones. It's a growing trend where ideological purity trumps the value of personal connection.

Many theories have been offered to explain this phenomenon. Yes, the isolation caused by the pandemic, the unhealthy influence of social media, and the extreme political divisiveness of recent years have all played a role, but what if the commonly assumed solution to this problem isn't the full story? What if the very people—professional therapists—who should be helping their patients escape the swamp of misery are, in fact, pushing them deeper into the morass?

What if therapists are fostering a culture of dependence and self-absorption—one that's making it harder for us to coexist as a functioning community? We need to ask: Is therapy truly making people stronger, or is it leaving them more divided and entrenched in emotional silos?

These are the questions I have set out to explore in this book.

Let me be clear: I'm not suggesting that no one needs therapy. Nor am I claiming that all therapists are failing their patients. What I am advocating for is therapy that functions more effectively for more people—therapy that doesn't stoke division but instead fosters resilience in both individuals and society.

Therapists must be held accountable for sustaining a system

that traps people in endless treatment, when what's truly needed is therapy that empowers them to break free from self-pity and dependence. The more we glorify victimhood, fragility, and relentless self-analysis, the more we cultivate patterns of emotional weakness—a culture that crumbles in the face of adversity. We're raising generations conditioned to seek constant validation and coddling instead of taking responsibility for their emotions and actions. And this culture of fragility isn't just personal—it's political. It fuels division, deepens polarization, and drives anxiety to unprecedented levels. The more therapists defend this broken system, the more they sustain it. That's exactly what happened to Amy. She was trapped in the therapy cycle—too conditioned, and too afraid, to see it for what it was, let alone break free. For nearly two decades, she cycled through therapists who kept her spinning in the same loop, endlessly rehashing the same old issues with no real progress.

It was made worse because so many of her friends were in similar situations and fed her perception that this was "normal"—as if therapy culture was as innocuous as morning yoga or weekend brunch.

Breaking the cycle wasn't easy. But once Amy saw the trap for what it was, she refused to stay stuck. She tapped into a strength she didn't know she had and used it to begin a new chapter of her life. That strength proved contagious.

I'm convinced most Americans have that same strength within them—despite an industry built on convincing us we don't.

Therapy Nation pulls back the curtain on this troubling reality. It's my job to use my insider's perspective to examine how therapy—once a powerful tool for genuine healing—has morphed into a force driving our broader societal decline. The widespread embrace of therapy as a universal solution has reshaped the way we view ourselves and one another, casting us all through the lens of illness, weakness, and division.

Throughout *Therapy Nation*, you'll find countless examples of patients like this. But through tough conversations, brutal honesty, and a clear commitment to change, they ultimately found their way back to real mental health.

This book is meant to spark a much-needed reckoning within the therapy industry—and a cultural shift beyond it. If this reframing makes you uncomfortable, if it doesn't align with your experience of therapy or that of people you know, take a closer look. The discomfort itself may point to the very mindset that needs rethinking. My hope is that this book will help show how to make that shift.

While many entrenched therapists will resist accountability, the rest of us must keep pushing forward. Patients and their families should demand more from those entrusted with one of our most vital national resources: the mental health of our people.

We need to build a society that's resilient—capable of facing personal and national challenges without relying on a therapist's validation. Even if you're not in therapy, have no plans to be, or even know anyone who is, I can promise you that an overtherapized, anxious, divided nation is your problem, too.

CHAPTER ONE

IS THERAPY MAKING US SICKER?

Jessica sat across from me, fingers knotted in her lap. Her eyes stayed fixed on the floor as she spoke, barely above a whisper. "I don't know what to do without my therapist's advice," she said, her voice tight with uncertainty.

She had been seeing the same therapist for years, and each week it felt like the same conversation—rehashing the same doubts, fears, and old wounds. What began as a temporary source of guidance had slowly become a crutch, leaving her unable to make decisions or move forward without first consulting her therapist. Whether it was a career move, a relationship question, or even weekend plans, she sought her therapist's approval. Somewhere along the way, she had stopped trusting herself altogether.

She's hardly alone. I've seen it countless times: smart, capable people stuck in an endless loop of therapy that left them weaker, not stronger. Therapy was meant to set them free, but instead it kept them dependent. Week after week, they circled the same fears and doubts, unable to move forward or make decisions without their therapist's hand to hold.

What should have built resilience became a form of avoidance. Instead of helping them grow more confident and self-reliant, therapy became the very thing holding them back.

And this isn't just Jessica's problem—it's a cultural one. Her story is a snapshot of a much bigger issue in American society. We've created an environment that encourages people to wallow in their struggles, to fixate on their weaknesses, and to wear their victimhood as a badge of honor. Mental health awareness, which should empower people to overcome challenges, has instead led them to cling to fragility, never moving beyond the past.

This mindset has spread from therapy offices into every sector of society. It's reshaping the world around us. In schools, academic standards are lowered to accommodate insecurities and self-esteem levels, which can often get conflated with real clinical deficiencies or disabilities. In the workplace, resilience is seen as less important than emotional accommodation. And in social movements, hardship is elevated into a form of absolute moral authority.

The result is a culture that rewards staying broken, instead of pushing people to become stronger.

The overtherapizing of America

The normalization of therapy would have been almost unimaginable a few decades ago. In the 1950s, seeing a "shrink" was either a luxury for the rich and famous or a last resort for the seriously unwell. Back then, if you'd polled your neighborhood, you'd have been hard-pressed to find even one person regularly seeing a therapist. Counseling and psychiatric help were often viewed with suspicion or stigma. Today, it's the opposite. More people are in therapy than at any point in human history.

All of that began to change dramatically as we entered the new millennium. Between 2011 and 2023, the number of people seeking mental health treatment nearly doubled, skyrocketing from 31.6 million to 59.2 million.[1, 2] Today, according to the Centers for Disease Control and Prevention (CDC), approximately one in five people are now receiving mental health treatment.[3] This sharp rise in therapy seekers has kept me and my colleagues busier than ever. According to data from the American Psychological Association (APA), most mental health professionals are consistently and fully booked, with little to no availability for new patients.

Many link these staggering rates to COVID-19 and the rise in mental stress, but the data tell a different story. By 2025, the average waitlist for new patients was even longer than it was during the early pandemic years. Psychologists are also working longer hours, struggling to keep up with overwhelming demand.[4]

There's no question that removing the stigma around therapy has been a positive step. No one should feel ashamed for seeing a therapist. But it would be reasonable to expect that, with all this treatment, mental illness rates would be declining—or at least not increasing. Unfortunately, that's not the reality.

Despite more people than ever in therapy, our nation's mental health continues to worsen. According to Gallup, the percentage of people who rate their mental health as "excellent" has been cratering.[5] Suicidal ideation has risen every year since 2011, with suicide now the second-highest cause of death among individuals aged twenty-five to thirty-four.[6] Rates of major depressive disorder and anxiety are also climbing. Today, 30% of people between eighteen and twenty-nine and 24% of those aged thirty to thirty-nine are affected by anxiety or depression—statistics that are nothing short of alarming.[7, 8]

Rates of loneliness and alienation are also on the rise, particularly among younger people in the United States, as highlighted by research published in the *American Psychologist*.[9] Even more concerning, according to American Psychiatric Association data, is the revelation that these days when people feel isolated they are less likely to reach out to others for support—even though that's proven to be the very thing that could help them feel better.

Instead, nearly half of individuals retreat into solitary distractions—binge-watching television, scrolling endlessly through social media, or playing games on their phones. These activities may offer a fleeting escape from uncomfortable emotions, but they often come at a cost: reinforcing avoidance, reducing real-world connection, and amplifying the rates of loneliness and dissatisfaction.[10]

A society torn apart

This epidemic of mental health problems extends far beyond the individual. It strains families, fractures communities, weakens institutions, and ultimately undermines the resilience of our nation.

A 2024 Gallup survey found that only 21% of Americans now attend religious services on a weekly basis, a sharp decline from 42% in the 1990s.[11] Membership in service organizations like the Rotary and Kiwanis clubs are also way down, with some of these clubs ceasing to exist entirely because of a lack of members.[12] Even youth sports, once a staple of community connection, are on the decline, further eroding the sense of shared purpose and engagement.[13]

In decades past, neighborhoods, apartment buildings, and city blocks were tight-knit communities where everyone knew one another. People kept spare keys to each other's homes. They shared groceries, watched one another's children, and offered rides to appointments. Today, that sense of connection has largely faded. People are much less likely to even know their neighbors.[14] Something as simple as a friendly "hello" has become a rare and noticeable gesture.

This growing sense of unfamiliarity breeds distrust. Instead of talking through their differences, some communities have seen neighbors call the police over minor misunderstandings. In the most tragic cases, those disputes have escalated into violence—even to the point of neighbors taking each other's lives over conflicts that could have been resolved peacefully. Reports of senseless violence—such as someone shooting another person over something as trivial as cutting in line at a taco truck or feeding squirrels[15]—seem to make headlines with alarming frequency.

Therapy's role in the problem

To me, it's no coincidence that the rise in people seeking therapy, the surge in societal problems, and the decline in mental health have all unfolded over the same period. The question is: How are they connected?

Many of my colleagues prefer to place the blame elsewhere, outside of the mental health profession. They argue that, over the past fifteen to twenty years, several external forces have converged to create the perfect storm for mental health issues. The standard narrative goes like this:

First, social media hijacked people's attention. Endless scrolling began to replace healthy habits like sleep, exercise, and in-person connection. As screens took over, real-life engagement faded, and with it, a sense of belonging. The result was a spike in loneliness, disconnection, and emotional isolation.

Then, political polarization took hold, straining relationships, deepening divisions, and fueling relentless anxiety. I see it daily in my practice—between friends and couples, across political parties, racial and religious groups, and socioeconomic classes. The gap between the rich and poor, the Left and the Right, and various communities is only widening, making meaningful connections harder to achieve and sustain.

Finally, the COVID-19 pandemic brought daily life to a grinding halt. And even after society reopened, something had shifted. Many people were left with what's been called "social rust"—a loss of confidence in how to connect, initiate friendships, or simply navigate everyday social interactions. The longer the isolation lasted, the harder it became to reengage.

But it's too simplistic to believe today's mental health crisis is the inevitable result of a simple equation: social media + political polarization + COVID-19 = emotional turmoil. That's not the full story. Yet there's a crucial factor left out of the narrative, especially by the therapy industry itself. That factor is bad therapy. It's not just failing people; in many cases, it's actively fueling personal distress and accelerating societal decline. This is the central argument of *Therapy Nation*: that we're caught in a therapy trap, and it's making us sicker, not stronger.

Therapy was once designed to help people improve their lives. Now it often fuels the very maladies it aims to cure. Combined with broader societal shifts, modern therapy culture has become a perfect storm for misery and fragmentation.

What is modern therapy culture?

Every day, millions of people flock to therapists, convinced they're doing what's best for their mental health. Constant therapy, once reserved for those struggling with severe issues, has become the norm—a go-to solution for every emotional or relational problem.

Celebrities and public figures have played a significant role in raising awareness. The concept of mental health is now woven into the lyrics and narratives of nearly every genre of entertainment. On television and in movies, we constantly see protagonists working through their issues in therapy. Shows like *Shrinking* on Apple TV and *In Treatment* on HBO even revolve around therapy as a central theme. Larry David's struggle with ending his relationship with his therapist was an entire storyline on *Curb Your Enthusiasm*. Therapy's reach goes even further: Hinge, a popular dating app where users post answers to various prompts about themselves, has one that says "My Therapist Would Say I . . ." When a friend is struggling, the common advice is "maybe you should talk to someone."

Again, on the surface, this shift seems positive—mental health care has become more accessible, and fewer people feel ashamed to seek help when they need it. Additionally, telehealth, app-based mental health services, and primary care physicians stepping in to address patients' mental health have all made it easier than ever to access therapy, receive diagnoses, and, in many cases, be prescribed medication.

While these advancements have brought real benefits, *Therapy Nation* reveals that they've also produced troubling—and at times dangerous—consequences.

The prevalence of bad therapy

Speak your truth. Practice self-care. Set boundaries. Find your safe space.

These platitudes can make a lot of sense if you don't examine them too closely. For some people, in certain situations, they can even be helpful.

However, when prescribed as hard-and-fast rules, as ineffective therapists find it easy to do, this advice can not only backfire but can also mire you in misery. What happens when your truth isn't the same truth as your spouse's, neighbor's, or child's? What do you do when your overly indulgent mindset hyper-focuses on self-care at the expense of your relationships? How do you grow closer to a romantic partner when your rigid emotional boundaries prevent you from listening to their opinion? How can you grow as a person when you only surround yourself with people who are carbon copies of you?

In modern therapy culture, this is exactly what's happening. Well-meaning advice, if misapplied, can do far more harm than good.

I once worked with a married couple dealing with serious relationship turmoil. After just a few sessions, the root of their issues became apparent. The woman was seeing another therapist on her own and, influenced by that therapist's advice, began setting boundaries—but in all the wrong ways. Her new mantra became, "Do what's best for yourself."

As she put this therapy advice into practice, the consequences were immediate and severe. She stopped attending her children's school activities, refused to share household responsibilities, and even stopped answering her mother's calls.

Boundaries can be healthy, as I'll explore later. When one spouse carries the lion's share of the housework and childcare, it's neither fair nor sustainable. But in any loving relationship, there must be balance, dialogue, and give-and-take. This woman's rigid boundaries allowed for none of that. Worse, they led to consequences she hadn't anticipated—including the near certainty of divorce.

This kind of thinking is parodied in an Instagram video that pokes fun at modern therapy culture. "All of her actions are justified by her therapist," a man says about his girlfriend. "It just seems like my girlfriend doesn't want to be held accountable for her actions, and she's paying a therapist to absolve her."

Like most good comedy, this has a kernel of truth—the real-life examples from my practice and beyond are numerous enough to bear this out.

They highlight a troubling trend: therapy increasingly used to validate personal narratives. Many patients are encouraged to see themselves as victims of external forces rather than as active participants in their own healing. Modern therapy culture often prizes self-validation to the point of self-absorption—sometimes knowingly, sometimes not. Sessions circle endlessly around the same people and the same problems. The result is more anxiety and depression, not less. Worse, it can drive individuals deeper into the very patterns they're trying to escape.

Time and again, I've seen the damage this mindset creates. Patients who've spent years in therapy remain trapped in toxic patterns because no one ever told them, "You are the problem."

Others have blown up marriages, friendships, and careers, only to be reassured by their therapists that it was all part of "finding themselves." That isn't therapy—it's self-destruction.

Surveys and research have indicated that this current system isn't working. One study found that one in twenty survey respondents reported lasting negative effects from mental health treatment.[16] Let that sink in for a moment—it's a damning statistic. If one in twenty cars had a defect that led to a crash, you'd be extremely hesitant to buy a car from that manufacturer. And somehow, people don't apply the same level of scrutiny when choosing a therapist.

Consider another data point: Fewer than 20% of colleagues in my profession actually track symptom changes over time.[17] In other words, they have no way of knowing whether their patients are improving or getting worse—and, disturbingly, many don't seem to care.

When therapy prioritizes short-term comfort over long-term growth and integrity, it fails the very people it is meant to help. When therapists avoid holding patients accountable—because being liked becomes more important than being effective—they are not merely failing professionally. They are promoting self-absorption and consequence-free living, where selfishness masquerades as empowerment.

This is how we arrived at our nation's current mental health crisis—and why we continue to struggle with it, both individually and collectively. In our relentless pursuit of mental wellness, self-validation, and "living our truths," we've abandoned the very qualities that sustain a healthy society: perseverance, resilience, and the capacity to engage opposing views without collapsing. These core values have been eclipsed by a cultural obsession with personal comfort at the expense of collective well-being.

In short, we've become overtherapized, overly fragile, and too quick to validate ourselves—often with little thought to how this affects our families, friends, coworkers, communities, or even our own long-term happiness. Meanwhile, countless books and opinion pieces dissect why certain people are "problematic" or "toxic" and why conflicts arise. These narratives drive people to seek solace in all the wrong places, deepening division instead of fostering resolution.

It's time for therapists to break this cycle of misery and self-absorption. They must start equipping patients with the tools to build genuine mental health, make sound decisions, and sustain meaningful relationships.

Beyond the therapist's office, as therapeutic language has seeped into social media, entertainment, and everyday life, it has fueled a broader crisis of meaning. Instead of helping people confront their problems, therapy culture often invites them to perform their pain—and remain trapped in it. We've become a society more invested in emotional expression than emotional resolution.

Therapy Nation argues that this isn't just a personal struggle—it's a cultural one. We are trapped in a cycle of perpetual self-analysis that leaves us weaker, not wiser. Breaking that cycle will require a new kind of therapy—one that restores resilience, responsibility, and genuine connection, both in our lives and in the nation itself.

CHAPTER TWO

SOCIAL MEDIA AND CULTURAL DECAY

I've lived in Manhattan long enough to know that you have to be ready for just about anything on the street. As a therapist, even a short walk can turn into a fascinating, eye-opening experience—one that no graduate school textbook could ever truly capture. As an observer, I've noticed one thing a lot more frequently in recent years, a phenomenon so widespread that there's now a name for it: "walking while distracted."

I've seen a man walk straight into traffic, completely oblivious to everything except his phone. One woman exited my building in front of me and was so intently scrolling that she let the door slam in my face. The rudeness was no big deal by New York standards, but my blood really started racing when I saw her almost walk straight into the intersection, stopped only by colliding with a man who was waiting for the light to change.

The people I've just described, and millions more like them, are absorbed in their own private worlds, oblivious to everything happening around them. Their distraction nearly put them in physical danger.

Even when you're physically safe—at home, scrolling on your phone or computer, far from busy traffic—the psychological effects of being fixated on a screen all day are real and damaging. Immersed in echo chambers designed to provoke anxiety and anger, people absorb stress without realizing it. A 2019 study found that increased screen time can negatively affect mental health by literally shrinking the cerebral cortex, the part of our brain we use to store memories and solve problems (including, for instance, whether to walk into traffic or not).[1] This is just one of many studies that confirm what's at stake with the social media addiction that's permeating every aspect of our culture.

That includes therapy. Nearly every problem that arises in human relationships—precisely what therapists are meant to help patients navigate—is intensified by social media. Lifelong friendships can now unravel over an errant "like" or comment. Words typed and posted without tone or inflection are easily misread, often with serious consequences. As therapists, we see these effects play out in our patients' lives every day.

Even more troubling is watching the influencer therapists—members of my own profession, or even some who are posing as professionals, actively fuel the problem. Instead of helping people work through their struggles, they exploit vulnerability for clicks, clout, and cash, offering shallow advice and serving up empty validation to strangers online.

In many ways, people being distracted while walking down a street is a relatively minor issue. Roughly two decades after the rise of modern social media, humans are more distracted, yes. But we're also divided, lonely, and prone to acts of rage. And that's far more dangerous for our society.

Lost on the information superhighway

Looking back at the early days of the internet feels almost like revisiting a different era. It was the turn of the millennium—an age of peace both at home and abroad. The economy was thriving. America's global influence seemed unquestioned. And we were on the brink of a revolution, with the "information superhighway" promising to replace outdated textbooks and provide free, real-time access to knowledge in science, history, literature, and beyond. Instead of driving to a library, people in rural areas could find answers to their questions from the comfort of their own homes.[2]

In many ways, it's astonishing. In just as many, it's sad, frustrating, confusing, and even unhealthy. For every question the internet can settle, it offers just as many ways to prolong doubt or fuel suspicion. Take the shape of the Earth. Anyone searching for the truth will quickly find overwhelming scientific evidence that the planet is round. Yet they will also encounter passionate communities devoted to arguing that the Earth is flat—or that its shape is somehow "impossible to know."

In a free society, there is a community for almost everyone, and everyone is entitled to their opinion no matter how bizarre or fringe it might seem. If someone prefers to spend their time meticulously debunking photos of the U.S. flag on the moon instead of collecting stamps, it is usually harmless.

But as we all know, the so-called information superhighway is chock full of many potholes, detours, missing or incorrect signs, and unlicensed back seat drivers.

The mental health and self-help space is no exception. In fact, it is uniquely primed for this kind of exploitation. Self-proclaimed experts prey on people's need for clarity and meaning, while the lure of quick fixes and trendy online solutions makes many especially vulnerable. It has never been easier to spread oversimplified—or outright false—messages that harm not only individuals seeking help, but the people around them. This flood of online pseudotherapy is wreaking havoc on society, making us sicker rather than healthier, weaker rather than stronger, and more divided rather than united.

False prophets go viral

For as long as the internet has existed, people have turned to it to research their medical problems. It's hard to blame them. Information can be accessed quickly and easily, and some of it at least is backed by legitimate medical review. And yet it's important to remember that around the time the internet came online, the public was growing increasingly distrustful of the medical establishment, occasionally for good reason. The media was awash with stories about medical malpractice. For example, in 1995, fifty-two-year-old Willie King underwent surgery to have a diseased leg amputated, only to have the surgeon accidentally amputate King's healthy leg instead.[3] Had this been a one-off, the public might have discussed it briefly, shrugged, and moved on. But the stories kept coming.

In early 2000, Allan Navarro, a former professional basketball player from the Philippines, walked into a Florida hospital. He told staff that he had nausea, headache, dizziness, and double vision. Several hours later and with no proper testing, an emergency room doctor diagnosed Navarro with sinusitis and prescribed him painkillers. It turned out that Navarro wasn't suffering from sinusitis; he was having a stroke. Eventually, Navarro returned to the hospital, where he underwent surgery to relieve swelling in his brain. He spent three months in a coma due to the delayed treatment and remained forever brain damaged. A jury awarded him $216.7 million.[4]

In 2003, Duke University Hospital performed a heart and lung transplant on a teenager without first checking her blood type. The teen went into shock, her organs shut down, and she suffered fatal brain damage. Duke quickly admitted error and reached a confidential settlement with the family. The hospital publicly accepted responsibility, and its CEO at the time, Dr. Ralph Snyderman, said: "We deeply regret what happened. This was a tragic error."

In 2007, neurosurgeons at Rhode Island Hospital performed surgery on the wrong side of an eighty-six-year-old's head. He died. The hospital acknowledged the error publicly within days. The Rhode Island Department of Health investigated and confirmed the mistake in its official report.

Those types of stories were hitting the press regularly, one after another. Hospitals were making fatal mistakes, surgeries were going wrong, and new drugs were being recalled almost as quickly as they were approved. Prescription medications once promoted as breakthroughs, like rofecoxib (Vioxx), were pulled after being linked to heart attacks and strokes. Others, like astemizole (Hismanal), were withdrawn when they were found to cause deadly heart rhythm disturbances. Each had been marketed as safe and transformative. Each, in time, revealed how fragile that promise could be.

As a result, more and more people began to lose faith in doctors and the medical system—or at least became more eager to seek a second opinion online. To some extent, the medical system adapted. Sites with legitimate backing, like WebMD or those run by the Mayo and Cleveland clinics, offered medically reviewed advice. While online forums remained full of people comparing symptoms and offering armchair diagnoses, these could, at least, be contained.

But a few years later, as the internet's superhighway expanded in 2004 to include Facebook, in 2005 for YouTube and Reddit, and 2006 for Twitter (later known as X), the underground medical information marketplace was supercharged. Instead of turning to credentialed experts, social media users increasingly sought answers from so-called influencers or micro-celebrities. And now our algorithms even serve us content and medical advice *without* us seeking it out. Having social media accounts means we almost can't help but be exposed. While there are undoubtedly many real professionals on social media, there are also plenty of charlatans with zero credentials and a never-ending stream of misleading health advice.

For instance, in 2017, actress Gwyneth Paltrow appeared on Goop promoting the idea that women could insert a $66 jade stone into their vaginas to improve "vaginal muscle tone, hormonal balance, and feminine energy." (Her company later settled a $145,000 truth-in-advertising lawsuit with the state of California, without admitting wrongdoing.[5]) Similarly, actor Josh Brolin shared a play-by-play of his experiment with the short-lived online trend of exposing one's backside to direct sunlight for supposed vitamin D benefits, which ended in an unfortunate sunburn.

On another site, Vani Hari, a computer scientist, was encouraging her Food Babe Army to avoid beer because, Hari claimed, it contained propylene glycol, a chemical in antifreeze. In reality, beer is brewed with propylene glycol alginate, which comes from kelp and is not used in antifreeze.[6]

As the years ticked by, these nonexpert "wellness influencers" grew in number and absurdity. In 2018, teens began filming themselves eating Tide Pods. In 2022, TikTokers were telling each other to boil chickens in the cold medicine Nyquil.[7] In 2023, Leah Anduiza told her 47,000 followers on TikTok to drink water mixed with borax, which is used to make laundry detergent. Her #boraxchallenge drew tens of millions of views and prompted widespread reports of vomiting and diarrhea.[8]

In the mental health space, wellness quacks began co-opting fragments of legitimate therapeutic advice—often absorbed from their own sessions—and layering them with distorted or bizarre interpretations. As more therapists joined social media and reinvented themselves as influencers, people's feeds became saturated with cute graphics and simplified therapy catchphrases. This, in turn, helped pave the way for the rise of ubiquitous therapy-speak, a phenomenon I examine more closely in a later chapter.

One example is the TikTok trend known as "bed rotting," which encourages people to lie in bed for hours—not to sleep, but to "get out of a bad place," as one TikToker explains. While the trend was initially framed as a way to find rest and combat burnout, in practice it often means eating, scrolling, watching movies, and spending entire days lounging in bed.

An inordinate number of social media users stumble on trends like this one, much like a patient of mine—a young professional woman in her twenties, who explained why she had no hesitation seeking mental health advice from her favorite TikTok influencer: "I've always found good recipes online," she said, "so I figured, why not try to fix my mental health there too?"

What was even more troubling was that this woman had been seeing another professional therapist before me—one who encouraged her to explore such online content without offering the critical guidance in their sessions that a therapist is supposed to provide.

In the real world, an occasional lazy day is perfectly fine; we've all had them. But when avoidance becomes the default, it's a problem. Bed rotting isn't just laziness—it's a pattern that encourages people to escape or go numb to their problems instead of engage with them, which only worsens anxiety and depression.

When behavior like this spreads as an online trend—or worse, is validated by licensed therapists—it creates far broader problems. People begin to see it as normal, even healthy. This cycle of avoidance doesn't just keep them stuck; it generates new mental health issues. Lying in bed with only a phone—no movement, no real rest, no meaningful connection—becomes a slow slide into emotional and physical decline, spent scrolling through other people's lives while neglecting their own.

True self-care isn't about being lazy in bed all day and indulging in unhealthy behaviors. In fact, what it promotes is exactly the opposite of what's good for your mental health. You should be doing what gets you out of your temporary comfort zone and taking action toward improving your life.

Helping patients address—and ideally solve—their problems is why most of us become therapists. That's always been the goal of the profession, or at least it should be. As a therapist practicing in this particular era, I take special satisfaction in helping patients disentangle themselves from bad online advice. Too many trends normalize unhealthy behaviors, yet people embrace them simply because they're endorsed by popular influencers. I've had countless patients ask about things they've seen online—supposed fixes for mood, productivity, or even sex. Most, if not all, lack any scientific basis. It's a familiar and disheartening cycle: People try the trend, it fails them, they feel worse, and then they look for the next quick fix.

To be clear, just because a piece of advice comes from someone without certain credentials doesn't mean it is automatically bad or wrong. For example, after Instagram influencer Rocio Romero told her followers about her years-long struggles with anorexia nervosa, she received hundreds of messages from people with the same condition who had been feeling alone and desperate. Unlike so many influencers, Romero refrained from offering health care advice. Instead, she shared her personal experience, which helped to reduce stigma and bias, and she encouraged her followers to seek treatment from licensed professionals.

This is a good example of how social media can help people with mental illness feel less alone, motivate them to seek help, and be better understood by those without their diagnosis. Efforts to reduce stigma are generally a good thing, and in many respects, they appear to be working.

But as a general rule, people tend to give undue credence to mental health influencers simply because they have amassed large followings. Many present one version of themselves online that bears little resemblance to how they live in reality. They urge followers to take digital detoxes while delivering that advice from a TikTok feed, or they preach sobriety while practicing what's often called "California sober"—replacing certain drugs with others they consider less addictive or dangerous.

Often, even their "lived experience" is suspect. A so-called dating influencer, for instance, may dispense relationship advice not from clinical training or meaningful insight, but from years of dating an endless stream of jerks. A man mired in depression might share mood-boosting tips that plainly haven't worked for him. These influencers can be entertaining and may help normalize conversations about mental health, but they lack real credibility. Their guidance often veers from hollow platitudes to outright nonsense—and at times, can even be harmful.

Digitally connected, socially alone

The British anthropologist Robin Dunbar proposed that humans can only effectively manage around 150 relationships, what is now known as "Dunbar's number." Before the internet, few would have argued with this concept. In the early 1990s, when Dunbar introduced his idea, communication was limited to more time-consuming methods: face-to-face interactions, phone calls, and letters.

With the rise of digital technology, the way we connect has evolved on a much larger scale. Today, we can have thousands of connections across platforms like Facebook, Instagram, and TikTok. At any time, we can find someone online willing to engage with us about any topic, from niche hobbies to shared frustrations.

Yet, as many experts have pointed out, despite these digital connections, people are more isolated than ever. Dunbar's number may still hold true: Our ability to maintain meaningful, real-life relationships remains limited. In my practice, I see many patients struggling with the consequences of these diluted connections.

When social media first emerged, I—and many in my field—anticipated its potential harm to mental health. By 2010, the concern had grown enough that *Fox & Friends* invited me on to discuss the dangers of social media addiction. Around that time, I was already seeing a steady stream of patients being drawn into the digital world in unhealthy ways.

"I can't stop scrolling," one patient admitted. "I know I should get up and do something else, but I can't."

For some, it's a distraction to numb themselves to the outside world, while others grow addicted to seeing the curated lives of friends or celebrities. Over time, I saw an increase in patients who had seemingly perfect lives but felt unexplainable sadness and inadequacy. For these people, the constant comparison left them feeling inadequate, especially those already prone to depression.

For example, in 2019 BuzzFeed wrote about a Fake Travel Challenge where people used common household objects to simulate being on an airplane along with fake backgrounds.[9] I've even seen people rent out lavish mansions for an hour just to use it as the backdrop for photos. This drives a narrative that happiness is tied to wealth and luxury, creating more dissatisfaction for those who measure their worth against these fabricated standards.

Missing out on life

Between 2003 and 2022, time spent at home jumped by ninety-nine minutes a day, according to an analysis of responses to the American Time Use Survey. For each additional hour spent at home, respondents spent twenty-one minutes alone and fewer than five minutes with friends. These trends were sharpest among millennials and Gen Z.[10]

It's no surprise that this shift coincides with the rise of technology. Rather than visiting a bank and chatting with a teller, we now handle transactions via apps. We can order groceries, connect with doctors, and even date—all without stepping outside. These conveniences have allowed us to save time, but they've also eroded the quality of our in-person connections.

Even when we gather with others, the pull of the digital world remains strong. Walk into almost any restaurant and you'll see people absorbed in their phones rather than engaging with those seated beside them. Conversation requires effort, but it is precisely this effort that builds real connection and supports long-term mental health.

For many, it's obvious in theory that humans are social animals, evolved to live in cooperative groups. Early humans hunted together, shared resources, and protected one another from predators. Today, when we interact with someone we care about—whether by holding hands or hugging—our brains release oxytocin and serotonin, chemicals that soothe anxiety and increase feelings of pleasure.[11] In fact, research shows that people with larger, more meaningful social networks tend to live longer, healthier, and happier lives. They're even less likely to develop colds after being exposed to viruses.[12]

But it's harder to take these truths into practice. Most of us know that compared to in-person relationships, online relationships lack richness and vitality. They're often shallow and also combative. This is likely because time spent online is highly correlated with loneliness,[13, 14] which has been shown to be as damaging to one's health as smoking a pack of cigarettes daily, drinking excessively, or being obese, according to the World Health Organization.[15, 16]

Whole books have even been published on the addictive nature of social media. Pursuing likes and follows are like playing a slot machine—you never know when you might hit the jackpot, and the randomness keeps you coming back. This is called "intermittent positive reinforcement," which is one of the most powerful motivators for human behavior, even when people know it's not good for them.

Many people have tried different strategies to combat these negative effects. Jonathan Haidt's book *The Anxious Generation* sparked a critical conversation about how social media impacts children's mental health, leading many schools to ban smartphones. For adults, though, the solutions are trickier.

Virtually fluent, verbally mute

Research shows that younger generations, especially Gen Z, excel at digital communication but often struggle with face-to-face interactions. I saw this firsthand while waiting with friends to check into a restaurant. After a long wait, one younger friend turned to me and said, "Could you ask the host what's going on?" I agreed but asked why she wanted me to do it. "I just don't like talking to people in person like that," she admitted.

That was when it struck me how much social media, texting, and emojis have replaced face-to-face exchanges and even phone calls and landlines.

It's a time-honored tradition for older generations to express skepticism about the communication abilities of younger ones. In fact, even in 1936, a British newspaper, the *Gloucester Citizen*, observed that young people "could not put their meaning into words and found the same difficulty when it came to writing."[17]

But research has measured differences in communication styles between baby boomers, Gen X, millennials, and Gen Z. Gen Z's proficiency with digital communication is well documented, with nearly a quarter of the members of this generation spending seven or more hours a day on social media, according to a Harris poll.[18] They're gifted at typing with their thumbs and using emojis to effectively convey emotions.

For Gen Zs and many millennials, in-person communication is a different story. They struggle to read and understand nonverbal cues. They don't like eye contact. Ask any middle-aged parent what it's like to get their teenager to make an actual call, and you'll get an earful. These parents describe a generation who, if the internet was down, would rather skip dinner than call a restaurant to order takeout over the phone.

In my own practice, I sometimes have parents calling to schedule an appointment for their twenty-something children. In most cases, I encourage them to have their child contact me directly.

One survey of two thousand people found that 25% of people aged eighteen to thirty-four never answer their phones, and 70% prefer text messages to phone calls.[19] For some younger folks, avoiding phone calls is more of a productivity hack than a phobia. Texting and instant messaging are faster and less disruptive, they claim.

I see a darker side in younger patients who struggle with phone and in-person communication; they are also more likely to experience real-life social anxiety. Over the years, researchers have tracked its prevalence using surveys like the Social Interaction Anxiety Scale, which asks people to rate, from 0 (not at all) to 4 (extremely), statements such as, "I get nervous speaking with someone in authority" or "I have difficulty making eye contact."

During the early 2000s, after asking just under ten thousand people to fill out this scale, researchers estimated that about 12% of people in the U.S. might experience social anxiety disorder at some point in their lifetimes.[20] By 2020, after researchers readministered the scale, however, that estimate had jumped to just under 58%.[21] That is a staggering increase, correlated directly with the rapid proliferation of social media.

All of this speaks volumes about how this has changed how we communicate and how we feel.

People with healthy communication skills can express themselves verbally and nonverbally, and they can quickly read a situation to grasp others' thoughts, feelings, and attitudes. Without these skills, face-to-face interactions can feel confusing and overwhelming. Rather than practicing and improving in-person communication, many retreat to the perceived safety of the online world. Digital spaces feel predictable and controlled. There, no one is judged by appearance, and the awkwardness of eye contact and small talk can be neatly avoided.

As someone who spends each day listening to and engaging with others, I don't struggle with small talk. Direct communication is central to my work, and years of daily practice have sharpened those skills. For someone who avoids face-to-face interaction because of social anxiety, however, those missed moments of casual conversation can deepen feelings of isolation, loneliness, and even persecution.

Without regular social feedback, their communication skills start to atrophy, making the real world feel increasingly daunting and unpredictable. This, in turn, leads them to retreat further into the online world, creating a vicious cycle of avoidance and anxiety.[22] In extreme cases, like the "hikkikomori" in Japan, some young people live entirely online, barely leaving their homes.

Paradoxically, many socially anxious people worry intensely about how they come across in person, yet give far less thought to what they say online. They can argue on Reddit or X for hours without concern that their digital footprint may follow them for life. Meanwhile, in everyday settings, they become hesitant and self-conscious about speaking to a restaurant host, fearing they will say or do the wrong thing, despite the simple reality that a host interacts with dozens of people each night and rarely remembers any single exchange.

Ultimately, most of us must learn to navigate both the real world and the digital one. As a therapist, my role is to help patients understand themselves, clarify their values, and learn how to show up authentically in both spaces. As confidence grows, they become better equipped to handle the challenges that arise online and offline alike. Encouraging further retreat into escapism, or framing avoidance as "self-care," may feel compassionate in the moment, but it ultimately hinders growth over the long term.

Feeding the outrage machine

In 2018, eight-year-old Jordan Rodgers set up on a sidewalk selling bottles of water to earn money for a trip to Disneyland. One woman appeared who threatened to call the police and report the child for selling without a permit. This encounter was filmed and "Permit Patty," as the woman came to be known, received death threats. Even many years later, the "Permit Patty" GIF still pops up in random corners of the internet.[23]

One client built a large following as a fashion influencer by posting photos of himself in different outfits. While visiting his parents one weekend, he came across a vintage fur coat in their basement and posted a picture of himself wearing it. Almost immediately, many of his followers turned on him, accusing him of being an "animal killer." Even animal rights groups joined the pile-on.

I've already mentioned the backlash to *The New York Times* opinion piece I wrote in 2012. I didn't receive death threats, but I did get hundreds of angry emails—and a few people went so far as to try to ruin my career.

In all these situations, the retaliation didn't match the offense.

Collective shaming has long existed as a form of social punishment. In modern online communities, however, shunning spreads and escalates in ways wildly disproportionate to the original norm violation. Most readers have encountered devastating stories of teenagers who took their own lives after being relentlessly targeted online, taunted with threats, and even urged to "go kill yourself."

This disgusting behavior, however, isn't limited only to teens. As we've seen in these examples, adults may have fully developed brains, but they're still susceptible to mob mentality. And sometimes they don't even have the facts right.

For example, as tiki torch–wielding neo-Nazis marched through Charlottesville, Virginia, in 2017, online sleuths identified one of the marchers as Kyle Quinn, an assistant professor at the University of Arkansas. But Professor Quinn wasn't at the Unite the Right rally. Rather, at that moment, he was at a museum in Bentonville, Arkansas. Soon, the sleuths posted Professor Quinn's contact information online. Vulgar and threatening messages flooded his email and work voicemail. Eventually, the real man in the photo, Andrew Dodson, came forward, expressing guilt and asking people to leave Professor Quinn alone.[24]

To some degree, the impulses in these situations are understandable. In my own case, my *New York Times* piece challenged a number of spoken and unspoken truths about my profession that many within it had held to for years. In these other cases, scolding kids running a sidewalk business probably wasn't necessary. Some individuals have strong opinions regarding the ethics of wearing fur, regardless of whether it is real or synthetic. Footage of torch-wielding neo-Nazis spouting offensive rhetoric is abhorrent, even (perhaps especially) in a society that values free speech.

But do any of these things justify online mobs taking justice into their own hands? In many of these cases, if crimes had been committed, justice would have been served. The organizers of the neo-Nazi rally in Charlottesville, as well as many who committed violence, quite rightly were prosecuted and went to jail. But did Professor Quinn deserve to be threatened and forced to defend his reputation? Was "Permit Patty" really worthy of death threats?

What is it about online spaces that cause human shaming to spiral out of control?

It's become widely known that social media algorithms reward and reinforce the extremes. These algorithms also tend to create an echo chamber. An analysis of one hundred million pieces of content on a wide range of controversial topics—gun control, vaccination, abortion—show that social media users tend to join groups and surround themselves with connections who share and reinforce their opinions.[25] While this is hardly a surprising statistic, slowly and over time, these echo chambers can lead to altered truths and realities. Virtual echo chambers have existed for years, but they still aren't going away—perhaps because people are vaguely aware this cycle occurs on a general level, but are convinced it doesn't apply to them and *their* echo chambers.

Holding a narrow view does not necessarily make someone bad or wrong. The real danger emerges when a dominant opinion turns out to be misguided or exaggerated, as often happens when an online mob sets its sights on someone to dox, attack, and humiliate. Although most of us are taught to avoid retaliation and revenge, these behaviors can still offer fleeting relief. When you retaliate against someone you perceive as a threat, your brain releases dopamine, a feel-good brain chemical. This dopamine burst causes you to *enjoy* the act of getting even. Because of this wiring, aggression can feel pleasant and cathartic, encouraging people to release anger through a violent outburst.[26]

Social media provides protection, an armor of sorts, that we don't have in real life, and makes it feel safer to lash out. That's why people may find themselves arguing and fighting back online in ways they would never do in offline life, calling people names or even wishing them bodily harm.[27]

Our online world has become a breeding ground for anger and absolutism, while sharply eroding empathy and nuance. Research from Indiana University found that heavy use of platforms like Facebook and Instagram correlates with lower levels of empathy, elevated narcissism, and increased personal distress.[28]

Pivotally, these emotional distortions don't stay online. They spill into therapy rooms, where patients arrive primed for conflict, validation seeking, and black-and-white thinking. Social media is nurturing the wrong emotional patterns, and good therapists are now tasked with pulling them out by the roots and fostering resilience, self-reflection, and nuance.[29]

CHAPTER THREE

WHEN POLITICS BECAME OUR IDENTITY

By 2015, the internet was functioning like the nearly lawless and often violent days of the early Wild West.

Our online spaces were becoming increasingly fraught. Group chats about seemingly mundane topics—knitting, dog ownership, self-employment—were morphing into a constant stream of arguments. Vegans were fighting with meat eaters. Owners of invisible fences were yelling at people who refused to leash their dogs. Lovers of the Oxford comma were feuding with people who refused to use it. Condescension brewed under the surface of nearly every online thread. The vector for much of this rage was politics, as it morphed during this period from providing a jolt of intensity every four years to a constant "new normal" of fractious anxiety and outrage.

It seemed like everyone—and especially the influencers and provocateurs who now made their living off the internet—wanted their content to go viral and would do just about anything to make that happen. To generate attention and shares, these influencers needed to appeal to the masses. Increasingly, their tweets, videos, and comments were carefully engineered to trigger strong negative emotions such as disgust and rage.[1] In the lead-up to the 2016 election, a meme depicting President Barack Obama as a chimpanzee appeared on the Facebook page of Linda Sorenson, the chairwoman of the Delta County Republican Party in Colorado. (She said she hadn't posted it and that her account was hacked). However, the post sparked outrage, drew national attention, and ultimately led to her resignation.[2]

Into this landscape entered a brash businessman and former reality TV star with zero political experience and zero fears of ruffling feathers. In June of 2015, Donald Trump rode down a golden escalator to the basement of Trump Tower in Manhattan, climbed onto a stage, and announced his candidacy for the GOP presidential nomination.[3] He soon launched into a statement on what would become the defining issue of his political career: immigration. He targeted Mexican illegal immigrants specifically.

"When Mexico sends its people, they're not sending their best," Trump said. "They're sending people that have lots of problems, and they're bringing those problems . . . They're bringing drugs; they're bringing crime; they're rapists. And some, I assume, are good people." By the time of Trump's second electoral victory in 2024, it was clear that the public had moved toward his tougher stance on illegal immigration. But Trump's rhetoric on the issue gave rise to much conflict. Many of my patients would describe their disdain for a friend or relative who sided with Trump on this issue, and it would tear families apart.

When Trump first ran, few pundits expected him to secure the Republican nomination, let alone win the presidency. But others, including myself, had a different sense of things. Time and again, patients would confide, "I kind of like this guy—he speaks my language—but I could never tell my wife." Trump's appeal went beyond his brash demeanor. For many of my patients, he symbolized a rejection of the status quo—a raw, unapologetic response to years of political correctness and a yearning to reassert an America that had once felt proud and powerful. While they didn't agree with everything he said, they were drawn to his willingness to speak plainly and express their frustrations in a way that felt real. He was a refreshing departure from the usual politics. "He can be a bit much at times," they'd admit. "But I'm okay with that."

Contrary to what many in mainstream media seemed to believe, these shy Trump supporters in 2015 were not limited to blue-collar workers or people without college degrees. Many were highly educated C-Suite executives and professionals who were fed up with the hyperfocus of the Left on progressive or "woke" politics, the permissiveness toward crime in cities, and the lack of focus on the economy. They were the kind of people who, although quietly supportive of Trump, would avoid speaking about their political views in social settings, choosing to stay silent rather than risk facing ridicule or social rejection.

But these shy Trump supporters were a specific subset. For other people, declaring their opposition to Trump became a badge of faith or belonging, one that shaped not only how people saw themselves but also how they engaged with others.

Politics was no longer confined to the voting booth; it had woven itself into personal identity. Friendships, marriages, and workplaces became battlegrounds, with each side of the aisle staking out territory in ways that were once unimaginable. This shift led to a reality where publicly supporting Trump could invite criticism or even ostracism. As public support of Trump became an invitation to outrage in many circles, Trump supporters became cautious, concealing their political beliefs to protect their social image and personal relationships. But this secrecy, while shielding them from judgment, also hindered genuine communication and strained relationships even further.

The phenomenon of the shy or closeted Trump supporter emerged in 2016 as well as 2024. Especially in 2024, patients who had previously voted for Democrats would tell me, "Sure, he's obnoxious sometimes, but this country is a mess, and I'm willing to put up with that character flaw if it means getting the economy back on track and securing our borders." I heard variations of this sentiment daily during the Trump vs. Harris campaign.

In the aftermath of both elections, many patients sought therapy to navigate a whirlwind of emotions—from confusion and fear to outright despair. They struggled to make sense of what these elections meant for the future of America. As one patient put it: "What does this say about America? Who are we as a country? Where did all these racists and immigrant haters come from?"

When I calmly explained that this was a normal election, like any other, and that there would be another opportunity to vote in four years, some patients became enraged. They accused me of being a MAGA Republican. For the record, I identify as a political moderate and have voted for both Republicans and Democrats for president. That perspective helps me understand competing viewpoints, but my personal politics have no place in the therapy room. That should be the professional standard.

It wasn't always this way. For most of my career, patients rarely asked about my political beliefs. Politics almost never entered the room at all. Increasingly, however, patients now raise it themselves, as if they expect therapy, like so many other areas of a polarized life, to align with a particular political identity. The expectation is no longer neutrality, but alignment.

Some patients talked about how they planned to withdraw all their investments because Trump would surely "tank the market and economy." They mentioned plans to flee the U.S. and head to Canada, Portugal, France, Italy, Panama, Costa Rica, Uruguay, Chile—just about any country where Donald J. Trump wasn't president.

What began as anxiety and hand-wringing quickly morphed into anger, resentment, and a desire to punish anyone and everyone they felt had contributed to what they saw as a disastrous election result. The rage and bitterness they expressed was ironic.

In many ways, they exhibited the very traits they claimed to despise in Trump and his supporters. They were angry, they felt society had turned against them, and they came to harbor contempt for those who didn't share their worldview. The supporters of the party that preached diversity, inclusion, and acceptance were now deviating wildly from those ideals.

I heard story after story about strained relationships, lifelong friendships ruined, and holiday gatherings on permanent hiatus due to political differences. Even in formerly apolitical spaces such as the gym and movie fandom forums, people were hurling insults at one another over disagreements about immigration, health care, and human rights. In 2017 a Scranton, Pennsylvania, YMCA banned cable news stations from all the TVs in the gym because it was causing fights to break out.[4] There was nowhere left to escape political controversy. Americans were consumed by politics—at work, at home, in restaurants, even during the hobbies they once used to unwind. For many, politics had become not just an interest but an identity.

American politics hasn't always been this fraught. To understand just how much we, as a society, transformed in 2016 and beyond, it's helpful to revisit another American period from several decades before.

An assassination attempt and an American reaction

The year was 1981. I was a happy-go-lucky, if awkwardly shy kid growing up in Connecticut who loved baseball and riding my bike. U.S. President Ronald Reagan had just finished giving a speech to five thousand members of the AFL-CIO. He was only seventy days into his first term, having won the presidency in a 489-vote landslide over Jimmy Carter.

As President Reagan emerged from the Hilton Hotel in Washington, D.C., he lifted his arm to wave at a crowd that had gathered outside. Not far away, John W. Hinckley Jr. raised an arm as well. A drifter and aspiring songwriter, Hinckley had become obsessed with the actress Jodie Foster. He'd tried calling her repeatedly, only to be rejected. To win Foster over, Hinckley's twisted mind determined to make a grand gesture that he would later describe as a "demonstration of love."

Hinckley aimed his .22 caliber revolver toward President Reagan.

One of the bullets ricocheted off the presidential limousine and into President Reagan's armpit, grazing a rib, piercing a lung, and narrowly missing his heart. Another bullet struck press secretary James Brady in the head. Secret Service agent Timothy McCarthy and police officer Thomas Delahanty were also wounded. In the hospital, as he was being wheeled into the operating room, President Reagan joked, "I hope you are all Republicans." Dr. Joseph Giordano, a liberal Democrat, replied, "Today, Mr. President, we are all Republicans."[5, 6]

I have vague memories of an announcement being made at my elementary school that day. As I grew older and studied history, I came to understand the gravity of presidential assassination attempts more clearly. President Reagan was neither the first nor the last American president to find himself on the business end of a gun.

As a mental health professional, I can now better appreciate the psychological forces that contributed to John Hinckley Jr.'s state of mind. Over the course of my career, especially early on when I worked in a hospital setting, I treated countless patients with severe psychiatric illness. I encountered delusions every bit as detached from reality as Hinckley's obsessive, violent fixation on an actress's attention.

From the vantage point of the mid-2020s, however, it's hard not to marvel at the public's reaction, especially as it's illustrated in the short dialogue between President Reagan and his surgeon. After the assassination attempt, the American public viewed Reagan as graceful and courageous. The press was awash with stories about how, at the hospital, Reagan had joked with his wife, "Honey, I forgot to duck." People gathered at work and in their neighborhoods, questioning how any person could do such a thing. There was no talk about false flags or evil liberals who'd somehow encouraged Hinkley to do the unspeakable. Even by 1981, national trauma of the John F. Kennedy assassination was still very much present in living memory. If anything, the general public seemed mystified that an American would commit such a heinous crime. They became united in their disdain for political violence.

Four years later, when President Reagan ran for a second term, he won by an even more significant margin, defeating Walter Mondale in every state except Mondale's own home state of Minnesota.

Today, more than forty years later, it's hard to imagine a similar public response to an assassination attempt on a candidate from either party. Partly, that's because we have a tragically recent case study in the 2024 attempt on President Trump that was quickly followed by extreme partisan rhetoric—which I'll explore in more detail later on. But there are larger forces at work that have changed how Americans treat one another in the new millennium versus the 1980s.

A nation of enemies

During President Reagan's tenure, the kind of rhetoric Americans hurl at each other today would be unthinkable. At the dinner table and in casual conversations, politics was considered a taboo topic, along with sex, money, and religion. Most people didn't know the political affiliations of their neighbors or coworkers. On those rare occasions when people did know one another's political leanings, they mostly respected their differences rather than demonized them.

The American television show *Family Ties* portrayed the 1980s with humor. It depicted two liberal hippie parents whose teenage son idolized supply-side economics, *The Wall Street Journal*, Richard Nixon, and Ronald Reagan. The differences between the parent's liberal views and their son's conservative ones often made for humorous episodes. The fictional Keaton family always got along despite their differences. It was the kind of loving family everyone wanted, so much so that the show launched a young Michael J. Fox, who played the teenage son, into stardom.

It's difficult to pinpoint an exact beginning, but the first era of intense political polarization seems to have taken shape around 2000, when the contested presidential election between George W. Bush and Al Gore was ultimately decided by the Supreme Court. The country briefly pulled together after the terrorist attacks of September 11, 2001. But that moment of unity was short-lived. By the time Bush ran for re-election in 2004, his decision to commit U.S. troops to Iraq and Afghanistan had made him an object of intense hostility on the left.

After him, Barack Obama, too, inspired vitriol from the Right. But there was still enough of the old civility left. Arizona Senator John McCain showed it in 2008 when he was running for president against Obama. During a town hall campaign event, McCain fielded several questions from concerned audience members who said they were terrified of his opponent, then–Illinois Senator Barack Obama, because, as they put it, he was "Arab."

"First of all, I want to be President of the United States, and obviously, I don't want Senator Obama to be," Senator McCain said, "But I have to tell you . . . He is a decent person, and a person that you do not have to be scared [of] as President of the United States."[7]

Loud boos erupted from the audience, but McCain continued.

"If I didn't think I would be a heck of a lot of a better President, I wouldn't be running."

The boos were silenced by an eruption of applause.

But since then, politicians like McCain have become fewer

and further between. More often than not, today's politicians intentionally inflame low-boiling resentments as they attempt to win voters and drive them to the polls. This leads to a vicious circle, as politicians quickly learn that social media rewards messages of hatred and disgust. In 2016, when Harvard researchers studied the Twitter (now X) activities of a variety of politicians, they found that those with extreme ideologies attracted larger followings than more moderate ones.[8]

Liberals refer to conservatives as Nazis, racists, homophobes, predators, and misogynists. In turn, conservatives call liberals libtards, elitists, America haters, baby killers, and children's-blood-drinking pedophiles. These are more than mere insults. This is politics as a form of warfare that pits good versus evil. People now see opposing voters as enemies rather than as fellow Americans. Social media and the echo chambers that I mentioned in Chapter Two, of course, are partly to blame. When you only hear one side of a story, it's easy to develop hatred toward the "other side." A report by New York University's Stern School of Business, among a substantial body of other academic research confirms that the siloing effect of tech platforms like YouTube and Facebook aggravates these deep political rifts.[9]

When added together—social media silos, extremist politics, and bad therapy—you end up with a recipe for division and rage. Consider the following survey results:[10, 11]

- About a third of respondents believe violence is usually or always justified to advance a political objective, such as preventing race discrimination or stopping an election from being stolen.
- Eight in ten Republicans say they believe socialists have taken over the Democratic Party.
- Eight in ten Democrats believe racists have hijacked the Republican Party.

- According to a 2020 YouGov poll, 38% of Democrats and 38% of Republicans indicated they would feel somewhat or very upset if their child married someone from the opposite political party, with one even notably saying, "I don't need that kind of stress in my life."[12]
- Two in five people say they would not date someone from the opposite political party.[13]
- Slightly more than one in four people admit they've ended a friendship over politics.[14]

The new religion

In many ways, politics has become the new religion. In my practice, prior to 2016, I would encounter many people in my couples counseling work who wanted to sort out religious differences they had with their partners. In many cases, they genuinely loved each other and were compatible in many areas, but they just could not see eye to eye on their personal faiths, which was enough to make the relationship eventually fall apart.

Since 2016, I've seen more people come into my practice struggling with political divisions, not just in romantic relationships, but also with family and friends. What's striking is the shift from people clashing over religion—where there was often sadness and reluctance on both sides—to now, where political differences lead individuals to summarily dismiss others, end friendships, and sever ties. It's done with almost a righteous zeal.

In the leadup to the 2024 presidential election, at least half of the patients I saw in any given week discussed their struggles reconciling political differences with friends and families. In many cases, they just couldn't handle the weight of these discrepancies, and they cut the person out of their lives. After Trump won, it was even more pronounced. One woman even told me she refused to bring her kids around her father and he "will absolutely not be allowed around his grandchildren."

Even long after the election, hardly a week passed without a patient expressing utter disdain for someone simply because they held different political views—or sharing their complete shock upon discovering that someone they had known for years, even decades, was a conservative or associated with conservatives.

I've appeared on a range of media outlets over the years, but it is my appearances on Fox News that tend to draw the most attention. Some patients expressed surprise. They struggled to reconcile the fact that a therapist they experienced as "nice" and "helpful" would willingly engage with a network they viewed as politically extreme. It wasn't only patients. Acquaintances reacted the same way.

This, to me, underscores the problem: Polarization has reached a point where we can no longer engage with people who think differently without losing our ability to empathize or even understand them.

What I've seen in my therapy sessions is a microcosm of a larger societal fracture. Political polarization is no longer just straining relationships; it is eroding trust, splintering families, and weakening the bonds that hold communities together. Even small disagreements are magnified. Loved ones are recast as adversaries, and nuanced conversation gives way to accusation and outrage.

That context helps explain why I agreed to appear on Fox News, along with many other outlets. I went because I was invited, the timing worked, and my background allowed me to offer a perspective their viewers might find useful or thought-provoking. It had nothing to do with politics. My goal was to turn the reaction itself into a teachable moment, and to remind people that the world, and the people in it, are rarely as black and white as our biases make them seem.

Now, we must ask ourselves: Are we willing to continue down this path of division, or are we ready to confront these underlying issues and rebuild the connections that make us stronger, together? It's a crucial question, one that goes beyond therapy and politics, and cuts to the heart of our shared humanity. What has become increasingly apparent is that political violence isn't just a societal threat—it's a mental health crisis. The work we do in therapy can either help heal the divides or, unintentionally, deepen them. This is the paradox that we must face as a nation.

This rise in political zealotry harms not only the nation as a whole but also individuals. An analysis of more than one hundred research papers and reviews found that as people drift away from the political center and toward the extremes—on either side—their individual and collective health declines. Part of the reason is mistrust: Extremists tend to reject medical guidance from institutions and authorities. Rather than follow a doctor's advice, they're more likely to turn to dubious remedies and modern-day snake oil.

Just as importantly, as people move to the extremes, they also become more isolated, with fewer friends and family to lean on for support. The online communities, which often foster extremism, eventually come to replace the real-life connections we need in order to feel a sense of belonging. Finally, the more extreme someone's political views, the more likely they are to embrace aggression and violence as a solution.[15]

The age of political polarization

"Political polarization" is a phrase that describes much more than simply not agreeing with the other side. And what I have seen in the most recent election cycle is the pathologizing of the election outcome.

"Trump will lead us into World War III; Nazis will take over

American streets." Or like the patient I mentioned who declared: "My dad will never see his granddaughter because he voted for Trump." People have made society sicker post-election, and mental health providers are in many ways responsible for this. They'll assure patients, "It's okay not to go to a holiday gathering if you're not okay with your Trump-voting uncle," or "Just avoid people who aren't like you." Many in my field have—in sessions and publicly—called for people to avoid others who voted for Donald Trump.

When individuals are politically polarized, they question not just an opposing party's ideology but their morality. From there, it's not a huge leap to view supporters of an opposing party as an existential threat to the country's way of life.

This obsession with morality rather than issues is, sadly, on the rise.[16, 17] One important study compared surveys from 1978 and 2020 where participants were asked to rate members of their own party and other parties on a "feeling thermometer" with a 0 to 100 scale. In 1978, the average person rated members of their same party 27.4 points more favorably than nonmembers. By 2020, this nearly doubled to 56.3%.[18]

In addition, between 1980 and 2008, Americans were more likely to say they "loved" their own political party than they were to say they "hated" an opposing party. By 2016, however, this had flipped. Americans were more likely to say they "hated" the opposing party than to say they "loved" their own party.[19] Political polarization has become so extreme that a 2021 report labeled the U.S. a "backsliding Democracy."[20, 21]

To be fair, some divisiveness is normal. Participating in a democracy involves people voicing their disagreement about various issues or topics ranging from taxation to immigration. By having these discussions, we should be able to better understand every angle of a problem, which makes it easier to solve. But when the sides become intransigent, all-consuming, and would rather score points than solve the problem, our whole cultural climate can shift in a negative direction.

Rather than feel a sense of belonging as "Americans," people identify much more narrowly as Democrats, Republicans, progressives, conservatives, and so on. Anyone who doesn't subscribe to the same identity is seen as an outsider who doesn't belong. Ultimately, a polarized person's ideal of democracy seems, by reason, to be a country where everyone agrees with and follows their ideas. However, that's not a democracy. It's a dictatorship.

Since 2016, this flavor of political polarization has woven its way into the American fabric with disastrous consequences.

The rise of political violence

America has faced political violence before, but, in recent years, these threats have increased. Between 2021 and 2024, the news outlet Reuters identified three hundred cases of political violence, including fifty-one in 2024 alone. The two attempts on Trump's life were notable examples, but others included the 2022 slaying of an Ohio man by his neighbor who "thought he was a Democrat;" and the 2024 injury of an eighty-one-year-old in Michigan who was rammed with an ATV while putting up a Trump yard sign.[22, 23] The violence showed no sign of abating in 2025, with high-profile incidents including an arson attack on the home of Pennsylvania Governor Josh Shapiro, the killing and attempted murder of Democratic politicians in Minnesota, and the killing of conservative activist Charlie Kirk at a public campus debating event in Utah.

It has been especially disturbing to note changes in the public's reaction to violent events over time. In my personal and professional experience, I've seen it shift from the "we're all in this together" attitude following the Kennedy, King, and Reagan shootings to many Americans responding to the Trump shooting in Pennsylvania by Thomas Crooks by saying "he should have shot straighter."

The seeds have been growing for some time. In 2011, after Arizona Representative Gabrielle Giffords was shot in the head outside a grocery store, public attention quickly turned to the broader climate of political rhetoric. Among the flash points was a map circulated by Sarah Palin's political action committee that marked several Democratic districts with stylized crosshairs. Her earlier slogan "Don't retreat. Reload." resurfaced in the conversation, not as evidence of causation but as an example of how political metaphors can be interpreted in charged ways. Investigators later found no evidence that the shooter had ever seen the map, yet the imagery and slogans became catalysts for a national conversation about symbolic language, responsibility, and collective blame. The moment showed how easily emotionally loaded interpretations can outpace what is actually known.

There is no indication that political slogans or imagery had anything to do with the shooting that permanently disabled Giffords and killed six others, including a nine-year-old girl. The gunman, Jared Lee Loughner, was later diagnosed with paranoid schizophrenia. What stands out is how different the public's reaction was compared with the aftermath of President Reagan's shooting. After Reagan was attacked, the country largely unified. After Giffords was shot, the country split along predictable lines. Many Democrats saw the event as part of a rising tide of inflammatory rhetoric, while many Republicans viewed that reaction as unfair and opportunistic. The tragedy became another moment when people sought confirmation of their existing narratives rather than common ground.

Political division and animosity have only deepened since then, with a marked escalation beginning around 2016. In 2017, James Thomas Hodgkinson—a Bernie Sanders supporter—opened fire on members of Congress practicing for the annual Congressional Baseball Game in Alexandria, Virginia. The sixty-six-year-old was a social outcast with a record of domestic violence and erratic behavior. His business had failed, his marriage was unraveling, and in the weeks before the shooting, he had been living out of his van.[24, 25, 26]

Hodgkinson is the textbook case of an aggrieved lone wolf who commits an inexplicable violent act. However, it's possible that were it not for his steady diet of highly partisan social media posts, in online groups like "Terminate the Republican Party" and "The Road to Hell is Paved with Republicans," he may never have launched his attack which wounded several people, including Representative Steve Scalise of Louisiana.[27]

Similarly, in 2020, the FBI foiled a plot to attack the Michigan State Capitol Building and kidnap officials, including Democratic Governor Gretchen Whitmer.[28, 29] Governor Whitmer blamed the planned attack on President Donald Trump, saying he failed to condemn far-right militia groups.[30] On the other extreme, Republicans claimed FBI agents had encouraged the men to kidnap the governor, referring to the whole story as fake news. Ultimately, nine people were convicted or pled guilty. Five others were acquitted.[31]

On January 6, 2021, a protest in Washington, D.C., against Trump's 2020 election loss turned violent when thousands of people overcame police barricades and stormed the U.S. Capitol. Members of Congress, and Vice President Pence, had to be evacuated or shelter in place, delaying the certification of the election results for several hours. Offices were raided and vandalized. The events of that day, like everything else in American politics, has been subject to fierce debate. *The New York Times* reported that one person was shot by police guarding the entrance to the House of Representatives' chamber, two others died of natural causes and one of an accidental overdose during the melee.[32] Dozens of police officers were injured; one suffered a stroke and died the next day, and others committed suicide in the aftermath.[33]

In 2022, David DePape broke into House Speaker Nancy Pelosi's California home. His goal: to hold Speaker Pelosi hostage, record his interrogation of her, and break her kneecaps.[34] Speaker

Pelosi, however, wasn't home. Instead, DePape found her husband, Paul Pelosi, dressed for bed in a pajama top and boxers. As police attempted to intervene, body cam footage captured DePape bludgeoning Paul Pelosi with a hammer. As the eighty-two-year-old Paul Pelosi recovered from his fractured skull in intensive care, right-wing commentators mused on social media that DePape might have been Paul Pelosi's "gay lover" or a "male prostitute."[35] DePape was later convicted on federal and state charges and sentenced to decades in prison.

Finally, in 2024, twenty-year-old Thomas Matthew Crooks fired multiple shots toward a stage where then former President Donald Trump was speaking in Butler, PA, killing a spectator, critically injuring two others, and wounding the former president in the ear.

News of the shooting rocketed through social media.

"It was the first attempted assassination of a current or former American president in the era of social media, and the conspiracy theories, finger-pointing, and campaign gamesmanship moved at the speed of the internet, far faster than the actual facts of what transpired," wrote Jonathan Weisman, who covers politics for *The New York Times*.[36]

Former President Trump called for unity, and Democratic leaders, including then-President Joe Biden, condemned the shooting. However, throughout social media, people predictably reacted based on their political affiliations. People on the right, for example, blamed the assassination attempt on Democratic rhetoric. Mike Collins, a Georgia Republican, said President Biden should have been charged with inciting the assassination attempt, and Georgia representative Marjorie Taylor Greene claimed, "Democrats wanted this to happen."

On the left, people were making crude jokes. Others were hatching conspiracy theories, calling the event a "false flag" attempt designed to elicit public sympathy and admiration for Trump. Those in the conspiracy camp even questioned whether

Trump was indeed injured. Perhaps the blood was fake, they suggested.

In the days after the assassination attempt, I started my therapy sessions as I always do, asking people about their week. That question invariably led patient after patient to bring up the events in Butler, PA.

"Well, my week would have gone better if that sniper had better aim," an attorney patient told me.

How could someone say something like that? I was incredulous. It was one thing to dislike a political candidate. It was another to wish that person dead.

"Don't you think it would be bad for our country if a president or nominee got assassinated? Think of the political unrest and chaos that would unfold as a result," I replied.

"I guess," he said, his arms crossed, visibly entrenched in his worldview.

"Do you think it might be unhealthy for you to spend so much time wishing for President Trump to die?"

"Well, I don't actually wish he got shot. I just wish he died, like in his sleep," the patient replied.

"What's behind this? Why do you want him to die?"

"Look," he said, "I'm bisexual, and Trump hates people like me. Everyone who supports Trump hates people like me. The whole Republican party hates people like me. They are going to round us up—like the Nazis did to the Jews—and put us into camps."

It was an outrageous belief that had no basis in fact, in Trump's rhetoric or campaign talking points, or anywhere else. I spent the rest of the session trying to help him sort facts from fiction. Yes, Trump did promise a crackdown on illegal immigration and crime, but none of that had anything to do with anyone's sexual orientation.

There's also been no evidence of Trump saying much at all about bisexual people. He appointed an openly gay member of his first administration, Richard Grenell, as the United States ambassador to Germany and later the acting director of National Intelligence. Grenell went on to serve a variety of roles in Trump's second term, which also included more openly gay officials such as Scott Bessent as the secretary of the treasury and Tammy Bruce as chief spokesperson for the State Department.

By the end of the session, I wasn't sure if I had made any impact. Like so many other patients that week, he seemed unwilling to entertain any alternative viewpoints. Yet his attitude was just as unsympathetic and uncompromising as the very people he accused of being intolerant. Wishing someone dead, I thought, is about as low as it gets.

Often, my patients claim that this inflexibility keeps them safe and allows them to plan for the future. Young women tell me, for example, that it protects them from predators and jerks. However, as I have gotten to know these patients from one session to another, it has become clear to me that this polarized and panicked worldview mostly functions to shrink their social circle, isolate them from their neighbors, and cause them to walk around with a pervasive sense of anxiety, dread, and anger. It also leads them to make gross generalizations about others based simply on their political leanings and miss out on potentially meaningful connections.

We saw further examples of this mentality on display several months later, when conservative commentator Charlie Kirk was killed on September 10, 2025. Kirk was famous for traveling to college campuses to rally conservative students and debate liberal ones, and it was during one of these open debate sessions that he was shot in the neck with a high-powered rifle.

Earlier incidents of political violence in 2025 received general condemnation. Democratic Governor Josh Shapiro's home in Pennsylvania was firebombed by a man apparently angered by "his plans for what he wants to do to the Palestinian people," according to NBC News, citing police reports (despite the governor of Pennsylvania having no official role in foreign policy).[37] The suspect, Cody Balmer, later pleaded guilty.[38] In Minnesota, Vince Boelter was arrested and charged in the shootings of Democratic state legislators and their families that left two dead and two injured. Boelter pleaded not guilty and has not been convicted of any of the charges. The Associated Press reported that Boelter's alleged "motivations remain murky," though "friends have described him as an evangelical Christian with politically conservative views" who "made long lists of politicians in Minnesota and other states—all or mostly Democrats."[39]

The Charlie Kirk killing, however, produced markedly different reactions. According to the Associated Press, the suspect, Tyler Robinson—whose DNA was allegedly found on the trigger of the rifle used in the killing—was characterized by his mother as someone whose "politics had shifted to the left in the last year," and he reportedly said of Kirk that "Some hate can't be negotiated out."[40] I saw some terrible comments online celebrating his death. Late-night TV host Jimmy Kimmel had his show suspended, with *The New York Times* reporting it was "over Mr. Kimmel's comments about the fatal shooting of the conservative activist Charlie Kirk."[41] The show was reinstated after about a week. The tasteless reactions were widespread and prompted pushback. As the aftershocks reverberated, NBC News observed: "In the days since the assassination of conservative figure Charlie Kirk, institutions from airlines to schools have moved quickly to discipline employees accused of celebrating or mocking his death, a reflection of the charged atmosphere surrounding the killing."[42]

Less than two months after Kirk's death, a poll was released that showed even more disturbing trends: Americans were getting more used to political violence, and perhaps more accepting of it. The Politico/Public First poll found that 55% of Americans expected increased political violence. Almost a quarter, 24%, said "there are some instances where violence is justified." And that feeling was more common the younger the respondent: "More than one in three Americans under the age of 45 agreed with that belief."[43]

Younger Americans growing more comfortable with political violence should concern everyone. Unfortunately, it's the younger generations that seem most willing to castigate others or cut them off (or worse) due to political differences. The effects of this new militancy appear to be spreading across wide swaths of our society.

Dating in the age of polarization

Decades ago, when two people first met, they often discussed topics unrelated to politics, marriage, money, or children. Instead, they explored whether their hobbies, sense of humor, and values were compatible. Did they both love (or hate) to travel? Did they share a taste in music, movies, or food? If not, could they find common ground? These were the questions that mattered most early on.

Today, dating apps prescreen people based on qualities that once wouldn't have been considered deal-breakers. Many now swipe right—or left—based on political alignment. For instance, a twenty-nine-year-old woman told CNN she brings up politics before anything else, declaring it a "100% deal breaker" if someone's political views differ from hers.[44] It's not just the Left—dating apps now cater to political preferences, with options like "Lefty" for progressives and "The Right Stuff" for conservatives.

Even when lefties and righties do somehow find one another on a dating app, their rigid political beliefs quickly end what could otherwise be a compatible relationship.

For example, when one man showed up for his counseling session in early 2024, he seemed stunned.

He had been messaging a woman on a dating app for weeks,

and things had been going well. They shared a lot in common—same college, religious beliefs, sports teams, and a love for stand-up comedy. They even had niche interests, like a mutual appreciation for certain cuisines.

He liked that she was physically active; she appreciated that he was career driven.

They had made plans to meet in person, ready to take things to the next level. That's when she asked him the question that ended it all.

> **Her:** "You're not a Trumper, are you?"
>
> **Him:** "No, I'm a moderate."
>
> **Her:** "What do you mean?"
>
> **Him:** "I don't have strong views—I'm more balanced than anything else."
>
> **Her:** "Of course you're moderate. You're a privileged white male. Only someone like you can afford not to take a stance."
>
> **Him:** "Where is this coming from?"
>
> **Her:** "Only minorities and women would understand what I'm talking about, so if you don't get it, just forget it."

And just like that, the romance was over before they even had the chance to meet in person.

Depending on your political views, you might think the woman dodged a bullet—or that my patient did. However, as a therapist with more than two decades of experience, I notice something else entirely. The conversation underscores the pervasive and dangerous political divide I've been exploring in this chapter, and sadly is driven by mental health professionals all in the name of "boundary setting" or any of the other mental health catchphrases du jour.

Fractured communities and families

Politics now shapes nearly every choice people make—even where they shop.

Some boycott Penzeys because of its outspoken support for liberal causes; others refuse to set foot in Hobby Lobby because of its donations to Republicans.

The day after Trump won the 2024 election and named X-owner Elon Musk to co-lead the Department of Government Efficiency, 115,000 people deleted their X (formerly Twitter) accounts. At the same time, sign-ups for Bluesky—a competing social media company created by Twitter co-founder Jack Dorsey—jumped by 2.5 million in the week after the election.[45, 46] At the time, the line seemed clear: Bluesky was for liberals. X was now for conservatives.

The tribal mindset extends to what people watch on television. Liberals flock to CNN and MSNBC; conservatives stick with Fox. The loyalty can surpass that of rival football fans.

This behavior—separate dating apps, separate stores, separate social media apps, and separate TV news shows—only solidifies and worsens the echo chamber effect.

Of course, you don't have to surround yourself with people you don't like. Setting boundaries is healthy—and sometimes even lifesaving. Abuse must be stopped; sarcasm and belittlement shouldn't be endured. And if every conversation with someone spirals into conflict, maybe it's time to walk away.

Similarly, maybe the election was merely the final step of a long "we're not compatible" awakening. I heard of one woman, for example, who decided to no longer associate with her brother, in part because he'd voted for Trump but also because, just a couple of years before, he'd refused to attend her gay daughter's wedding.

I'm not arguing with any of that. I am, however, questioning why someone would heed the advice of so many mental health professionals and refuse to say hello to a neighbor just because that person installed a yard sign promoting the opposing party. Isn't it possible that such a neighbor offers other redeeming qualities beyond who they support politically? Maybe they're active in the Rotary Club. Or perhaps each winter this person uses his snow blower to clear your driveway because "I figured I'd do yours while I was already out here doing mine." Does that person wholly deserve to be shunned for one part of their ideology? Why walk away from someone you like in real life?

The shared interests that bring people together before an election should endure long after the ballots are counted, even if they supported different candidates. These relationships ought to transcend any election, politician, or party.

Just as importantly, about half of the U.S. population votes differently than you do. That's a lot of people to hate—and a lot of life to miss out on.

Therapists as boundary police

Therapists can and should serve as voices of reason during these fractured times. We should be helping people overcome their differences and find common ground. After all, that's what's *good* for our patients, mentally and physically. According to a study of 2,752 people, the more politically polarized someone is, the more likely they are to report worse health outcomes.[47] The more isolated someone is, the worse their mental and physical health.[48, 49] In addition, people with no strong social connections were more than twice as likely to believe political violence is justified than are people with one to four strong social connections.[50]

However, increasingly and inexplicably, my colleagues are driving people apart rather than working to bring them together.

A few days after the 2024 election, Dr. Amanda Calhoun, chief resident in psychiatry at the Yale School of Medicine, appeared on MSNBC to offer her version of mental health advice as Americans prepared to spend the upcoming Thanksgiving holidays with relatives of different political persuasions. Host Joy Reid listed some of Trump's controversial statements from the campaign and implied that anyone who voted for Republicans approved of them, before asking Dr. Calhoun what her viewers should do if they "know someone voted that way."

"Do you recommend, from a psychological standpoint, being around them?" Reid asked.

Dr. Calhoun responded, "Absolutely not." She explained: "If you are going through a situation where you have family members or close friends who you know have voted in ways that are against you, against your livelihood, it is completely fine to not be around those people and to tell them why."

She even provided a sample script for how to respond to conservative relatives' invitations to holiday festivities: "You can say, 'I have a problem with the way that you voted because it went against my very livelihood, and I'm not going to be around you this holiday. I need to take some space for me.' "

The particular focus on "livelihood" notwithstanding, Dr. Calhoun seemed to be recommending viewers not only cut off family members based solely on how they voted, but she seemed to be actively encouraging greater conflict by suggesting her viewers "tell them why," thereby potentially starting a political argument themselves.

The basis for this advice was the concept of "boundaries," one of many ideas which are often applied with the best of intentions in therapeutic settings, but which have escaped the clinician's office to become part of pop psychology and taken on outsized and distorted meanings. In Dr. Calhoun's view: "There is a need to establish boundaries, and if you feel like you need to establish boundaries with people, whether they are family or not, you should absolutely be entitled to do so. It may be essential for your mental health."[51]

As I've mentioned, healthy boundaries are crucial in certain situations and relationships. These self-imposed limits allow you to distance yourself from draining people and circumstances, giving you the space to practice other positive behaviors and prioritize your well-being.

However, therapists are increasingly encouraging people to set rigid, inflexible boundaries for the wrong reasons. For example, I'd have no issue advising a patient to distance themselves from a relative with differing political views if that relative had been aggressive, abusive, or made personally offensive remarks based on those views. But if the only "offense" is that the relative voted differently, and they've otherwise behaved in healthy, respectful ways, I would generally advise against cutting them off over that alone. I would also question Dr. Calhoun's recommendation to "tell them why" and, in doing so, make yourself the instigator of a political argument.

By encouraging clients to wall off anyone who thinks or votes differently, some therapists are pushing them to overreact in ways that ultimately do more harm than good. It's one thing to avoid Cousin Lester's antisemitic or racist rants at family gatherings, but before cutting ties, I would urge people to carefully consider what their relatives have actually said or done. Given the way humans are socially wired, shrinking your circle of friends and family is rarely beneficial. Making such drastic decisions can leave you with fewer people to turn to when things get tough. On Thanksgiving, you might find yourself scrolling through social media, eating a bland, frozen turkey dinner alone. But hey, at least you never have to see anything that challenges your views.

To truly improve their mental health, people often need to do the opposite of what many of my colleagues are recommending. Exposure to diverse viewpoints is not harmful; it's how people grow and develop deeper character. It's entirely possible to maintain meaningful, supportive relationships in real life while disengaging from the most divisive content online. Doing so also strengthens the capacity to recognize the humanity in others, something people on all sides claim to value. And this isn't just my opinion. Psychologists and social scientists have studied this extensively, and the evidence supports it.

In one experiment, 1,661 people deactivated their Facebook accounts in the run-up to the 2018 U.S. midterm election while simultaneously increasing offline activities such as socializing with family. After four weeks, study participants reported increased well-being and fewer experiences of anxiety or depression. By plugging into real life and unplugging from online life, they also scored lower on tests of political polarization. As the researchers wrote, "deactivation moves both Democrats and Republicans visibly toward the center."[52]

In addition, as I mentioned earlier, mental health professionals are fueling polarization by pathologizing politics. For example, the day after Trump won the 2024 election, several mental health providers in a networking listserv formed emergency support groups. They referred to Trump's win as "these objectively difficult times," pointing to an "acute need" for their clients who are "politically stressed." They hoped that their emergency support groups would give clients a sense of hope and agency. Other therapists offered free sessions for "anyone who doesn't know how they will face the next four years."

The advertisements for these workshops and support groups framed the moment as apocalyptic, as though the country were facing the end of the world. But was Trump's victory truly a national tragedy, one that warranted such an intense therapeutic response?

If terrorists had just attacked the United States, like on September 11, or if there had been a mass shooting or devastating natural disaster, the hyperbole might have been more understandable. Those are moments when intense therapy and support are often needed. But a routine election? It didn't measure up.

In the United States, we hold elections regularly. We have a free and fair system that produces a consistent outcome: one person wins, and one person loses. For a democracy, elections are a healthy, normal event—they're something to celebrate! Yet my colleagues were pathologizing this election, framing it as a mental health crisis. I couldn't help but wonder: If Harris had won instead, would they have offered the same kind of extra support to the disappointed half of the country that voted for Trump?

My colleagues aren't alone. A broader impulse to pathologize ordinary experiences has taken hold across society. In the days leading up to the 2024 election, for example, several elite private schools preemptively gave students the day off after Election Day. Some Ivy League institutions also canceled classes and postponed exams. These gestures were framed as compassionate, but they did more harm than good, reinforcing the idea that disappointment and discomfort are psychological emergencies that require therapeutic intervention. If anything, schools could have offered a straightforward forum for students to talk about how they felt and then return to routine. By canceling classes or substituting them with therapeutic programming, schools amplified collective anxiety rather than helping students regulate it.

These examples show how badly my profession missed the moment in 2024. Therapists, the very people entrusted to help others, ended up fueling anxiety, division, and dysfunction. Instead of addressing patients' fears and guiding them toward strength, many joined in the panic. I have seen it firsthand: therapists urging patients to cut off family members over political differences and venting in professional forums about their own inability to cope. Rather than leading, they are hopping on the anxiety bandwagon, "trauma bonding" with their patients, and calling it therapy. In their desperate attempt to create "safe spaces" and validate every feeling, they are doing the opposite of what good therapy demands. They are reinforcing weakness instead of building resilience. Too often, the therapist's own need to feel important, agreed with, or in control overshadows what the patient needs. When the provider-patient dynamic becomes this muddled, you have to wonder: Who is really the patient? The true purpose of therapy—teaching people to face life head-on and grow stronger—is being drowned out by wallowing, grievance, and fear. This isn't just bad for patients. It's bad for the profession. And it's bad for America.

Healing the nation

The way out of political polarization will not be shown to us by politicians. Politicians react to what people, especially their base, want. If appealing to emotions like fear and anger is successful at rallying support (not to mention donations), then politicians will keep selling fear and anger. Plenty of politicians set out to run a "positive" campaign, but it doesn't typically last too long. Negative emotions can be especially more motivating in the short term. We cannot wait for them to pull back from polarization. We have to do it ourselves.

We can all see that the current state of affairs isn't working. Too many people now view those who vote differently as not just wrong, but evil—or even a threat to their way of life. Friendships have ended. Families have fractured. Politics now influences who we date, where we shop, what shows we watch, and even which restaurants we're willing to support.

And none of it is making us happier. If anything, it's leaving more and more people exhausted and miserable.

For many, this change accelerated somewhere around 2016. The world of 2014 or 2015 seems like an entirely different lifetime. America wasn't perfect—no society ever is or will be—but there was a distinct feeling in the air.

In the decade since, despite economic growth and progress, individual Americans and the general population have not become happier, healthier, or more peaceful. Instead, most of us are angrier, more anxious, and more suspicious of other people's motives. For many of us, this has led our worlds to shrink as we get older, rather than expand. We willingly cut ourselves off from people and businesses, or even entire cities, states, or countries—

because we have convinced ourselves it is the righteous thing to do for "our side."

Polarization is making people and society sicker, and with no corresponding payoff. It doesn't have to be this way.

Some argue that a democracy without division isn't a democracy—and that's fair. In a free society, disagreement is inevitable. But we can stand on different sides and still work together to solve problems and move forward. We have to relearn how to discuss our differences civilly, or at least agree to disagree. If more people focused on strengthening their own mental health—by examining how they think about themselves and others—we might slowly, but surely, begin to bridge some of the deep divisions that define our time.

Consider that the person who voted differently than you may hold their convictions just as sincerely—and for reasons that feel just as legitimate—as your own. They see themselves as good people, just as you do. And neither of you is inherently more moral than the other. People simply prioritize different values, and that difference is not a moral failure. For some, the overriding concern is climate change and environmental protection. For others, it's feeding their children or keeping their families safe from crime.

To find some common ground, consider that we all likely have more in common than we may, at first, realize. For example, a survey of more than eight thousand people determined that most Americans feel exhausted by political divisions and the "us versus them" mindset. Three in four people indicated that differences aren't so great that people can't work together. Hidden Tribes, which conducted the survey, referred to this segment of society as "the exhausted majority."[53]

It's time for the party that preaches diversity, inclusivity, and acceptance to start doing exactly that when it comes to people who have different political ideas. And it's time for the party that values family, free speech, and individual liberties to honor just that and see beyond electoral differences. Chances are, no matter which political party you affiliate with, you want peace, safety, security, and a healthy economy.

It's easy, and sometimes tempting, to call someone names or label them as a "Crazy Liberal" or "Alt-Right." Such labels can escalate tensions and further the "us vs. them" dynamic. Instead, we ought to focus on specific ideas and policies—and challenge those. Contrary to the modern trend of ideological purity, which encourages you to cut off even people who believe 90% of the same things as you just because of that 10%, you don't have to agree. You don't have to agree with everything your friend, colleague, relative, or online acquaintance says, but it's important to respect their perspective. Acknowledging differing views can reduce tension and foster a more civil dialogue.

It will take a long time to tear down some of the walls that Americans have set up around themselves. But I can think of one place to start: the therapist's office. This should be a place free of discord, not an incubator of it. My colleagues in the profession who encourage patients to engage in behaviors that prolong and enhance individual polarization in their patients' worlds are contributing to the larger divisions that grip our nation. We should know better, and do better. If people seeking help are consistently told by therapists they trust and rely on to wall themselves off, or start political arguments themselves, the cycle of anxiety and anger will continue. If that cycle is allowed to continue unchecked, the division of today might seem like a Sunday picnic compared to the bitterness that lies ahead.

CHAPTER FOUR

COVID AND THE ISOLATION TRAP

Try to remember late 2019. Any mention of a new and concerning virus was still weeks in the future. No one was obsessing about public health, vaccines, masks, or washing their hands.

Instead, in the United States, Donald Trump was finishing the third year of his first term as president. Political partisanship now consumed everything and everyone—dividing Americans far more than age, race, ethnicity, gender, education, religion, or any other factor.[1]

In the U.S. House of Representatives, Democrats called for a vote on two articles of impeachment. All but two Democrats voted in favor. All House Republicans opposed the measure.

Mere days after the impeachment, however, reports of a strange, flu-like virus hit the press. Far away, in Wuhan, China, increasing numbers of people were hospitalized for pneumonia. Public health experts seemed especially concerned. However, these same experts had warned Americans about countless other potential plagues that seemed to peter out before doing any noticeable harm. Most Americans shrugged their shoulders and went on with their lives.

The rise of therapy culture in recent years has coincided with a growing trend of emotional fragility. We live in a time when people are increasingly encouraged to view themselves as victims of their circumstances, unable to navigate challenges without outside help. But no moment in recent history has magnified this vulnerability like the COVID-19 pandemic.

By March 2020, the world was thrown into chaos by a deadly new virus. In Manhattan, where I was living, we found ourselves at the epicenter of it all. President Trump declared a nationwide public health emergency, ushering in a period of isolation and uncertainty. Schools, businesses, and restaurants shut their doors, while the rest of us stayed indoors, maintaining a strict six-foot social distance. Even when we dared to step outside, a sense of pervasive fear and separation hung in the air. This isolation, heightened by a constant flow of negative news, intensified feelings of vulnerability and helplessness.

And in this climate, therapy, already a booming industry, was positioned to become a lifeline for many who were struggling to cope with the emotional fallout of this crisis.

Initially—and considering what came later, paradoxically—COVID-19 served as a healing balm for our deeply fractured country. Democrats and Republicans came together in a shared mission to save lives and eradicate the virus. Everyone seemed to unite against a common enemy.

In those early days, stories of hope, resilience, and goodwill flooded social media feeds, websites, and the nightly news.

Throughout the United States, after a frantic surge of shopping—people scrambling to stock up on essentials—many store shelves were left bare. In particular, toilet paper and yeast were nowhere to be found. Some stores even raised prices, fearing they wouldn't be able to restock. I remember paying $12 for a small bottle of hand sanitizer that typically cost $4. Despite the uncertainty, neighbors did their best to support one another, sharing what rations they had left. One woman, for instance, posted on social media about her longing to bake bread—but she was out of the necessary ingredients. Within the hour, a neighbor had dropped a package of yeast on her doorstep.

NBA players donated hundreds of thousands of dollars to cover the wages of out-of-work ticket takers, food vendors, and other arena workers. Two New York City residents organized more than one thousand volunteers to deliver food and medicine to anyone too immunocompromised to venture into crowded public grocery stores.

So many of these acts of kindness populated nightly newscasts that someone coined a new word: *caremongering.* It was considered the opposite of *fearmongering*, and it described humans coming together to help other humans in crisis.

In my virtual therapy sessions with patients, the initially positive COVID effect was stunning. People were less anxious, less depressed, less agitated, and less angry. Couples were finally spending time together, some even falling back in love.

At first, many people said they enjoyed being home. They no longer had to tolerate annoying coworkers, battle crowds on the subway, or change out of their sleep clothes. Without the daily commute, they had more time to get in shape, learn new skills like playing a musical instrument, bake, cook, and reconnect with simpler things in life. For them, their homes became a safe sanctuary, offering protection from the potentially deadly virus lurking outside.

For a while, it almost felt as though the rage-filled, highly partisan world I'd experienced just months earlier was a thing of the past. Finally, there seemed to be one topic—public health—that everyone could either agree on or, at the very least, discuss civilly.

Then, it all fell apart. The brief unity unraveled, and the old divisions surged back. But this time, they were filtered through therapy-speak and identity politics. What began as shared anxiety quickly morphed into competing narratives of victimhood, with therapists often reinforcing the divide.

By June 2020, the political polarization I described in Chapter Three had woven itself into how Americans perceived the virus and the measures to contain it. Once again, everyone retreated into separate camps.

On one side, people on the right of the political spectrum argued that COVID was a hoax—no more dangerous than the common cold. They contended that the immune system needed to be exposed to germs in order to function properly. In their view, staying home and wearing masks was the real danger. This belief fueled their push to end lockdowns, stay-at-home orders, and mask mandates. They even called for Dr. Anthony S. Fauci—the then-director of the National Institute of Allergy and Infectious Diseases, who supported containment measures—to be fired, or worse, jailed.

Meanwhile on the left, fueled by the macabre "COVID death counter" ever-present on CNN, they boasted about how much they excelled at following public health protocols and publicly attacked anyone who strayed. "Trust the science!" they chanted almost ritualistically. They not only masked, but sometimes double masked. They ordered delivery groceries, and they wiped them down with disinfectant.[2] They bragged about not leaving their house to comply with regulations, many with callous disregard for the delivery people who sustained their cocoon lifestyle.

These partisan differences were more than mere opinions. They affected how people interacted with one another.

At one point, in the late spring or early summer of 2020, I was taking an evening walk in a park by the Hudson River. I kept my distance from everyone I could see, when I suddenly felt a sneeze coming on. I covered it up, and before I knew it, a woman who was easily ten or fifteen feet away from me marched up and started screaming. She claimed my sneeze "hit her" and took out her cell phone, raised it to my face and started recording. She demanded my name and number. I swiftly walked away, seeing no point in trying to talk to someone in a state like that.

The impulse wasn't limited to confrontations in the park. I heard from people who saw themselves as neighborhood public health enforcers. They'd take note of any local business with unmasked employees, report them to health bureaus, leave scathing one-star reviews online, and warn their social media networks to steer clear.

These encounters only grew more intense as mental health issues and destructive behavior surged to unheard-of rates.[3] People felt trapped, deprived of their usual coping mechanisms, and lashed out in ways they never had before. Online comment sections overflowed with insults and vitriol. Fistfights erupted in grocery stores and convenience stores. Furious individuals confronted teachers, health care workers, and public officials. It seemed as if adult temper tantrums, rudeness, and rule breaking had become the new norm, rather than the exception.

These deep fractures lasted long after the restrictions ended.

Why did the pandemic have such a profound impact on mental health and society? There isn't a single, simple explanation. It's likely that a combination of factors, including ineffective therapy and the rigid dogma promoted by some therapists, converged to create the perfect storm of division, hostility, and worsening mental health.

You're a social animal

Regardless of whether you see yourself as a loner or a people person, you need a community. That's because, over time, humans evolved to connect, communicate, and cooperate. After exploring regions of the world where people live longer than average, the journalist Dan Buettner, author of the best-selling *The Blue Zones*, identified several key factors contributing to increased longevity. A sense of community was one of them.[4]

Even with so many stories of kindness and unity circulating in the media, the truth remains: When humans spend too much time alone, and so many of us did during the early days of the pandemic, our mental and physical health suffers. Long before the pandemic, when I counseled people with depression, I suggested engaging and interacting with others as a way to improve their mood.

Even in less extreme conditions than a pandemic, people who are lonely or socially isolated are still more likely to become depressed, sleep poorly, develop heart disease and dementia, and die prematurely. To reiterate a statistic I mentioned earlier, loneliness's health-harming effects are comparable to smoking fifteen cigarettes a day.[5, 6] The percentage of people who reported feeling isolated nearly doubled after the pandemic, jumping from 27% in 2018 to 56% in 2020.[7, 8] This increased isolation likely drove many other mental health problems, including skyrocketing rates of anxiety.

Several months into the pandemic, it seemed as if most of my patients started our sessions by talking about their anxiety.

"I'm freaking out," one patient told me. "I can't do this much longer."

At night, the patient couldn't sleep. Often, she told me, she spent hours on her phone, doomscrolling through story after story about the pandemic. Eventually, she'd finally nod off, only to startle back awake, sometimes with such intense panic that she felt physically sick.

"My chest is so tight. Are you sure this is anxiety? It feels like I'm having a heart attack," she said. I knew the signs: She was having a panic attack. These were already common before COVID, but increased during the pandemic. Many of my patients who experience panic attacks mistake them for cardiac episodes, and for good reasons. The symptoms can be strikingly similar to a heart attack. Your chest tightens like a vice. Your heart pounds so hard you can hear it in your ears. A sudden wave of dizziness washes over you, and for a moment, you're convinced—this is it. You struggle to catch your breath, each one shallow and as if your lungs are no longer working properly. A cold sweat might break out across your body and thoughts might race through your mind.

But the causes are quite different: While a heart attack is caused by a physical blockage in the arteries, a panic attack begins in the head with thoughts and leads to a surge of adrenaline which sets off the body's fight-or-flight response. The fear of the unknown amplifies the sensation, making it feel even more life-threatening. The more you focus on the symptoms, the worse they seem to get. I've experienced it myself, right before I ever went on national television for the first time.

Many of my clients who were struggling with anxiety, including panic attacks, before the pandemic were plunged into a much worse state. Such patients hyper-focused on physical things—a slight cough, an itch, a rash—that they erroneously thought was a symptom of COVID-19. Some were now almost incapacitated by their desire to avoid all germs. One, for example, couldn't stop worrying about the valets in the garage where he parked his car. "They touch the key, and then I touch it, and what if they have COVID and it gets on the key?" This worry seemed to operate on repeat in his mind, leaving little room for any other thoughts.

To calm his nerves, I said, "You wash your hands when you get home. That would wash off the germs, wouldn't it?"

"But I have to touch the door on my way into the apartment as well as the handle to the sink so that I would be transferring the germs to those surfaces," he worried. No matter how much I tried to soothe his fears, he found more things to worry about.

I heard countless stories just like this. The worry was reaching a fever pitch. Nothing I said seemed to help. My patient load almost doubled, and every session was dominated by talk of COVID-19 despite my best efforts to get these anxious minds to think about something—anything—else.

According to the World Health Organization, rates of anxiety and depression jumped 25% during the first year after the start of the pandemic.[9] Mental health issues were most severe in areas with the strictest stay-at-home orders. In regions of the country with strict lockdowns, for instance, the use of mental health facilities increased by 18%. In contrast, in areas without strict lockdowns, the use of mental health facilities *dropped* by 1% during the same period. Rates of insomnia, burnout, and stress were all higher in areas with lockdowns as well.[10]

One might expect that, as the lockdowns lifted and life began to resemble "normal" again, mental health would stabilize and return to pre-pandemic levels. For comparison, in the middle of 2019, just 8.1% of American adults reported symptoms of anxiety and just 6.5% reported symptoms of depression.[11] But we haven't even come close to those 2019 levels in recent years. According to CNN and Kaiser Family Foundation surveys:

- **In 2021**, four in ten adults reported symptoms of anxiety and depression.
- **In 2022**, this declined slightly to three in ten adults.
- **In 2023**, rates of anxiety and depression remained steady at three in ten adults.

Like anxiety and depression, drug overdose and alcohol-related deaths also rose in 2021 and remained elevated in 2022 and 2023.[12]

These increases in poor mental health were the sharpest in our young adults, up to half of whom were reporting increased anxiety or depression.[13] Between March 2020 and December 2022, the use of antidepressants jumped 63.5% in teens and young adults, according to the American Psychological Association.[14] By May 2023, then-Surgeon General Vivek Murthy had declared loneliness a national epidemic.

Rage against the vaccine

Animal behaviorists have long observed a phenomenon known as *cage rage*, a term used to describe the aggression exhibited by animals—whether hamsters, dogs, or parrots—who spend too much time in confined spaces. This frustration, born from feeling cornered and trapped, leads to destructive and violent behavior. The same principle applies to humans, especially during the pandemic. As isolation heightened, many felt their mental and emotional "cages" growing smaller, and, just like the animals, some lashed out in a way that felt like a desperate form of self-defense.

The same reaction can occur in humans, especially if they feel threatened. When someone is socially isolated—as so many people were during the pandemic—their brain becomes hypervigilant, continually scanning their environment for danger. As they fixate on these threats, they can feel even more under attack. Then, if they lash out, they view their actions as a justified form of self-defense and retribution.[15]

In certain experiments, participants who have been excluded in some way—for example, not being passed a ball during a game—are more likely to agree to harm other humans by administering loud noises.[16] At the extremes, this increased hostility can be deadly. Someone who turned feelings of exclusion into murderous rage was Elliot Rodger, who murdered six people and injured fourteen others in 2014 at the age of twenty-two before turning his gun on himself.[17] As he claimed in a YouTube video before the event, he was sick of being rejected by women. Inexplicably, he saw himself—and not the people he set out to kill—as the real victim. In a 137-page manifesto that he left behind, Rodger refers over and over again to being "cast out," "rejected," and "lonely."

Rodger's actions were despicable and irrational, the product of severe mental illness. They also illustrate that an extreme example of social isolation and rejection can lead humans down the road to hostility, aggression, and violence. Many school shooters and other killers have expressed similar sentiments about feeling excluded from society.

During the pandemic, people stuck in isolation and thereby excluded from social activity, would sometimes lash out when they found themselves back in the presence of others.

Consider what happened in a Safeway grocery store in San Francisco in March 2020, just after a three-week shelter-in-place order went into effect. Someone wheeled a bicycle into the store, irritating another shopper who felt it crowded an already tight space. Shoppers quickly took sides, and a large fistfight broke out between multiple patrons.[18]

In April 2020, a disgruntled Pittsburgh shopper leaned under a plexiglass barrier and spit on a grocery store employee.[19] In a Colorado Springs Walmart, two women got into a fistfight over social distancing.[20] On an American Airlines flight, two passengers brawled over the airline's face mask policy.[21]

This animosity spilled over into all public spaces. One woman who believed COVID was a hoax deliberately coughed on produce, prompting a Pennsylvania grocery store to throw out $35,000 worth of food. Fistfights broke out at meetings about masking in schools. A new phrase entered our lexicon: "COVID rage." This undercurrent of fury was not isolated to grocery stores and flights, it would soon manifest in more organized expressions of discontent. As time wore on, more and more people began taking their anger out on teachers, elected officials, and health care professionals.[22]

These small outbursts of rage were more than just random acts of frustration. They were the culmination of a nation's collective isolation and anxiety, unleashed when people were pushed to their breaking point. Social tension had been building for months, and when people were allowed back into the world they did not return with calm composure. They returned with the anger and fear they'd cultivated in isolation, eager to release it.

Then, as April 2020 turned into May, everything boiled over.

In Michigan on April 30, hundreds of armed people stormed the Michigan statehouse. At that time, about 3,789 people had died from COVID-19 in Michigan. It was the third highest COVID death toll in the country, and then-Governor Gretchen Whitmer had recently extended the state's stay-at-home order. For five hours, the mob of those opposed to the order banged on the closed doors to the legislative chamber as they shouted, "Let us in!"[23]

Later the same month, the media continually showed footage of a Minneapolis police officer kneeling on the neck of George Floyd, a Black man, ultimately killing him. Protests and unrest rocked Minneapolis and soon spread to over two thousand cities and sixty countries.

Though some protests were peaceful, others turned destructive and violent. Police vehicles were defaced with graffiti, businesses were looted and set on fire, freeways were blocked, and cars were ransacked. That summer, while dining outdoors in Greenwich Village—a practice that had become popular by then—a group of several hundred people suddenly charged down the street, shouting and throwing objects. They grabbed bottles of wine from restaurant tables, and the smell of marijuana hung in the air. Some chanted and yelled things like "F★★k you, whitey!" at Caucasian diners. A woman at the next table began to cry. Police officers were nearby, but they were outnumbered and appeared powerless to intervene. It felt like an eternity before this protest, which was anything but peaceful, finally moved on.

But my experience was tame compared to many others. In Detroit, someone opened fire into a crowd, killing a nineteen-year-old young man. In St. Louis and Las Vegas, officers were wounded by gunfire. In other cities, perpetrators rammed their vehicles into police and crowds, injuring officers, protesters, and bystanders. The National Guard was activated in just under half of the states.

The year 2021 would emerge as the most violent year in two decades. Homicides were up 24%.[24] On July 4 of that year, more than 180 people were killed by shootings across the country in just one weekend.[25] Rates of aggressive driving and road rage were up, too.[26]

Do as I say, not as I do

Primatologists and anthropologists believe humans evolved with an innate belief in fairness—that equal efforts deserve equal rewards. When fairness is violated—for example, because someone takes more than their "fair" share—we become irate, which functions to reinforce cooperation.[27]

During the pandemic, perceptions of hypocrisy and injustice multiplied. In May 2020, British Prime Minister Boris Johnson and his staff held a wine-and-cheese gathering at Downing Street while the rest of Britain remained under strict stay-at-home orders. It was one of several lockdown-era parties later confirmed by investigators, a scandal that became known as "Partygate." The episode—emblematic of elite double standards—would ultimately contribute to Johnson's downfall as prime minister.

Over here in the United States, Democratic Speaker of the House Nancy Pelosi found herself in a similar scandal. While the rest of nonessential San Francisco businesses were shuttered, Pelosi went to a salon to style her hair. The salon's owner, who wasn't present, became irate, calling Pelosi's actions "a slap in the face."[28] Then California Governor Gavin Newsom attended a fancy dinner party at The French Laundry, one of the world's most exclusive restaurants, to celebrate a friend's birthday while the citizens of his state were in lockdown per his orders.

The hypocritical actions of Pelosi, Johnson, and Newsom infuriated many, and for good reason. When elected officials and leaders violate the strict rules they impose on others, it creates a "rules for thee but not for me." This breach leads to immense feelings of betrayal and resentment. This was brewing in the American psyche at the time.

This sense of betrayal extended beyond politicians. For example, when the George Floyd protests first erupted, the very public health officials who'd recommended strict stay-at-home policies quickly changed their stance. More than 1,200 medical professionals signed a letter saying the protests were "vital to the national public health and to the threatened health specifically of Black people in the United States." They declared: "We do not condemn these gatherings as risky for COVID-19 transmission."[29] These were the same officials who'd warned Americans against heading to the beaches for spring break, attending church on Sundays, and gathering at funerals to mourn loved ones.

Effective leadership during a crisis relies on modeling the behavior you expect from others. During the lockdowns, citizens were asked to make significant sacrifices—closing businesses, canceling celebrations, and isolating from loved ones. These sacrifices formed an implicit social contract where everyone was expected to follow the same rules. High-profile violations by leaders undermined this contract, fueling widespread anger.

The pandemic was already a time of heightened stress, anxiety, and frustration. The self-interested actions of Johnson, Pelosi, and Newsom—along with the sudden recalibration of rules for certain political protests—served as a lightning rod for those emotions. It provided a clear focus for people's frustrations about the broader challenges of lockdown life. It also eroded the moral authority of political and public health leaders who had set the rules for everyone, making it harder for people to trust or comply with restrictions moving forward. Decision-makers appeared to be out of touch with the struggles of ordinary people, further widening the gap between the public and those in positions of power.

Logged into rage

Another lasting effect of the pandemic centers on our online behavior. Public outrage can be contagious, and stories spread over social media can often provoke visceral reactions that resonate widely.

During the initial stay-at-home orders, many people turned to online communities to maintain a sense of connectedness. This behavior wasn't necessarily wrong or bad. When used during a time of crisis as a way to shore up social support, research shows that social media can improve how people cope, helping to alleviate anger, anxiety, and loneliness.[30]

As I've noted, social media also has a built-in dark side. During the pandemic, that dark side became especially pronounced. Platforms that promised connection often intensified anxiety, keeping people glued to a nonstop stream of alarming news and fueling anger as users argued over social distancing, masks, and vaccines.

The most lasting damage, however, may be how much time people learned to spend online. Instead of engaging in restorative activities like sleep, exercise, or real connection, many became absorbed by their screens. Today, countless people tell me they're on their phones nearly all the time, often from the moment they wake up until they go to bed.

In addition to being addicted to scrolling, they're experiencing what's been called "social rust": they've forgotten how to make friends in real life.[31] This issue is compounded by remote work, which took off during the pandemic. Because it saves money on overhead—and, frankly, because many workers demand the option—many companies maintained remote work as an option long after the pandemic ended. However, these work policies have further contributed to social rust. According to a 2024 ResumeBuilder survey, 25% of remote employees admit that their social skills have worsened since they began working from home.[32]

Therapy, therapy everywhere

Before the pandemic, many people struggled to access mental health care—even in places like New York City, where therapists are plentiful. Some couldn't physically make it to in-person sessions. Then, during the first wave of stay-at-home orders, the mental health industry rapidly shifted to online appointments.

Private insurance and Medicaid began covering telehealth, which helped expand access. I kept my office during that time, mainly to maintain a workspace separate from my apartment. But over time, I found less and less use for it and eventually decided to give it up. The transition made my work more efficient: Without a commute, I could see more patients each day.

The RAND Corporation found that tele–mental health services surged sixteen- to twenty-fold during the COVID pandemic—boosting overall mental health treatment by 10% to 20%. In 2020, telehealth visits made up 13% of mental health and substance abuse sessions.

By 2021, 40% of all mental health services and substance use disorder outpatient services were delivered virtually.[33]

Ultimately, this is a positive development, allowing more people to access the therapy they need. Telehealth *should* have positioned mental health professionals to guide lonely, isolated people toward better health and stronger connections. It *should* have provided an opportunity for therapists to heal divisions, not deepen them. If only that had been the case.

Don't get me wrong—I'm sure many therapists did remarkable work during the pandemic. Countless professionals used every tool available to help people cope and heal.

However, with the surge in demand for therapy and the convenience of telehealth, some have found no shortage of clients even while providing subpar care. I know of one therapist who encouraged followers to fight loneliness by talking to their furniture. Another advised people to adopt imaginary friends. These are the kinds of suggestions I'd expect from a third grader, not from someone holding a license to practice therapy.

The rapid expansion and accessibility of therapy during and after the pandemic was not without impact.

Between 2020 and 2023, COVID-19 consumed every corner of our culture, including my industry. Many therapists began to attribute every symptom to the virus. Some patients even told me that their previous therapists focused solely on COVID-19. One patient confided that he often felt as though he was counseling his therapist, who, for much of their time together, repeatedly mentioned how lonely she felt.

A patient of Asian descent told me her previous therapist spent an entire session focused on "microaggressions and Asian hate." The therapist was convinced the patient "must be feeling anxious," given the many news stories about Asian people being attacked and harassed by strangers who seemed to blame Eastern Asian people for the COVID-19 virus and resulting restrictions. However, this client wasn't worried about these attacks—at least, not until the therapist began focusing on them during their sessions. Ultimately, this therapist made the person feel worse, not better.

Another client told me about a previous therapist who kept bringing up far-fetched conspiracies regarding the origins of COVID-19. Yet a different patient shared how his therapist lectured him about vaccines and restrictions, making him feel guilty for not adhering. This therapist imposed strict rules and even refused to see any client who wasn't compliant with CDC guidelines, even though the sessions were remote. My patient was bewildered by this approach.

This hyperfocus by therapists often escalated the anxiety, loneliness, and anger people were already grappling with, deepening existing problems and divisions rather than easing them. Instead of fostering resilience, too much of the response encouraged fear, catastrophizing, and a constant sense of threat. In some cases, this went further, with unnecessary sessions framed as treatment for "pandemic trauma," blurring the line between care and financial self-interest.

Therapists can get caught up in that world of doomsaying themselves, and unfortunately, they can also use it to keep the schedules full.

In times of crisis, some therapists take advantage of the moment. They may instill fear in their patients to test their reactions—

a tendency I wrote about in my 2012 op-ed. Within the profession, I heard of therapists who projected their own uncertainty onto clients, saying things like, "We've never seen anything like this, so you need to see me more." It was hard to know whether they genuinely believed the world was collapsing and that the answer was three sessions a week—or whether they were simply protecting their billable hours. Both possibilities are damaging, and unfortunately, both are likely true.

Ultimately, therapists must remember their responsibility: to help patients build the emotional strength to face life's challenges, not to fuel hopelessness. The line between support and exploitation is a fine one and therapists must tread it carefully. Helping patients heal does not mean validating every fear or leaning into their anxieties. It means challenging them to rise above those fears and grow stronger.

It's crucial to be a voice of reason, not lean into the catastrophe. Remind them that while bad things have happened before, we've made it through just fine. There's so much in our world that feeds into catastrophizing; you shouldn't need your therapist to do that, too.

CHAPTER FIVE

THE RISE OF THERAPY NATION

Many years ago, those struggling with depression and anxiety often kept it hidden, weighed down by societal stigma and feelings of shame. Today, however, psychotherapy is discussed as casually as weight lifting or Pilates—it's entered the mainstream. Slogans like "find your center," "let it go," and "it's okay to not be okay" dominate social media feeds. Celebrities—including Olympic gymnast Simone Biles, swimmer Michael Phelps, tennis star Naomi Osaka, singer Selena Gomez, and rapper Megan Thee Stallion—have all publicly shared their mental health journeys.

Mental health influencers now claim that regular therapy sessions are as essential to well-being as hitting ten thousand steps, getting eight hours of sleep, or eating five servings of vegetables a day. Conversations with coworkers, friends, and even casual acquaintances frequently revolve around the latest insights from their therapy sessions.

This presents a unique opportunity for my profession. The need for healing has never been greater—whether it's mending societal divisions, fostering healthy friendships and human connections, revitalizing civil discourse, or equipping people with the tools to truly heal and thrive.

Sadly, as I have noted, many in my field are missing this critical moment. Instead of helping to unite people, a significant number of my colleagues—whether intentionally or not—are doing the opposite. Today, the phrase "My therapist says" has become an all-too-common excuse for bad behavior and poor decision-making.

- "My therapist says I have ADHD. That's why I'm always late." Translation: Rather than acknowledging that there might be underlying ADHD symptoms at play contributing to my chronic lateness (overscheduling, distraction), I'm accepting a label, hiding behind it, and never actually changing the behavior.
- "My therapist says my severe anxiety stems from my parents divorcing when I was a teenager. I really can't help it, so if you want to date me, you're going to have to get used to it." Translation: I had some hardships as a child that affected me deeply. But rather than trying to understand and improve, others must revolve around me and my issues.
- "My therapist says my entitlement stems from being an only child and used to getting my own way." Translation: I'm selfish and have a hard time relating to other people, and I blame it on childhood circumstances rather than taking action and trying to learn how to deal with things in a healthier way.

Similarly, "maybe you should talk to someone" is often a well-intentioned suggestion, but it has become so overused it is almost a cliché. Our culture seems to have forgotten the crucial difference between needing a professional therapist and simply needing a friend or a sympathetic ear when facing everyday challenges. Not every problem in life needs to be pathologized. Venting endlessly can reinforce problems rather than resolve them. Going in for a session might feel good in the moment, but it doesn't always provide direction or the tools to truly improve. In some ways, it's a form of positive reinforcement.

This distinction lies at the heart of the current issue in our nation of therapists and those they treat. In my practice, the goal is to help patients reach a point where they no longer need me. To achieve that, my approach isn't just about providing insight and a sounding board, as many of my colleagues do. Instead, it's about equipping patients with the tools, skills, and confidence they need to persevere and thrive on their own.

Therapy goes mainstream

Before the COVID-19 pandemic, a third of people who wanted mental health treatment couldn't access it. Instead, they white-knuckled their way through extreme bouts of depression and anxiety.[1]

These treatment gaps were especially prominent in rural areas, where there weren't enough therapists and other health care professionals. The poor also struggled, but for different reasons. They couldn't afford the therapy they needed and deserved.

Long before COVID-19 entered our lives, I believed that virtual mental health therapy—delivered via phone or computer—could close some of the service gaps in mental health care. The virtual shift could make it more affordable and accessible, especially for those with mobility issues or physical disabilities. My conviction grew even stronger in late 2023 and early 2024, after I was hit by a car while biking. I broke my leg and couldn't walk for ten weeks, which was a challenge not only for my body but also for my mental health. This experience gave me a deeper understanding of what life is like for those with mobility challenges or who are homebound.

Before COVID-19, only 2% of psychiatric and psychology services offered virtual therapy. The pandemic, however, forced practitioners to quickly pivot from in-person counseling to teletherapy. Health insurance companies were also forced to accept this new reality and cover virtual services provided by mental health providers. This could be due to the greater availability of online therapy, or the greater need caused by the unique stress of the pandemic—or most likely, both.

Undoubtedly, increased access to mental health treatment is a positive development. However, as more therapists have moved online in recent years, this has also produced unintended consequences. The unchecked rise of teletherapy has amplified some of the industry's long-standing problems—and created troubling new ones.

This rapid expansion of mental health therapy has also created space for underqualified practitioners peddling oversimplified, cookie-cutter advice. Some tell patients to count to ten whenever they feel anxious, as if that alone could solve life's deeper struggles. Others reduce every major issue to the same hollow mantra: "Just breathe." One therapist I know even suggested a patient tattoo those words on their inner wrist, a bizarrely permanent solution to a problem a sticky note could easily address.

While deep breathing can be helpful in managing stress, reducing complex problems to simple slogans does a disservice to patients who need real solutions.

Furthermore, the increased access has turned therapy into a kind of status symbol, one that disincentivizes true mental wellness and independence. More and more, patients proudly wear their poor mental health like a badge of honor. They flood social media with videos and status updates about their struggles, bragging about working eighty hours a week, sleeping only four hours a night, and managing endless stress. Many obnoxiously proclaim a slew of diagnoses—bipolar disorder, generalized anxiety disorder (GAD), post-traumatic stress disorder (PTSD), panic disorder, attention deficit hyperactivity disorder (ADHD)—often without any formal diagnosis at all.

It's beyond the point of people taking solace in mutual struggle—now, people are almost competitive about it. The constant stream of likes, shares, and attention reinforces the idea that being unwell is not only acceptable but admirable. In this environment, genuine recovery and resilience are no longer the goal; victimhood is.

This behavior also sends a message that mental health issues are more common than they are, encouraging people to self-diagnose conditions they don't have. One patient, after watching an online video about ADHD, insisted he had it, even though he had never been screened. Following a thorough evaluation, I concluded that he was simply overwhelmed by a sudden increase in workload after a colleague's departure.

Failing to complete tasks is one symptom of ADHD, but a diagnosis requires at least five of nine symptoms persisting for six months or more. Context matters, too. In this case, the patient was facing an unexpected spike in responsibilities, a normal reaction, not a disorder. The real solution involved helping him organize his work and advocate for additional support, not chasing a self-diagnosis or medication.

I've seen patients insist they have a range of conditions without formal diagnosis, and when an excess of people claim these labels because it "feels right," it diminishes and dilutes the experience of those who are truly diagnosed.

Invariably, I find myself reminding them that having a bad day—or even a rough few days—does not amount to a diagnosis of major depression. Feeling anxious before a deadline or starting a new job is normal; it doesn't mean you have GAD. Struggling to finish your work during a busy period doesn't mean you have ADHD. Often, it simply means you need better organizational and time management skills.

The pros and cons of online mental health care

During a traditional in-person session, you meet with your therapist in a private office for forty-five to fifty minutes.

In contrast, tele–mental health sessions are typically offered in one of three ways: video calls, phone calls, or live (or delayed) chats via text or email.

I'm not opposed to these options. They make therapy more convenient and accessible. You don't have to spend half an hour commuting to your appointment, and it's easier to fit therapy into a busy workday. For those living in areas with few mental health resources, virtual therapy provides access that might not have been available otherwise.

Those are real advantages. Still, some remote options are more effective than others.

Video Therapy

For people interested in teletherapy, video sessions are closest to in-person appointments. That's because therapy delivered through a computer screen can be as effective as in-person, as research tells us.[2, 3] Video-based sessions tend to follow the same format as in-person therapy sessions. They allow both the therapist and the patient to hear one another's tone of voice and see one another's facial expressions and body language. That matters. Your therapist can use those cues to decide when to push you to go deeper—as well as know whether it's time to back off. Over time, this give and take draws you and the therapist closer, creating a trusting space where you feel welcome to share what's on your mind.

Referred to as the "therapeutic alliance," this rapport is critical to treatment success. According to research, having a relationship with a warm, respectful therapist with high expectations for patient success is the most essential ingredient for healing—and it's what all effective therapies share in common.[4]

Phone-Based Therapy

Like video sessions, phone therapy allows you and your therapist to pick up on one another's tone of voice. However, because you can't see each other's facial expressions, it can be harder to build the all-important therapeutic alliance I mentioned earlier.

That said, some patients prefer phone therapy. It gives them the freedom to take a session while on the move—such as walking outdoors, where they can speak freely without worrying about prying ears at home or work. Many of my clients favor this method for exactly that reason.

Text-Based Therapy

Are you okay having a therapy session the same way you handle online tech support (and possibly provided by the same foreign call centers)? Therapy by text involves messaging your therapist in a secure chat window whenever needed. Depending on the setup, the therapist generally responds once or twice a day.

In some cases, text-based therapy is delivered by therapists who follow standardized templates—a system not unlike those used by telemarketers or help desk attendants. I discovered this firsthand when I applied to one of these online therapy companies, not to work there but to see how it operated. Rather than relying on my clinical training and judgment, I was told I'd be expected to respond to client messages using preapproved scripts that followed a set formula. A typical exchange might look something like this:

Therapist: "How do you feel today?"

Client: "I'm pretty depressed."

Therapist: "I'm sorry you are depressed. How long have you felt that way?"

And on it went. There was no room for improvisation, and nothing was tailored to the unique needs of the client. It was a prefabricated, one-size-fits-all approach that attempted to standardize therapy.

In other cases, this prescribed set of responses isn't delivered by humans. Instead, you interact with a chatbot trained to provide mental health information and support. These artificial intelligence (AI) bots check in on people during set intervals. They then process and respond to your texts and emojis by using a computerized decision tree.

The people who design these tools say they help reduce the feeling of being judged, allowing patients to be more forthcoming than they would be with a human therapist. However, in my opinion, they're no substitute for an actual human. Keep in mind that, in Belgium, a man died by suicide after conversing with a chatbot named ELIZA about his climate change anxieties—and she clearly brought him little comfort.[5] (The chatbot company was not charged with any wrongdoing in connection with his death). "Without these conversations with the chatbot, my husband would still be here," the man's widow told the Belgian news outlet La Libre.

Even more troubling is the rise of AI in the hands of inexperienced therapists. Several just a few years into their careers have told me they rely on AI apps to diagnose patients and even script their responses. This strips therapy of its most essential element: human connection. It sends both patient and therapist down a dangerous path.

But the rise of AI therapy isn't random. It's a direct response to how ineffective much of modern therapy has become. AI offers what many human therapists don't—clarity, structure, and outcomes. In a field increasingly defined by aimless validation and endless process, people are turning to machines simply because they want results. According to a 2023 PEW study, 23% of adults report using an AI based therapist. In 2025 this increased to 50%.[6]

Unlike therapy delivered via video, text-based therapy with a human hasn't been well studied—and chatbot therapy even less so. Of the scant research studies on text-based therapy with a human, most were poorly designed. They either lacked a control group, had very small sample sizes, or were sponsored by a text-based mental health company.[7, 8, 9] Studies on chatbot therapy are even more rare. Because of design issues with the few studies we have, it's difficult to know whether text-based mental health services offer any true benefits.

On the other hand, there's lots of evidence showing this form of therapy may pose real harm.

However, the biggest issue with text therapy is the business model behind it. Text-based mental health therapy tends to be offered by start-ups that are owned by private equity firms. These companies often incentivize profit and growth over evidence and excellence.

According to whistleblowers who have worked for these companies, therapists are often forced to manage an overwhelming client load, making it hard to remember and document details from one session to the next.[10, 11, 12] Unlike tech support, your therapist, whether human or an AI chatbot, should be entirely focused on you. If they are juggling multiple patients, you will not get the attention you need and deserve. This only adds to the poor quality of "therapy" you are receiving.

It's not that text-based therapy is necessarily always harmful. Writing can be therapeutic, and in some cases, communicating by text may offer temporary relief. But for real healing and meaningful progress, in-person sessions—or at minimum, video or phone sessions—are usually necessary.

Therapeutic overuse and dependency

Constant, around-the-clock access to a therapist may sound reassuring, but it can have troubling consequences. The first is that it fosters dependence. To see how this plays out, consider how we approach problems of the body rather than the mind.

If you saw a physical therapist for knee pain, they would likely give you a set of exercises and stretches. During your sessions, they'd show you how to perform them properly. Over time, they'd monitor your progress, correcting your technique as needed. As your pain decreased and your mastery of the rehab plan grew, your therapist would eventually discharge you—leaving you responsible for maintaining your progress on your own. After I broke my leg, my physical therapist made the goal clear: Build strength, restore mobility, and regain flexibility. With consistent effort, I recovered—and we parted ways when my therapy was no longer necessary.

That's how psychotherapy should work, too. In the first session, the therapist should conduct a comprehensive evaluation. For example, during an initial session with a patient, I ask dozens of questions to better understand them—their problems, their history, and their goals. I inquire about medical issues, medications, lifestyle habits (diet, exercise, sleep, and substance use), support systems, career, family, and, of course, mental health. I then summarize my impressions to give the patient a clear understanding of what's happening. Together, we establish specific, reasonable, actionable goals for treatment.

In the sessions that follow, I provide suggestions and tools to help the patient move toward those goals, while carefully monitoring their progress. As they improve, I deliberately space out our meetings—weekly sessions become biweekly, then monthly. This gradual transition helps patients build autonomy and confidence, so they no longer feel dependent on me. Eventually, they graduate from therapy and move forward on their own.

This pattern should be the norm for most patients. But I've heard enough from so many different clients that I'm concerned this is now the exception. And it's not just the patients who have told me this. Some colleagues have told me about their "deep work with clients that goes on for years"—but they're describing an average anxious client, not someone with profound mental health issues. To many people, psychotherapy is increasingly becoming an open-ended saga from which they never escape. There's no treatment plan and no end date in sight. Instead, the client shows up session after session to vent and be heard, but makes no actual progress.

Some therapists instill fear in patients if they want to leave, saying, "If you stop therapy, you'll become more depressed," or "If you stop seeing me, you'll fall apart." This could even be characterized as psychological extortion. Others even force patients to commit to rigid, routine weekly sessions for an extended time, and then once these dates are locked in, patients who try to postpone or cancel any of them can face financial penalties. Let's be honest: How can someone know how they might feel months from now? Things change, and ideally, patients feel better much sooner! My advice: If you have a therapist who uses these practices, fire him or her.

This endless therapy issue is especially rampant when the service is offered by large online practices. Rather than pay for each session as you go, these app-based therapy options charge weekly or monthly fees. In exchange, you get an unlimited amount of therapy. You can message or chat with your therapist at any time. These offers are deceptive because they seem like the deals of a lifetime. In reality, like the fourth trip to an all-you-can-eat buffet, there can be too much of a good thing.

The all-you-can-talk therapy model encourages patients to lean on their therapists way too much. By continually turning to a therapist for help every single time a need arises, a patient may feel unequipped to make decisions, take risks, try tools, and manage symptoms *without the hand-holding of their therapist.* There's no space for building confidence. Instead, they continually second-guess themselves and fear doing anything before consulting with their therapist. They might even think of their therapist constantly, repeatedly wondering what they might think of what they just experienced. This therapy fosters dependence and makes them weaker, not stronger.

On TikTok, Instagram, and YouTube, you'll find video clip after video clip of people admitting that they consult their therapist before making just about any decision in life.

Not sure if you should cancel lunch plans with a friend? Ask your therapist.

Not sure how to handle a work situation? Ask your therapist.

Not sure whether to send your mother a birthday card or a bouquet of flowers? Ask your therapist.

In many ways, people are unknowingly held hostage by the all-you-can-talk therapy model. Instead of practicing the tools discussed in sessions—such as reframing negative thoughts or using grounding techniques—patients often reach out to their therapist at the first sign of distress, no matter how minor. True healing requires practice and perseverance outside the therapy room. But increasingly, therapy is becoming the instinctual (and often only) response to everyday struggles. This dynamic fosters a cycle of dependence that keeps patients stuck rather than helping them move forward.

But that, of course, is the plan. This dependence is exactly what the financial backers of these apps and services aim to create—they want you to keep paying for access to something you've come to rely on almost like a lifeline. In this regard, it mirrors the worst practices of in-person therapy, but with the added dopamine hits from a glowing screen.

By turning therapy into yet another activity performed while staring at a phone, they have reduced it to bite-sized content and shallow interactions. These social media–style traps are designed to monetize real anxieties and emotional struggles, exploiting vulnerability for clicks and revenue. What gets lost in the process is the depth and rigor of real therapy, including careful listening, nuanced guidance, and the hard work that leads to meaningful change.

Therapizing the well

Therapy is now widely viewed as a lifelong habit, a routine part of maintaining mental and physical health. Its constant presence, and the casual way it is discussed and assumed to be universal, carries consequences of its own. While this normalization can encourage people to seek help when they need it, it has also fueled a troubling trend: the rise of amateur diagnosis. Clinical terms and mental health labels are now tossed around casually, often by people with no training and little appreciation for their weight or potential harm.

Healing for the mind should be approached like medicine for the body: only when something is truly wrong. Just as we do not take antibiotics for a minor scrape, therapy should not be treated as a default response to life's ordinary discomforts. By shifting how you view therapy and how you engage with your therapist, you could not only feel better but also build true independence and avoid the financial and emotional costs of overtreatment. For most people, treating mental health checkups like an annual physical, with a wellness visit to a qualified therapist once a year, makes sense. This allows for perspective, early detection of real issues, and practical guidance without creating dependency.

The problem begins when therapy is overused. Without a serious mental health condition, repeated sessions can paradoxically make people feel worse. You might walk in one day feeling like you have had a productive, happy week, only to have your therapist dig into your childhood, workplace grievances, or relationships, searching for hidden problems that may not exist. What begins as a positive encounter can spiral into an excavation of pain and negativity, reinforcing the idea that you are never finished or capable on your own.

I have heard therapists say, "There is always work to be done." That mindset does not empower patients; it traps them in perpetual self-analysis and dependency. Therapy should give people the tools to move forward on their own, not keep them locked in an endless cycle of self-examination.

As a result, you might endlessly ruminate about that time during childhood when your brother read your diary out loud in front of your friends. As you dissect this ancient memory, you find yourself feeling enraged. "I thought I forgave him," you might tell the therapist. Now you see there's still anger, and the more you talk about it and focus on it, the bigger the anger gets. Perhaps this incident takes on a greater importance, and you begin to blame your brother as the root of other issues in your own life. This line of thinking is often a recipe for more problems.

That's because rumination—the repetitive dwelling on negative feelings and experiences—has been linked with increased rates of depression and anxiety. When people ruminate, they focus more on negative events and less on positive ones, and become preoccupied with problems. But expending all of this brain energy on problems doesn't usually come up with creative ways to solve them. Ultimately, it just leads to most people feeling hopeless.[13]

Instead of therapy-endorsed rumination, often what you most need to do is the opposite. To feel better, you should *stop* thinking about the adverse event, especially if you've already processed it and made amends. But that's hard to remember when your therapist keeps asking you about it, session after session. That's what most therapists are trained to do.[14]

In this way, overtherapizing can make people sicker, not better. It can worsen grudges, lead to new obsessions, and cause people to endlessly self-reflect over childhood experiences and pain that bring them no new understanding or productive value. By endlessly dissecting anger, grief, loneliness, trauma, anxiety, and other negativities, patients make these problems bigger and more intense, continually feeling worse as a result.

Therapy can be one of the most effective ways to help someone feel better when it is guided by a solid plan of action. But it is not healthy to keep deep-diving into the same issues and leaving each session feeling worse. If you find yourself caught in that spiral, it may be time to step back, call it quits, or seek out a therapist who offers a more practical and results-focused approach.

Trapping people in endless therapy

With many wellness pursuits—including healthy eating, exercise, or getting adequate sleep—the benefits add up the longer and more intensely you do them. For example, for overall health and longevity, three daily servings of veggies are better than two, two are better than one, and one is better than none. Another example: Walking for thirty minutes daily for two weeks will likely benefit your health a little. However, walking thirty minutes every day for a year will benefit your health a lot more.

In contrast, there's no measurable benefit of long-term (or endless) psychotherapy over short-term or time-limited therapy.

Of course, the time needed in therapy will vary from one patient to another. Those with more intense problems may need more sessions, others fewer. According to the American Psychological Association, about half of people undergo fifteen to twenty sessions, with some staying in therapy much, much longer.[15] You likely know someone, even with mild psychological issues, who has been in therapy seemingly forever, with no end date. As I pointed out back in my 2012 *Times* article, this long-term use of therapy often turns into a dead-end relationship.

Contrary to what many believe, the longer therapy lasts, the less likely it is to be effective. There's abundant research that explains this. For a study published in the *Journal of Consulting and Clinical Psychology*, researchers assessed mental health in 1,868 patients before and after a set number of therapy sessions. The percentage of clients who got better *decreased* as the number of therapy sessions *increased*. A stunning 88% were improved after one session of therapy, but that percentage dropped to 62% after twelve sessions.[16]

Another analysis of 26,430 patients who completed questionnaires at the start and end of therapy determined that shorter treatment was more likely to lead to recovery than longer-term treatment.[17] Additionally, a review of nineteen studies involving 3,447 people determined that shorter-term therapy and longer-term therapy led to similar results—in other words, being in therapy for twelve months offered no added benefit over being in therapy for six, for example. Three years of therapy was no better than twenty weeks. Anxiety and depression symptoms were similar regardless of time spent.[18] Think about the massive strain on society this all has. Just extrapolate those rates of success across the entire population of people in therapy and imagine how many anxious, frustrated people bad therapy has unleashed on the world.

Proponents of long-term therapy tend to argue that severe psychological disorders require years to manage. That may be true, but many therapy patients don't suffer severe disorders. Instead, they seek help for discrete, treatable issues. They're stuck in unfulfilling jobs or relationships. Maybe they can't reach their goals, are fearful of change, and are depressed as a result. It doesn't take years of therapy to get to the bottom of those kinds of problems.

While there's no one-size-fits-all, and no one knows the ideal amount of time needed for beneficial psychotherapy, one thing is clear: Endless psychotherapy is a waste of time and money at best, and harmful at worst.

Still, therapists seem to cling to their clients, despite them making little to no progress. I continually hear from clients who were encouraged by previous therapists to stay in therapy long-term. One forty-five-year-old woman was having communication issues with her spouse. Instead of looking objectively at the relationship and teaching the client to more effectively communicate, the therapist went down a path of blaming the patient's mother for her problems. During each session, the patient was encouraged to hyper-focus on how badly her mom raised her. As a result, hatred and resentment grew.

The tactic of identifying a "nemesis" on whom to blame all their patient's problems is a common tactic for bad therapists. They may do it out of laziness or lack of skill, or because they never challenge their patient's initial assertions about this person in order to get to the real root of the patient's problem. Ultimately, this doesn't do any good—it doesn't help the patient with their own issues, and it certainly doesn't help them fix their relationship with their supposed nemesis. The family dynamic, and everyone in it, remains stuck.

In the case of the forty-five-year-old woman, her therapist began to position herself as a maternal figure, reinforcing the patient's growing sense of animosity. Over time, the woman started to wear her "traumatic" childhood like a badge of honor, central to her identity. After four years of endlessly dissecting her past, she decided it was time to scale back on therapy. When she raised the idea, her therapist warned, "You need to keep seeing me, or your marriage will fall apart."

At that point, a friend referred the patient to me. During our first session together, it became clear that the patient didn't have the best relationship with her mother, who often commented negatively on the patient's hair, weight, and clothing. Her mother wasn't perfect—and while it's hard for any parent to be perfect, perhaps she was even hypercritical. However, as everything came out, it appeared that mother's behavior fell mostly into the category of insensitive and curt. It wasn't abusive.

After initially discussing it, I told the patient I did not want to spend multiple sessions rehashing her childhood or dissecting every grievance she had with her mother. The goal was not to defend or excuse her mother's behavior, but to help the patient stop ruminating in a way that was damaging her life, particularly her marriage. I wanted her to shift her focus away from her mother and toward her relationship with her spouse, as well as on the changes she could make within herself.

After the patient learned and practiced assertive communication skills, she was able to ask her mother to stop commenting on her weight, and her mother agreed. In her marriage, she eventually admitted she had not been the best listener, largely because she was so preoccupied with herself and her issues with her mother. This had left her spouse feeling unheard and misunderstood. Within a few months of therapy, the patient told me she was feeling much better. All her relationships had improved, including those with her spouse and mother. At that point, I discharged her because she no longer needed my help.

Another case was a thirty-year-old man who had been seeing his therapist for six months. By this point, he expected to feel at least somewhat less anxious and better overall, but he didn't. His therapist acted as a sounding board, offering nothing more than the occasional "How does that make you feel?" without providing any insight or actionable steps to help him address his anxiety. After each session, the therapist would say, "See you next week," with no progress made. Frustrated with the lack of direction, the man finally asked for tools to manage his anxiety. The therapist responded with the same phrase: "See you next week." At that point, the patient attempted to end the relationship, but the therapist warned him with a familiar refrain: "If you stop seeing me, you'll sink into a deep depression, and your anxiety will get worse."

The man Googled "How long should people be in therapy?" and came across my 2012 *New York Times* opinion piece, "In

Therapy Forever? Enough Already." Intrigued, he searched for my name, found my contact information, and reached out to set up an appointment.

In our sessions, we focused on his anxiety—how often it occurred, and how it affected him. We quickly pinpointed the source: his work. His industry was cybersecurity sales, a high-pressure field where making presentations to colleagues and potential clients on the latest technologies was crucial for career success. The anxiety stemmed from a fear of judgment and criticism, causing him to tense up before and during his presentations. As a result, his performance faltered, which further eroded his self-esteem and broader sense of identity.

We decided to focus on a specific, trainable skill: public speaking. I believed that if he could gain more confidence in delivering the presentations central to his job, his satisfaction at work and his overall sense of self-worth would improve. After a few sessions honing his skills, he approached his sales presentations with a completely new mindset.

The results were nearly immediate. He successfully landed key clients and was eventually promoted to a senior role. After about eight sessions, I felt he had reached the point where he no longer needed me, so we concluded our work together.

I've seen similar stories countless times—patients who remain stuck in therapy far past the point of meaningful progress, endlessly spinning their wheels, only to end up with worsened mental health.

Why continue to see a so-called expert if you're not getting better? Would you continue to see a hairdresser if you didn't like the cut you received? Would you continue to see the same mechanic if they weren't fixing your car?

Psychotherapists should operate like other health professionals—creating clear treatment plans with an end date.

If a client falls apart the moment they don't have constant access to their therapist, the therapist is most likely the problem. It's a sign they've failed to equip the client with the tools necessary to function independently. Therapy should not just be about alleviating distress—it's about empowering clients to handle their challenges on their own. In the early stages, clients may rely heavily on their therapists, particularly if they're recovering from bad therapy or have never had effective treatment before. But as sessions progress, the role of the therapist should shift toward teaching clients how to make their own decisions, solve their own problems, and navigate life's challenges with confidence.

Clients should not need to seek their therapist's approval on trivial matters—like what to wear to a party or where to take a friend for dinner. They should be able to handle ordinary anxiety without rushing to schedule an emergency session. Real growth only happens when clients have the freedom to stumble, fall, and learn from their mistakes. The true mark of success for a therapist is not the length of time a client remains in therapy, but when they are able to leave, stronger, more resilient, and capable of facing life's challenges without looking back.

Sadly, some therapists fear this outcome and view it as a threat to their practice. That mentality must change. It is not only possible but deeply rewarding to witness a client's journey to independence. Seeing them graduate from therapy and step into the world as a stronger, more secure version of themselves is one of the greatest successes a therapist can achieve.

CHAPTER SIX

HOW THERAPY TURNED INTO A SOCIAL JUSTICE CRUSADE

Imagine a woman who has a near miss with an 18-wheeler on the highway. Shaken but unharmed, she brushes it off, until the anxiety sets in. At first, it's only near the site of the incident. Then it spreads. Soon she can't drive on highways at all. Eventually, she stops driving altogether.

With public transportation spotty, she's forced to quit her job. She can't visit her mother, who lives two hours away. Her world shrinks.

Determined to reclaim her independence, she finds a therapist with stellar reviews. Too anxious to drive, she calls a taxi to the appointment, hopeful this will be the first step back to freedom.

She isn't prepared, though, for what happens next. Instead of focusing on her fear of driving, the therapist launches into a series of questions about her gender and race:

"How do you feel as a woman driver on the road with all those aggressive guy drivers?"

"What is it like for you, a White woman, to get behind the wheel of a car?"

"How do negative stereotypes about women drivers affect how you feel on the road?"

Eventually, the therapist even asks:

"I'm sure you have a lot on your mind given all of these antiabortion bills being passed in our state. Do you feel they are contributing to your oppressed status as a woman?"

Confused, the woman says, "I'm sorry. I'm not trying to be disrespectful, but I don't understand what those questions have to do with my desire to conquer my fear of driving."

That's when the therapist snaps: "Are you here to do the work? Because if you're not, I have plenty of other patients who are. We need to dismantle the system of white supremacy if we ever want to see positive change. I'm running a White affinity group. You should join. It will help you understand your privileged role as a White woman and how that impacts systems of oppression."

Bewildered and deflated, she leaves feeling worse than when she arrived.

As bizarre as this may sound, it really happened to someone I know. And sadly, it's not an isolated case. Stories like this are becoming alarmingly common, and they reveal a disturbing trend inside the world of therapy. And I hear more and more stories from patients and others who share similar experiences with therapists intensely focused on issues of race and gender, tying everything back to oppression.

It's not surprising to hear that therapists take this tack. After all, graduate school counseling programs are training the next generation of practitioners to focus *more* on social justice and dismantling what they label as systems of oppression, while paying less attention to the actual goals that bring patients into therapy.

Universities are, in part, responsible for turning out woke ideologues masquerading as therapists. Regardless of whether someone is struggling to communicate with their spouse or face a difficult situation at work, these social justice therapists continually steer in-therapy conversations toward race, gender, sex, sexual orientation, ability, religion, and other identities. The goal: Force clients to awaken to their privileged or oppressed status. This growing social justice movement has taken over school curriculums, continuing education credit programs, training sessions, and treatment programs—and they're doing an incredible amount of harm.

A brief and unsettling history of woke therapy

If you go far enough back in time, you'll find many examples of mental health professionals being on the wrong side of history.

For example, in the 1840s, some mental health professionals claimed that free Black people who lived in northern cities experienced higher rates of mental illness than enslaved Black people. According to this argument, Black people lacked the fortitude to deal with owning property, running businesses, civic engagement, and the other stressors of free life. These mental health professionals even coined an official diagnosis—Drapetomania, or runaway slave syndrome—to describe this phenomenon. These professionals then argued that freedom was too much for Black people to bear. Therefore, it was more humane to round up free Black people and re-enslave them.[1]

There are, of course, many other embarrassing and regretful historical instances of this. During the Civil Rights Movement of the 1960s, many psychiatrists diagnosed their Black clients in the Jim Crow South as having "neurotic hostility" rather than taking the time to understand their unique experiences. (The American Psychiatric Association has since issued an apology.)[2]

These stains on the psychological profession eventually led to "multicultural counseling," which recommended mental health specialists undergo cultural competency training to better understand and be empathetic to the experiences of a diverse range of clients. According to research, these types of training sessions do have some benefit for patients. Data from seventy-eight studies involving 13,998 participants found that people who saw culturally competent therapists were 4.7 times more likely to experience remission from their symptoms.[3] Because of this data, multicultural counseling went from fringe to mainstream. The American Psychological Association and American Counseling Association now require accredited graduate programs to include classes on multicultural topics.

This was a well-intentioned idea meant to address real historical wrongs. The mental health profession cannot be effective for all patients unless we recognize everyone's shared humanity. Empathy is at the core of what we do. But over time, like many good ideas, this one has become dangerously distorted in parts of the profession. Cultural competency is important, but when it grows into an exercise in evaluating and categorizing therapists and patients based on demographics or "privilege," the trust and empathy that is so central to good therapy can start to break down. When therapists are taught to base their practice around categorizing themselves and others, the profession can become a divisive force, and we can start to lose the focus on shared humanity that cultural competencies were first intended to protect. And the effects from that can ripple out into the wider society in negative ways.

"The center of all counseling"

Standards for multicultural counseling were first developed in the 1990s and today have morphed into the Multicultural and Social Justice Counseling Competencies (MSJCC). They are expressed in a sacred text of modern therapy, developed by a committee of academics and adopted by the American Counseling Association in 2015. "At the core," the authors state, "is the belief that multiculturalism and social justice should be at the center of all counseling."[4]

To do this, therapists are instructed to consult an elaborate rubric that sorts both them and their patients into "privileged" and "marginalized" categories. These designations are then supposed to guide how the two relate. One MSJCC example describes a heterosexual woman of color seeking treatment from a gay man of color. The framework suggests they may share a "common experience" around racism because of their racial identities. But then the rubric requires them to factor in their relative "privilege." The client, they note, might feel "displaced and at a disadvantage because of the counselor's male privilege." Or, just as the model allows, "the counselor may be placed at a disadvantage because of the client's heterosexual privileges."[5]

This absurd exercise is inherently divisive. Slapping labels on each other and forcing people to view one another through those lenses risks damaging the therapist-patient relationship before it even begins. Not to mention, it's a colossal waste of time. My job when meeting a patient for the first time is to understand them as an individual—not to compare our relative privilege or marginalization based on demographic characteristics. I want to know what's bothering the person in front of me and what they need help with. If their race or gender factors into the issue for which they've sought my help, they'll bring it up, and we'll incorporate that into our work together. But plotting each other on a privilege chart before we even begin the session is not going to help.

That, of course, is not how social justice counselors see it. They view the role of therapy entirely differently. In addition to framing the patient-therapist relationship around their respective privileges, the MSJCC includes an exhaustive list of what they believe the duties of a social justice–minded counselor should be. These include "seeking out formal and informal opportunities to engage in discourse about historical events and current issues that shape the worldview, cultural background, values, beliefs, biases, and experiences of privileged and marginalized clients."[6] This suggests that if the client doesn't bring up issues of identity, it's the therapist's job to do so for them.

They advocate for "empowerment-based theories" that will supposedly "address internalized privilege experienced by privileged clients and internalized oppression experienced by marginalized clients."[7] Presumably, everyone's relative "privilege" or "marginalization" can be determined by MSJCC's own elaborate rubric. They direct therapists to examine "the degree to which historical events, current issues, and power, privilege and oppression contribute to the presenting problems expressed by privileged and marginalized clients."[8] If a patient thinks some aspect of history is directly impacting them and wants to talk about it, I would be happy to address it, but in most cases I would generally work to reframe the discussion about concrete actions they can take in their life in the present. But if I, in my practice, followed the MSJCC recommendations and proactively tried to turn my sessions into history lessons, I would imagine most of my patients would—quite understandably—ask for their money back.

Some of the MSJCC ideas could be interpreted as instigating or worsening the kind of societal fracturing we see around us, and about which I've warned in this book. They want therapists to "take initiative to explore with privileged and marginalized clients regarding how community norms, values, and regulations are embedded in society that hinder and contribute to their growth and development."[9] Again, my approach is to focus on aspects of my patients' inner and outer lives that they can control. If someone wants to spend their time advocating for changing "norms, values, and regulations" in society, they're welcome to—but I would be doing my patients a disservice if I focused blame for their problems on those things. That won't help them in their daily life. And just what hindering "norms" do they want to change? It's a societal norm, for instance, to maintain good relations with family members despite differences of opinion. When mental health professionals like Dr. Amanda Calhoun publicly advocate for cutting off family members because of how they vote, is this the sort of norm challenging that the MSJCC seems to endorse?

I can't see how more divisive behavior for the sake of challenging "norms, values, and regulations" will make things any better.

Perhaps most damagingly, the MSJCC guidelines advocate blatantly for bringing political activism into the counseling profession. They want us to "initiate discussions with privileged and marginalized clients regarding how they shape and are shaped by local, state, and federal laws and policies."[10] They again make it the therapist's duty to "initiate" these conversations, pivoting blame to an outside system and working to tie that to our patients' everyday problems with jobs, relationships, and the like. They want therapists to take on an activist role outside the office, too, urging them to "engage in social action to alter the local, state, and federal laws and policies that benefit privileged clients at the expense of marginalized clients" and "assist with creating local, state, and federal laws and policies that promote multiculturalism and social justice."[11] Therapists, like everyone else, of course have the right and freedom to support any cause they choose. If a patient gained positive feelings of power and purpose from engaging in political activity, any good therapist would support them in that. But everything I've seen at both the clinical and national level suggests that turning the therapist's office itself into an incubator of political activism—as the MSJCC guidelines seem to suggest—is making things worse, not better.

In the full MSJCC guide, there are more than one hundred such demands. In the years since these were adopted, we have seen a greater emphasis on social justice in counseling and psychology programs at the expense of clinical skills. This shift has made counseling more politically charged, biased, and heavy-handed, prioritizing societal change over client well-being.

Therapists are increasingly taught to view patients not as individuals, but as members of societal groups. Rather than focusing on a patient's specific issues, social justice counseling (SJC) therapists diagnose them based on their perceived oppressed or privileged status. These therapists often steer conversations with Black patients toward racism, with female patients toward sexism, and with disabled patients toward ableism. For queer patients, the focus shifts to homophobia or transphobia, and so on. By framing their clients' problems within a "system of oppression," these therapists aim to help clients achieve what they call "critical consciousness"—a fancy way of saying that their struggles are rooted in their oppressed status.

You might wonder: What happens if a patient is wealthy, White, and straight? In that case, an SJC therapist typically directs the conversation toward the patient's privileged status and their role as an oppressor. This framework isn't limited to wealthy individuals, either. Even poor or working-class White people are often still viewed as race privileged in the SJC model.

No doubt those who developed these guidelines believed they were fostering empathy, which is, of course, essential in the patient-therapist relationship. But mandating division and shifting the focus from the individual patient to "historical events and current issues" as a routine part of therapy is not the answer. While there are certainly scenarios where these factors are relevant to a patient's concerns, assuming they apply to everyone based solely on their demographics is highly reductive and nonsensical.

The vast majority of people will not benefit from "engaging in discourse" about history or politics with their therapist, or from exploring how "community norms, values, and regulations embedded in society" are to blame for their personal problems.

Similarly, if colleagues of mine want to use their off-work hours to "engage in social action" or try to change laws they find oppressive, that's their right as Americans.

But the therapy office isn't a political battleground. Inside those four walls, the focus should remain entirely on the patient's needs—not the therapist's personal activism or agenda. I feel it's more important that my profession focus on changing lives, rather than changing laws.

The more people who are subjected to therapy steeped in this rhetoric, the more divided and unhappy our society will become.

The politicization of counseling education

If you had looked at the web pages and marketing materials for counseling schools across the United States in early 2025, you would have been able to quickly see how SJC had woven its way into curricula. For example, at that time, the University of Vermont in Burlington's counseling program webpage stated that graduates "believe that our role of counseling in the community is to identify and redress processes of oppression to promote equity and justice. These core beliefs are emulated throughout our program objectives and curricular experiences."[12]

But that statement mysteriously disappeared from the school's website during the spring of 2025. This may be due to many institutions' reconsidering their "woke" or DEI-based programming in response to Donald Trump's reelection and his administration's subsequent actions. At least, they made certain public-facing changes. However, the University of Vermont student handbook from the 2024–2025 year lists a three-credit course in Diversity & Intersectionality described as follows:

> This course is designed to assist students in recognizing and acknowledging diversity in society, and developing the knowledge and skills to recognize, interrupt and redress inequity within their spheres of influence. Specifically, we will take an intersectional lens to examine the cultural forces and legacies that shape our view of others and systemically advantage some while disadvantaging others. We will explore theories and models that address alterity and identify and develop individual counseling skills and systemic advocacy processes needed to address institutional and social barriers that impede access, equity, and success

> for clients and students. This course is relational, experiential, and designed to engender discomfort as well as empowerment.[13]

At that time, Vanderbilt University's Master's program in Human Development Counseling affirmed: "We integrate diversity, social justice, and multicultural competence into our courses, clinical supervision, and co-curricular activities. Our training emphasizes core counseling values, unconditional positive regard, cultural humility, developmental sensitivity, avoiding harm and value imposition, decolonizing counseling, and advocating for social justice at individual, group, institutional, and societal levels to support growth and development."[14]

Like the University of Vermont, these statements have since been removed from the website.

At Rollins College in Winter Park, Florida, social justice is one of the main principles listed for the Master's in Clinical Mental Health Counseling program.[15]

At Columbia University's Teachers College in New York City, marketing materials boast that the faculty "place significant emphasis on the importance of social justice, multiculturalism, and diversity."[16]

The Wright Institute in Berkeley, California, says its Master's in Counseling program is "Grounded in principles of social justice" and offers "a profoundly multicultural perspective."[17]

In several other graduate counseling programs I've encountered, the marketing materials emphasize social justice, multiculturalism, and diversity. A colleague of mine, Alexandra, who completed one such program in New York City, recalled professors urging her to examine "the violence of whiteness" and her "need to protect white men." When she questioned that framing, she felt she was viewed as "problematic" and even told she might be "better suited for corporate America."

Finally, Antioch University—which has six campuses that specialize in eight academic areas, including counseling, education, and nursing—claims it provides "learner-centered education to empower students with the knowledge and skills to lead meaningful lives and to advance social, racial, economic, and environmental justice."[18]

Antioch University's Master's in Clinical Mental Health Counseling program says its mission is devoted to "endorsing the principles of social justice by confronting oppression and injustice and working with underserved populations."[19]

Unfortunately, I believe these schools *aren't* helping future counselors understand their clients better. Arguably, in our current climate, they're doing the opposite—teaching them to automatically sort patients who belong to any minority group as victims and those who are White, wealthy, or straight (or some combination) as oppressors. Instead of fostering real understanding, they're equipping students with what I view as a narrow, reductionist view that promotes and perpetuates harmful stereotypes.

At schools like Antioch, social justice is much more than an elective available to interested students. In 2024, the topic was *required*, and it infiltrated the curriculum. So, rather than primarily training future *counselors*, these schools are arguably training future *activists*—and that's problematic.

In 2023, a former Antioch graduate student, Leslie Elliott, filed a $4.32 million civil rights lawsuit, claiming Antioch retaliated against her for criticizing the school's diversity, equity, and inclusion (DEI) policies. After she'd already enrolled, Elliott claims Antioch changed its policies to require students to adhere to DEI principles and to sign a civility pledge as a requirement to graduate.[20, 21] After refusing to sign the pledge, Elliott released a series of YouTube videos critical of Antioch's curriculum. In one, Elliott claims, "Antioch has almost entirely replaced classical notions of education and psychology with social justice ideology."[22, 23, 24]

According to Elliott, the school teaches students to:

- Be an activist for social justice.
- Use Pamela Hays's "the addressing model." In this model, the word *addressing* stands for age, developmental and acquired disability, religion and spirituality, ethnic and racial identity, socioeconomic status, sexual orientation, indigenous heritage, national origin, and gender. According to Elliot, Antioch teaches counselors to use those identities to determine whether patients are "privileged" or "oppressed." If they're privileged, the counselor must help them confront their white supremacy. If they're oppressed, the counselor should help them see how that oppression is contributing to their mental health problems.
- Bring up race and other identities early in any counseling relationship, no matter the client's stated goals.

Elliot's allegations depict an institution whose curriculum has abandoned the foundational principles of psychotherapy. Instead of focusing on evidence-based practices—cognitive behavioral therapy, exposure therapy, and dialectical behavioral therapy, to name a few—Antioch's curriculum now revolves around unproven and unstudied techniques and woke ideology, according to Elliot. Antioch disputed this characterization and maintained that its program remains grounded in accredited counseling standards and evidence-based clinical training. Antioch denied Elliot's allegations and the lawsuit and all of Elliot's claims were dismissed.

It's easy to see how little evidence there is that backs any of this up. The National Library of Medicine is an online repository of scientific studies run by the National Institutes of Health (NIH). A search in their archives for something like "cognitive behavioral therapy"—a well-regarded practice—will show you thousands of scientific papers, along with opinion pieces and other materials discussing this method. Even if you narrow the search only to include randomized controlled trials—which are the scientific gold standard for research—you'll still find some 13,000 studies that show how this style of therapy helps people with depression, anxiety, post-traumatic stress disorder (PTSD), and so on.

Searching the National Library of Medicine for "social justice counseling" yields a telling result: nothing. When I attempted this, the search engine returned an error notice, indicating that the phrase isn't found in the NLM's index. In other words, the search engine of the central government research database can't find a single research paper to back up the importance or effectiveness of the SJC method, yet it dominates many programs that are producing tomorrow's therapists.

Research aside, you need only read a few of the more than two thousand comments on one of Elliott's videos to understand that this kind of ideology harms the very people it claims to help. I've captured just a few of those comments below.

- "When I was a young Black person getting psychotherapy, it would have been incredibly stressful to have a White therapist ask me a question like 'how does it feel talking to a White therapist like me?' And if she then kept directing the conversation to race while I talked about other things, I'd think she thought of me solely as a Black person and not as a person. This would have undermined my feeling of being seen or understood by her, since I see myself as a person who has many characteristics, including being Black."
- "I had a similar experience as a college student going to therapy as a Muslim. It wasn't comforting AT ALL when some therapists centered questions around culture and religion. I ended up being put in a position to defend my background, saying that I'm not being oppressed."
- "I'm grateful as a woman of color that none of the white therapists I ever saw forced me to obsess about the least

> interesting thing about me: my race. If a client wants to discuss that, wonderful. But to assume "BIPOC" (hate that acronym) are all just walking wounded race cripples is, well, pretty racist."

Again, these are just internet comments. But the videos commenting on Antioch's alleged practices seem to have struck a nerve with a diverse array of people who take issue with woke therapy. And the claims made against Antioch are far from an isolated case. In Elliott's videos, dozens of commenters say they've undergone similar programming at other schools.

Social justice ideology has also infiltrated continuing education offerings and post-graduate training opportunities. As I was working on this book, several of my colleagues, for example, advertised a ten-session "anti-racism group" for White therapists, aimed at helping them become more effective allies to the Black community. The training included a stunning thirty hours of demonstrations and discussions designed to help participants "explore their White identities." The price tag: $1500.[25] If you'd like to save a little money, you can opt for the $600, six-session course "Getting Free From Whiteness," an "embodiment group for white folks to bridge the gap between theory and practice in this era of racial reckoning."[26] It's offered by a New Jersey–based therapist who "uses metaphors, archetypal symbols, and dreams to help clients access their inner wisdom."[27]

Offerings like this flood the private networking listservs for therapists that I'm part of. I don't doubt that many of my colleagues mean well. They believe these trainings will help therapists avoid making false assumptions about their clients' experiences—a worthy goal. But in practice, they often do the opposite, encouraging therapists to trade one set of assumptions for another, alienate patients, and deepen societal divides. Therapists need to wake up to the damage caused by this obsessive focus on demographics.

Therapy sessions aren't meant to be political. Therapists should help people overcome problems, manage stress, and cope with depression, anxiety, loneliness, and other painful emotions. Yet many of my colleagues have become social justice warriors—and it's harming not only their patients but society at large. It's pitting one group against another.

One patient shared his frustration after thirteen months of couples counseling following an incident of infidelity on his wife's part. "I've had enough," he told me, describing his experience with their couples therapist. "I'm not going to sit there and listen to the therapist and my wife talk about gender issues while my marriage is falling apart." Instead of helping them confront the betrayal and rebuild trust, their therapist seemed to steer the sessions toward broader social themes—discussions about gender identity, power dynamics, and even workplace equity—topics that may have been well-intentioned but were far removed from the crisis at hand.

Consider the case of another man who, following the 2024 assassination attempt on President Trump, posted to his social media account the now-iconic photo of Trump raising his hands in the air, shouting, "Fight, fight, fight." His girlfriend saw the post and immediately began calling him a "MAGA Republican," even though he had never voted for Trump and historically identified as politically moderate. When the girlfriend brought up the issue with their couples therapist, the therapist strongly took her side. The therapist even suggested that the man atone for being a "MAGA Republican" and asked, "Is there something you can do to make it seem like you're fighting for justice?" The therapist went on to say, "We need to vote for Kamala Harris because she is a woman." The man left that session feeling far worse than when he entered, with a deeper rift between him and his girlfriend. He later came to me for individual counseling, expressing how grossly misunderstood and ganged up on he felt.

The many downsides of woke therapy

Sometimes, a patient's therapy goals do align with aspects of their identity, such as their race, sex, ability, or another characteristic. For instance, a woman might seek counseling after experiencing sexual harassment at work, or a Black man might schedule an appointment after surviving a hate crime. A gay or transgender individual might seek therapy to process their feelings about parents who disowned them after they came out.

At times, encouraging a client to engage in politics can be appropriate for a therapist. In 2024, during many therapy sessions with Kamala Harris supporters who expressed frustration about Donald Trump, I encouraged them to regain a sense of control and agency. I suggested they contact their elected officials, organize voters, or even exercise their right to peacefully protest. These actions can help people strengthen their "locus of control"—a psychological concept that refers to how much control individuals believe they have over the events in their lives. It is categorized as internal when someone believes their actions influence their future, and external when they feel that outside forces control their destiny.

However, it's important to note that this approach works for some patients in specific situations. After more than two decades of counseling people from diverse backgrounds, I can confidently say that not everyone in marginalized groups feels victimized, or oppressed. In fact, the vast majority of people seek therapy for reasons unrelated to their age, ability, race, sex, gender identity, sexual orientation, or religion. I once worked with a successful CEO who struggled with maintaining work-life balance. He was also Hispanic. If I had consistently brought his ethnicity into every session, I wouldn't have helped him address his work-life balance concerns. On the contrary, I would have likely alienated him, disrespected him, and undermined the therapeutic relationship that is key to successful outcomes. He might have even fired me—and rightfully so.

Just as importantly, the last thing a White person with a phobia of bridges or relationship issues needs—or wants—from a therapist is a lengthy, finger-wagging lecture on their societal privilege. More generally, I've lost count of how many new patients have told me that their previous therapists fixated on their race, age, disability, sexual orientation, or another characteristic, even when that had nothing to do with why they sought therapy in the first place.

"My past therapist kept bringing all of my problems back to me being gay," one man told me. He was dealing with anxiety at work, in part because he was up for a major promotion that a backstabbing coworker was trying to steal from him. None of this anxiety had anything to do with his sexual orientation. His previous therapist kept assuming that all of his problems stemmed from discrimination due to his sexuality. By hyper-focusing on this single aspect of his identity, the therapist completely overlooked the true source of the man's anxiety. As a result, the man ended up wasting one therapy session after another without making any real progress.

Another patient, a Black executive in a marketing role, shared that he was experiencing conflicts at work between a superior and a subordinate. To make matters worse, his previous therapist kept redirecting every conversation back to his race. "It must be so difficult to be Black in corporate America," the therapist would say, repeatedly. The client pushed back each time, explaining that his issues had nothing to do with the color of his skin. However, the therapist refused to let it go.

During their final session together, the therapist launched into a rant about the evils of tokenism—the practice of hiring a small number of minorities to create the illusion of fairness. This executive didn't see himself as a "token hire." He believed he deserved every promotion he had received. By persistently bringing up "tokenism," the therapist only fueled his frustration and anger.

"Sure, I'm a Black guy, but I'm also a highly educated professional who's worked my butt off to get to where I am," he told me. "Being Black doesn't define everything I do."

I'm consistently struck by how often patients share stories like this with me. It's not always about race, but frequently, something a previous therapist decided made that patient "different." This is the outcome when everything is viewed through the lens of woke ideology, categorizing and dividing people, obsessing over their differences. By the time these patients come to me, they're understandably exhausted. They've spent sessions with a therapist who's fixated on what they see as the defining characteristic of the patient, even if that's not how the patient sees themselves.

Fundamentally, those kinds of therapists just aren't listening. Instead, they say things like:

"You must have had a trauma to be experiencing so many panic attacks," one therapist told a non-traumatized client session after session.

"Your parents' divorce must have affected you. Is this why you can't form relationships now?" another client heard too many times to count. While divorces can absolutely be difficult and have long-lasting effects, this client had made peace with it long ago and was in therapy for very specific issues.

"It's so hard for people with your physical limitations. Are you sure you want to be shouldering so much responsibility?" another therapist unhelpfully asked someone else, who relied on a cane due to a recent injury, but was seeking therapy for unrelated problems at work.

Rather than helping counselors better understand their patients, the SJC philosophy overcorrects, leading therapists to focus on details that may or may not be relevant to the clients' concerns. Some patients embrace this victimhood, becoming trapped in a cycle of therapy that their practitioner is often only too eager to prolong. Either way, patients suffer, and society grows more divided. Others grow frustrated and abandon therapy altogether.

As I've mentioned, I believe many of my colleagues who use SJC therapy and similar approaches genuinely think they are on a mission to change the world for the better. No one wants a patient to feel misunderstood, unheard, or discriminated against. Every therapist should be sensitive to the real-life struggles people face. However, in practice, this overcorrection often leaves individuals feeling even more misunderstood. Becoming preoccupied with issues of identity can obscure and set back the solution of the patient's specific concerns.

The unfortunate truth about diversity training

The SJC mindset has also infused countless corporate antibias training programs—with disastrous consequences.

Similar to SJC therapy, diversity training sessions began popping up during the 1960s as a well-intentioned response to the Civil Rights Movement. The Civil Rights Act of 1964 and Title VII made it illegal for employers with more than fifteen employees to discriminate based on race, religion, sex, or national origin. At the same time, more people of color and women were flooding workplaces. Corporate leaders felt the need to run training sessions to ensure employees treated one another with respect—and that they didn't run afoul of this new legislation.[28]

Today, nearly all Fortune 500 companies offer diversity training for employees.[29] In many cases, they are mandated.

While a good idea in theory, the unfortunate reality is that these trainings often accomplish nothing. In surveys, two-thirds of human resources leaders admit that the diversity training sessions their companies offer have led to no positive effects.[30] Dozens of studies show that the attitude and behavior changes prompted by diversity training often fade within days.[31, 32, 33]

While all training courses vary, many force-feed participants a steady stream of blame and shame. A White gay patient in his forties shared the outrage he felt during a diversity training when the leader pointed to him and declared, "You are an example of a White supremacist. Because of your whiteness and maleness, you're privileged. You were born with access to power and resources that women and people of color don't have."

Fuming and shocked, the man tried to explain to the facilitator of this mandatory training all the adversity he had faced—being bullied in school, having some family members disown him when he came out, and not talking about his partner at work for fear of being judged by his coworkers. "What are you all talking about? I'm a gay forty-year-old man who has faced a lot of discrimination and adversity!"

But no one listened. Instead, another participant quipped, "Your privilege is showing."

Both inside the workplace and out, one area where this routinely surfaces is personal pronouns. Gender identity has become one of the most charged cultural issues of our time, as more people identify outside the traditional male-female categories. Pronouns, once a mundane part of grammar, have become a flash point in larger cultural battles. While some view them as a tool for advancing broader societal change, most people are simply not versed in the latest gender theory and should not be vilified for defaulting to pronouns that until very recently were considered standard.

This does not mean pronouns are unimportant to those who use them. They matter. But the current cultural climate treats even honest mistakes as evidence of malice. Instead of fostering understanding, this creates a chilling effect where people feel afraid to speak at all. In therapy, I have watched patients—kind, well-intentioned people—retreat from workplaces and friendships not because they oppose inclusion but because they fear they will say the wrong thing and be publicly shamed.

I had a patient, an executive in her early fifties, who was reprimanded during a workplace training session for referring to a colleague as "she." The colleague had recently adopted they/

them pronouns, something my patient didn't know. She wasn't hostile, just unaware. But the fallout left her anxious, isolated, and hesitant to speak up in meetings. What started as a push for inclusion has morphed into a kind of cultural intimidation. Instead of promoting understanding, in cases like these, it punishes mistakes and shuts down honest conversation.

Racial issues have also increased tension in recent years. In the early 2020s, following the death of George Floyd at the hands of a Minneapolis police officer, mandatory training seminars exploded across corporate America and governmental agencies. Many patients of mine, even those who embraced these training initiatives, were shocked to find themselves labeled "racists" or "oppressors." These labels left them confused and anxious. They reached a point where they felt they had to watch every word they said to colleagues, fearing that well-intended compliments might be misconstrued as "cultural appropriation" or "racist." These trainings, meant to bring people together, had the exact opposite effect. Instead of fostering unity, they increased division and heightened racial tension. Even a progressive friend who sat through one of these trainings sarcastically told me later: "I never knew I was a racist until they told me today at work."

As participants were pressured to adopt certain labels and values, their unease grew into anxiety. Many felt uncomfortable and unsure how to respond without risking backlash. The tension in the room was palpable. And that was the point.

These practices push blame and shame tactics, insisting they're needed to "make people uncomfortable." According to this line of thought, putting people on the defensive is the only way to dismantle "systems of oppression." That idea might earn more support if it were based on a shred of data. In reality, however, the evidence shows that mandatory, negative, shame-based trainings that single out so-called privileged attendees almost universally backfire.[34] Attendees feel defensive and then rebel, refusing to consider the viewpoints of others. This is the opposite effect you want if you're trying to create a workplace where people recognize one another's humanity.

These moral shaming tactics can also be deadly. In Toronto, Canada, in 2021, a school principal submitted a harassment complaint against his school district after an anti-racism training session. The leader of the training suggested that Canada was more racist than the United States because it had "never reckoned with its anti-Black history." The principal—who had previously lived in the United States—pushed back, arguing that Canada was a more just society. The training leader allegedly then accused the principal of supporting white supremacy and of being a racist.

Canada's Workplace Safety and Insurance Board found that the conduct of the person leading the training "was abusive, egregious and vexatious, and rises to the level of workplace harassment and bullying." But the principal continued to suffer after the incident, and in 2023, he took his own life. Suicide is always profoundly sad and complex, and it is often impossible to tell exactly what motivates someone to take such a drastic step. But in this case, the principal's attorney alleged in a statement that "the stress and effects of these incidents continued to plague" his client, who eventually "succumbed to this distress."[35]

Even well-designed trainings that avoid the blame and shame mentality still offer little real benefit. In one study, researchers created three one-hour online diversity trainings and offered them to ten thousand employees at a large multinational organization. One training focused exclusively on gender biases. Another addressed multiple biases—gender, age, race, sexual orientation, and religion. The final training served as a control and explored the importance of psychological safety within teams. The researchers went to great lengths to design training sessions that avoided these tactics. Instead, participants filled out assessments that helped them understand their own biases. While the bias-focused training initially seemed to change the attitudes of some of the employees, it didn't lead to measurable changes in behavior.[36]

"We found very little evidence that diversity training affected the behavior of men or White employees overall—the two groups who typically hold the most power in organizations and are often the primary targets of these interventions," wrote the research team in *Harvard Business Review*.[37]

Despite substantial evidence against their effectiveness, these trainings persist—likely because they allow executives to feel good about themselves. White executives, in particular, may have internalized the notion of White guilt due to their positions. At the very least, they view these sessions as an easy way to check a box and shield themselves from accusations of racism—often leveled by the very organizations profiting from the trainings.

No company leader wants a workplace where employees hurl racial slurs or treat each other with disrespect. But fostering division by pitting employees against each other is not the solution. By continuing to mandate these ineffective sessions, companies overlook more impactful initiatives—such as mentoring programs—that research has shown deliver real, lasting benefits.

In conclusion, the well-meaning intent behind diversity training has been undermined by ineffective methods that often foster division rather than unity. Blame and shame tactics alienate participants, fueling defensiveness and resentment, which only heighten racial tensions. Even trainings that avoid these tactics show minimal, short-lived results. Yet, despite overwhelming evidence of their failure, diversity training persists, offering a convenient but superficial solution for companies wanting to appear socially responsible. Real progress will only come when companies invest in initiatives that build genuine connection and systemic change rather than relying on flawed training models.

This problem extends into therapy, where the rise of "woke" therapists and graduate training programs fuels the crisis. Many therapists now push ideologies aligned with the woke movement, focusing more on identity politics than on evidence-based practices. This shift often reinforces guilt and shame, rather than facilitating real self-reflection and growth. Graduate programs that prioritize these ideologies over therapeutic fundamentals are training future clinicians to perpetuate divisiveness, ultimately undermining the therapeutic process.

At a deeper level, this approach contradicts a core principle of human psychology: the need for connection. Humans are naturally social creatures, wired to collaborate in groups for survival and progress. When we focus on dividing people by identity, we fracture our ability to work together and support one another. Rather than fostering understanding and empathy, these ideologies breed a culture of competition and defensiveness. By pitting people against each other based on labels, we undermine our shared human experience. Whether in the workplace or therapy, this culture of division damages the psychological bonds that allow us to thrive together. To heal and move forward, we need to focus on what connects us, not what sets us apart.

CHAPTER SEVEN

MUNCHAUSEN'S BY GOOGLE

Ask any mental health professional you know and they'll tell you that the American Psychiatric Association's Diagnostic and Statistical Manual of Mental Health Disorders (DSM) is hardly a light read.

Much like *Gray's Anatomy* (the book, not the TV show) for aspiring doctors, the DSM, spanning over one thousand pages and priced above $100, has long been a crucial reference for mental health professionals. Its primary readership consists of those who rely on it for its central function: diagnosing a wide array of mental health conditions, from depression and anxiety to schizophrenia and personality disorders.

But in the summer of 2022, something strange occurred.

When the American Psychiatric Association released an update to the DSM, the e-book version was downloaded so many times that it earned a spot on *The Wall Street Journal*'s e-book bestseller list.[1]

This was perhaps the clearest sign yet that psychiatry had gone mainstream. Mental health disorders, like major depression, bipolar disorder, and obsessive-compulsive disorder (OCD), were no longer stigmatized or obscure. Instead, people living with these conditions were sharing their experiences online, gaining massive followings in the process. Everywhere I went, I overheard conversations where complex mental health diagnoses were mentioned as casually as the weather.

"Oh, your friend must have borderline personality disorder!"

"He sounds like a narcissist."

"Not another screaming infant in a restaurant. My PTSD can't handle it!"

In addition, people increasingly were making appointments for conditions that were mild at best and nonexistent at worst. When I first started my private practice in the mid-2000s, people mainly sought help from therapists for psychological problems that caused them extreme distress. They might, for example, feel significant depression and a repetitive lack of motivation even to shower, brush their teeth, get out of bed, go to work, or perform other routine activities of daily living. Or they might feel so incapacitated by their anxiety that they barely left their homes out of fear.

Over the years, I've noticed a growing trend: People with relatively mild or short-lived concerns are increasingly seeking therapy. At the time of writing this book, for instance, a man came to see me because he felt stuck in his role at his firm and wanted guidance on how to approach his executive team about moving up. In his case, our work centered on identifying his strengths and accomplishments, developing the confidence to articulate them, and learning how to ask directly for the promotion he deserved.

Seeking help for this kind of challenge isn't necessarily a bad thing. The hit series *Billions* even portrays it through Wendy Rhoades, the in-house clinician turned performance coach at a Wall Street hedge fund. I appeared in the real-life counterpart to that world—the 2010 Academy Award–winning documentary *Inside Job*—offering perspective on the mindset and culture of top Wall Street professionals. (It won the Oscar, though probably not because of me.)

They sought me out because, alongside my clinical work, I

also coach people who want a performance edge. Many therapists operate in both roles, and that's perfectly appropriate. What's different—and increasingly troubling—is the growing tendency, among both clients and some therapists, to label ordinary life challenges as mental health disorders.

Consider the following reactions that are all too common these days.

Example	**How Someone Would Have Described It During the 1990s**	**How People Describe It Today**
Waking up tired and unmotivated	"I woke up on the wrong side of the bed."	"I'm depressed."
Losing their cool during a confrontation.	"I lost my temper."	"That was my bipolar disorder coming out."
Zoning out during conversations	"I missed what you said, could you repeat it?"	"I have attention deficit hyperactivity disorder, so I may tune you out from time to time."
Noticing sweaty palms before a presentation	"I'm a little nervous about this."	"My panic disorder is out of control right now."

Not everyone who uses these phrases truly believes they have a psychological disorder. Terms like *depression* and *trauma* have become so common that people often use them as stand-ins for ordinary sadness or discomfort. But as we'll see in this chapter, that shift in language is far from harmless.

If you genuinely believe something deeper is going on, it's important to seek professional help. A good therapist will explore the issue with you and, in many cases, put your mind at ease. Their role is to evaluate what's driving your symptoms and determine the best course of treatment.

But not all therapists do that. As online self-diagnosis has exploded, some clinicians have followed suit, adopting a "give the people what they want" approach. In an age of online reviews and TikTok therapy stars, a growing number have shifted from treating patients to catering to customers. Instead of questioning a patient's self-diagnosis, they accept it without hesitation. Sometimes this stems from misplaced empathy or poor diagnostic skill; other times it's a matter of convenience, deference to Google, or a desire to keep a paying client. Whatever the reason, by reflexively affirming hasty, unverified labels, these therapists are not helping—they're deepening the problem.

While self-diagnosing minor ailments might seem relatively harmless, there's a much darker side to the impulse.

The modern Munchausen

The story of Gypsy-Rose Blanchard likely brought the once-obscure term *Munchausen syndrome by proxy* into the public consciousness. In 1991, shortly after giving birth, Dee Dee Blanchard convinced doctors that her infant daughter, Gypsy-Rose, suffered from sleep apnea. The fabricated diagnoses piled up: leukemia, muscular dystrophy, seizures, asthma, and even hearing and visual impairments. As news of her daughter's supposed illnesses spread, Dee Dee garnered financial donations, including a free trip to Disney World.

To maintain the illusion, Dee Dee shaved Gypsy-Rose's head and forced her into a wheelchair. Dee Dee's lies even led to unnecessary medical procedures, including a feeding tube insertion and the removal of Gypsy-Rose's salivary glands.

This went on for years until 2015 when, in an attempt to escape her mother, Gypsy-Rose convinced an online boyfriend, Nicholas Godejohn, to kill Dee Dee. She pled guilty in 2016 to second-degree murder and served eight years in prison and is now out on parole.[2] Godejohn was convicted of first-degree murder and is serving a life sentence.

The details of this tragic story have led many to speculate that Dee Dee Blanchard suffered from a rare mental health condition once known as Munchausen syndrome by proxy. It describes a bizarre condition that drives caregivers to inflict harm in an attempt to seek sympathy and attention, as well as be perceived as intelligent, caring, selfless, and in control.[3]

The phrase "Munchausen" arose in the early 1950s when British physician Richard Asher, MD, was studying data showing that a tiny fraction of patients monopolized hospital resources. These patients continually showed up in medical settings complaining of a wide range of vague symptoms, often talking their doctors into performing incredibly invasive and expensive tests. Yet, no matter how carefully a physician investigated these patient complaints, they could find nothing amiss.

He referenced the fantastical tales of Baron von Munchausen, a fictional character first introduced in 1785. Based on a real aristocrat and military officer, the fictional Munchausen was famous for telling outrageous stories, such as wrestling a forty-foot crocodile, traveling to the moon without a rocket, and riding cannonballs over the Thames River.

Dr. Asher noted that people with Munchausen syndrome, like the fictional Munchausen, can sometimes tell dramatic and false stories. However, unlike the adventurous tales of the historical Munchausen, those with the condition fabricate stories centered around poor health.

Over the years, Munchausen syndrome has evolved in both name and understanding, with clearer triggers and diagnostic criteria. Today, the DSM refers to similar symptoms as "*factitious disorder imposed on self.*" Dee Dee Blanchard's actions align with a closely related diagnosis: "*factitious disorder imposed on another.*" The term *factitious* means something artificially created—manufactured through human action—a word often used in scientific contexts.

The hallmarks of factitious disorder include:

- A deep knowledge of medical terms and diseases
- Vague, inconsistent symptoms
- Worsening health without clear cause
- Symptoms unresponsive to treatment
- Using fake names to seek care
- Resisting efforts to gather information from family or friends
- Frequent requests for tests or invasive procedures

This factitious disorder is thought to stem from an intense emotional need—to be cared for, or to exert power and control. Some individuals may fear abandonment and use illness as a way to draw attention or maintain relationships. Or, as Ferris Bueller observes in one of my favorite 1980s movies, *Ferris Bueller's Day Off*, "He's the only guy I know who feels better when he's sick." It's a throwaway line in a comedy, but it captures something real: For some, illness provides a strange sense of safety, purpose, or even identity.

The long and strange history of hypochondria

The official term *Munchausen syndrome* didn't emerge until the 1950s, but the strange symptoms it describes were noticed centuries earlier.

Hippocrates, the father of medicine, and other healers of his time (around 460 to 370 BC) believed that black bile could seep into and infect various parts of the body, leading to symptoms like belching, flatulence, cold sweats, dizziness, ringing in the ears, and emotional distress. They concluded that an excess of black bile could cause feelings of fear, sadness, and anxiety.[4] Hippocrates referred to this condition as *hypochondria,* with *hypo* meaning *under* and *khondros* meaning *cartilage.* The term referred to the soft area under the ribs, where Hippocrates believed this bile originated.

Eventually, after slicing into enough abdomens and discovering no black bile, physicians began to speculate that the mysterious set of symptoms might be more psychological than physical.

Over the years, the term *hypochondria* was replaced with *Illness Anxiety Disorder (IAD),* a phrase that more accurately describes its set of symptoms. People with IAD tend to label typical and widely experienced bodily sensations as abnormal.[5] For example, someone with a mild headache might not see their symptoms as harmless and fleeting. Instead, they might automatically jump to, "I'm dying from a brain tumor."

In my practice, I've seen this pattern again and again: symptoms that appear under stress and vanish once the stress resolves. One young woman began experiencing tingling in her hands just as she was deciding whether to buy her first home. After searching her symptoms online, she became convinced she had multiple sclerosis (MS), a chronic neurological disorder. "I can't buy a house if I have MS," she told me. "How will I pay my mortgage if the disease forces me to stop working?"

Seeking answers, she visited several doctors and pushed for invasive tests, including a spinal tap. One after another, each confirmed that she did *not* have MS. For most people, that would have been a relief. For her, it only deepened her frustration. She told anyone who would listen that every doctor she'd seen was incompetent. Then, after she finally closed on her new home, the tingling disappeared—just as suddenly as it had begun.

Unlike those with factitious disorder, people like the woman I just described genuinely believe they're ill. It usually begins with mild, ordinary sensations—an ache, a flutter, a tingle. They start researching their symptoms, consulting doctors, and searching for explanations. The more they focus on these sensations, the more intense and convincing they become.

To understand this phenomenon, think about how hunger fades when you're deeply engaged in something—a video game, a conversation, a project. Without distractions, though, that same hunger can start to dominate your thoughts until you "treat" it with food. Other bodily sensations—fatigue, stomach aches, anxiety—work the same way: The more attention you give them, the stronger they feel.

That's why I teach grounding exercises to patients with anxiety. When they notice their heart racing, I ask them to redirect their attention to the present moment: five things they can see, four they can touch, three they can hear, two they can smell, and one they can taste. This simple practice pulls their focus away from the sensations of panic and back into their environment, helping them feel calmer and more in control.

An epidemic of cyberchondria

IAD is a type of health anxiety, and it used to be quite rare. Today, however, it's becoming disturbingly more common, in part thanks to the internet. Though it's not an official DSM disorder, many people in the mental health field refer to this intersection of health anxiety and the internet as *cyberchondria*.[6] The internet is free, always accessible, and capable of answering questions in seconds, assuming you're using a modern connection. Compare this convenience to visiting a health care professional in person. You need insurance, you have to find the right professional, and once you've located one, you may wait weeks or even months for an appointment.

Given the comparative ease of use, it's understandable that increasing numbers of people consult Google before—and often instead of—seeking help from a trained professional. According to some estimates, one in four people have self-diagnosed themselves with a condition with the support of Google. Fewer than half have followed up with a medical professional to check to see if their diagnosis is accurate.[7, 8]

Among mental health self-diagnoses, attention deficit hyperactivity disorder (ADHD) and autism are the most common, especially among teens and young adults who frequently use video-based social media sites like TikTok, Instagram, and YouTube. One study found that TikTok videos associated with an autism hashtag have billions of views. However, only 27% of the most-watched videos provided accurate information, while the rest were either inaccurate or overly generalized.[9]

Once people watch, like, and share mental health content, social media algorithms begin to deliver more of it. This results in increasingly tailored content, such as "10 signs you might have ADHD" and similar posts. As individuals begin to identify with these signs, they may come to believe they do, in fact, have ADHD. So, they follow and connect with others who also identify with the condition. Over time, self-diagnosed individuals join private online chats and groups dedicated to their perceived condition, which only reinforces their belief in the diagnosis, perpetuating the cycle. This creates a dangerous echo chamber where individuals are further convinced of a diagnosis that may not be accurate or even real.

To some extent, for as long as there's been medicine, there have been people who have self-diagnosed themselves with conditions they don't have. But when people couldn't access their doctors or friends during the COVID-19 pandemic, this harmful behavior mushroomed. People had too much time on their hands, many unanswered questions, and were cut off from people in real life who could help find answers. As a result, when an essential health-related question arose—*What are the symptoms of COVID-19?*—people understandably turned to the internet, where they sometimes found factual information and other times uncovered anything but.[10] For many, this habit remained stubbornly in place long after the pandemic restrictions were lifted.

As researchers from Banaras Hindu University in India wrote in a review article for *Frontiers in Psychiatry*: "The Internet has crawled into people's lives and has gradually become an umbilical to the peripheral world."[11]

Actual doctors vs. the internet

When it comes to diagnosing mental health conditions, clinicians like me are trained to remain objective. Our role isn't to confirm a particular outcome but to help people understand what's really happening with their mental health. We don't hope you have a condition, nor do we hope you don't. Our job is to clarify the complexities behind your symptoms.

Mental health disorders often overlap, which can make identifying a single cause or diagnosis difficult. Someone who withdraws socially, for instance, might be experiencing depression—or anxiety, ADHD, or simply the exhaustion that comes from stress. As professionals, we're trained to navigate these nuances and consider context. Unlike social media influencers who offer quick labels and sweeping advice, we rely on evidence-based tools and clinical assessments to build a full picture of what's going on.

In my practice, I consider both psychological and physical causes when evaluating mental health concerns. Depression, for instance, may arise from life circumstances or negative thinking patterns, but it can also signal an underlying medical issue such as hypothyroidism or a vitamin B12 deficiency. That's why I encourage patients to get a full checkup and annual blood work to rule out physical factors that may affect their mood and energy.

A quick Google search, on the other hand, offers only surface-level answers. It might satisfy momentary curiosity, but without professional context, it's easy to spiral down digital rabbit holes. This kind of self-diagnosis breeds confusion and unnecessary worry. Worse, seeing a therapist who doesn't challenge those assumptions can reinforce them—leaving patients not only stuck but further misled about their own mental health.

The confirmation trap

When people use the internet to self-diagnose, they often fall into familiar cognitive traps—chief among them, *confirmation bias.* This is the tendency to seek out, interpret, and remember information that supports what we already believe while ignoring evidence that challenges it.

You can see this bias in action with a simple experiment: Google something you strongly believe, then search for the opposite. If you think divorce harms children, look up "benefits of divorce for children." If you believe divorce has little effect, try "harms of divorce for children." If you're like most people, you'll feel a flicker of discomfort when reading arguments that contradict your view. That feeling is *cognitive dissonance*—the mental tension that arises when reality collides with our beliefs.

Confirmation bias is especially risky in mental health. When scrolling through online symptom lists, we tend to focus on what fits and ignore what doesn't. Because psychological symptoms often exist on a spectrum—from normal to pathological—it's easy to mistake everyday experiences for disorders. Algorithms only worsen the problem by showing us more of what we already believe and less of what might correct us.

In this way, it's surprisingly easy to convince yourself you have a mental health condition, when in fact, you're simply experiencing what it means to be human.

The Barnum Effect

In high school, I vividly remember one of my teachers posing a provocative question:

"Do any of you believe in astrology?"

A fellow student eagerly raised her hand and responded, "I do! I lead my life by it."

That student explained she was an Aries, and the teacher then proceeded to open that day's newspaper and read out the Aries horoscope.

"That's so me!" my classmate exclaimed. "It's spot on. I'm textbook Aries."

The teacher paused for a moment, letting the anticipation build. Then, with a slight smile, he revealed, "That wasn't the horoscope for Aries. I read the one for Gemini. I'm trying to prove a point. When presented with vague, generalized descriptions that could apply to almost anyone, the human tendency is to assume the information applies *only* to us."

This tendency to interpret vague, generalized statements as deeply personal truths lies at the heart of what's known as the Barnum Effect, a psychological phenomenon that can lead to misguided beliefs—especially in contexts like self-diagnosis and therapy.

At the time, I didn't know it, but my teacher had adapted an experiment popularized by American psychologist Bertram R. Forer in the late 1940s to illustrate the Barnum Effect—named after showman P.T. Barnum, who famously claimed, "There's a sucker born every minute."

In 1948, Forer's students begged him to administer a personality test. Though initially reluctant, he eventually agreed and asked the thirty-nine students in his Intro to Psychology class to complete what he called a *Diagnostic Interest Blank* (DIB). At the next session, he handed each student a personality sketch, claiming it reflected their unique results.

After reading their sketches, students were asked to rate how accurately the DIB described their personalities on a scale of zero (poor) to five (perfect), and to mark each statement as "true" or "false." The descriptions included lines like:

> *"You have a great need for other people to like and admire you."*
>
> *"You tend to be critical of yourself."*
>
> *"While you have some personality weaknesses, you can generally compensate for them."*

The professor then asked the students to raise their hands if they felt the Diagnostic Interest Blank had been accurate. Every hand shot up. Finally, he asked one student to read their personality assessment aloud. That's when the class discovered that they hadn't received individualized assessments at all. Instead, the professor had handed out the same one to every single student. He had loosely based the one-size-fits-all description on statements taken from an astrology book.[12]

Tarot decks, horoscopes, palm readers, and fortune tellers all exploit the Barnum Effect to keep people coming back for more. When you receive a "reading," it often feels like you're getting personalized insights. In reality, however, you're being presented with vague, general statements that could apply to almost anyone.

The self-fulfilling prophecy effect

The Barnum Effect explains why so many people fall victim to vague diagnoses, but it doesn't stop there. The self-fulfilling prophecy takes this concept further by demonstrating how our beliefs about ourselves can influence our actions and, ultimately, shape our reality.

In 1948, sociologist Robert K. Merton defined self-fulfilling prophecies as "a false definition of the situation evoking a behavior which makes the originally false conception come true."[13] In simpler terms, a self-fulfilling prophecy is a prediction that becomes true, at least in part, because the person believes or expects it to happen.

I often see this in my patients when they predict negative outcomes. For instance, a patient might say, "I know I won't get promoted at work." By embracing this belief, they may start lacking confidence, which shows in how they interact with their manager and colleagues. They may even stop putting in effort at their job. In doing so, the patient inadvertently brings about the very outcome they feared.

This effect is powerful. For example, when people believed they were "old," they tended to walk more slowly than people of the same age who didn't think of themselves as old, found a 2015 study published in *PloS One*.[14]

In mental health, the self-fulfilling prophecy can cause individuals to act out the condition they believe they have. For example, someone who believes they have ADHD might stop using helpful reminders to stay on track with appointments. A person who self-diagnoses with social anxiety may begin avoiding social events. If someone believes they're depressed, they may internalize that, thinking no one wants to be around them. By staying home instead of engaging with others, they reinforce their feelings of isolation, which only deepens their sense of despair. What might have started as mild sadness can escalate into a persistent sense of doom, further validating their initial belief. Even more concerning, if this person continues to seek answers online, they may feel less motivated to consult professionals in real life, allowing their mental health struggles—both the initial and self-fulfilled ones—to linger.

The ADHD challenge

If you're like most people, myself included, you likely don't want to believe that you could ever fall victim to the thinking traps I just mentioned—but it's impacting our minds in ways that are far more pervasive and sinister than most of us realize.

For example, if any of us tried a simple internet search for "symptoms of ADHD," we would encounter information from several reputable organizations, including Britain's National Health Service (NHS), the U.S. Centers for Disease Control and Prevention (CDC), Mayo Clinic, the American Psychiatric Association (APA), and others. However, even from these reputable sources, we would find symptom lists and descriptions that overlap with typical human experiences. For example, according to the APA, some of the hallmark symptoms of the inattentive type of ADHD include:[15]

- Not paying close attention to details
- Not following through on instructions
- Struggling with organization
- Avoiding activities that require sustained mental effort, such as completing forms
- Losing things, such as keys
- Forgetting to do daily tasks

Much like the Barnum Effect, many of these symptoms could apply to most people at some point.

Behaviors often associated with ADHD—like misplacing keys or missing appointments—are common human experiences. But when social media and personal bias amplify them, people may start to self-diagnose based on fleeting or superficial traits.

Because of how algorithms work, once you search for ADHD, your feeds will be filled with ADHD-related content designed to hold your attention and sell you targeted ads. Soon you're following influencers who "specialize" in ADHD, watching videos of people describing how they went undiagnosed for years, and scrolling through memes listing "hidden signs of ADHD" or "five traits doctors won't tell you about." Some of this content is AI generated; others come from influencers who claim that overexplaining, running late, quick wit, buying unused notebooks, or abandoning an Etsy shop are all proof of ADHD.

Over time, this flood of content can narrow your focus. You start noticing only the traits that resonate—like losing things—and disregarding the rest. Eventually, when you miss a meeting, forget a lunch date, or misplace your phone, it's easy to blame your "undiagnosed ADHD" instead of recognizing the far more likely explanation: ordinary distraction, stress, or simple human error.

The downsides of self-diagnosis

I hope it's becoming clear how harmful it can be to buy into an online diagnosis. At best, these labels become convenient excuses for certain behaviors. Instead of addressing traits or habits that could improve their lives, people hide behind a social media–inspired self-diagnosis that feels validating but ultimately stalls growth.

Too often, a patient's firm belief in a false diagnosis pulls the therapist into the same trap. Rather than relying on evidence-based tools and careful clinical evaluation, some therapists simply take patients at their word, assuming they are helping by affirming the latest diagnosis du jour. This approach helps no one. I have even seen clinicians promote certain diagnoses because they are trending online, mistaking popularity for accuracy.

For example, terms like *narcissist*, *borderline*, and *bipolar* are tossed around in popular culture but rather than educating patients on their true meanings, some therapists adopt them, applying them inaccurately. This could be due to a lack of understanding of the actual clinical definitions or a misguided attempt to align with the patient's existing beliefs, driven by an unproductive and warped interpretation of empathy.

If you show up for a therapy appointment and say you have depression, anxiety, panic disorder, or some other diagnosis, a good therapist will ask a simple question: "Why do you think that?" If your answer is that the belief comes from a quiz you found on social media, a good therapist will not give that result much weight. Instead, they will set it aside and rely on proven, reliable methods of assessment to understand what is going on.

By contrast, bad therapists fail to verify whether a patient actually meets the criteria for the conditions they claim to have. Instead, they take those claims at face value, validating pre-existing beliefs rather than testing them. By repeatedly centering therapy around a supposed disorder, these therapists reinforce false assumptions, heightening health anxiety and locking patients into a self-perpetuating cycle.

Over time, this cycle can actively interfere with improvement. Rather than challenging patients to build resilience, change habits, or tolerate frustration, bad therapists enable avoidance. As a false diagnosis becomes woven into a person's identity, it is increasingly used as an excuse to sidestep responsibility and justify behavior that would otherwise need to be confronted.

This then leads to an accommodation-driven mentality. Over the past few years, I've seen this trap play out in many ways. Some therapists, for example, have turned their practices into accommodation mills for people who've self-diagnosed themselves with cognitive and psychological disabilities. Students, in particular, will seek out these therapists, claim to have a "diagnosed" cognitive or psychological disability, and ask the therapist to write a letter recommending a list of needed accommodations under the Americans with Disabilities Act (ADA). Without checking to see if these students actually have a true diagnosis, these therapists will recommend students be offered any or all of the following:

- Extra time to take tests
- The ability to turn in work late without being penalized
- The ability to not participate in class discussions
- The need for a private note taker to assist the student in class

For someone with a genuine condition that impairs their ability to learn, these accommodations can be the key to success. However, the abuse of this system has become so widespread that individuals with legitimate mental health disorders are now being questioned, as others, without a true diagnosis, take advantage of the accommodations offered by schools.

This problem extends well beyond the classroom. I am frequently asked to write accommodation letters so someone can bring a pet on a flight without paying the standard fee. When the need is legitimate, I will provide one. But it would be unethical to issue such a letter for a stranger whose sole goal is to bypass airline rules, whether the pet is a dog, a cat, or something more exotic. Accommodation letters are meant to address real disabilities, not to serve as loopholes for convenience.

By avoiding the hard work involved in growth, people who self-diagnose end up trapping themselves in an ongoing cycle that makes them continually weaker. In addition, they could theoretically be missing what's truly going on. They might think, for example, that they have ADHD or generalized anxiety disorder when, in reality, they have a thyroid condition that is 100% treatable. To have a therapist who doesn't assist them in solving the problem, but only endlessly indulges the patients' confused ideas, makes the problem infinitely worse and sometimes interminable.

This "everyone must accommodate my needs" mindset is like expecting the entire Earth to be covered in soft fabric, rather than just wearing a pair of sneakers to protect your feet from sharp objects.

Escaping the trap

I understand that most people will turn to Google at some point. The key is to set guardrails.

First, consider the source. Rely less on social media personalities and more on reputable health organizations such as Mayo Clinic, Cleveland Clinic, and the National Institutes of Health. Always ask what the site wants from you. Is it a nonprofit providing information, or is it trying to sell you something—like an expensive supplement? If it's the latter, read with caution. Treat online mental health quizzes the way you'd treat a palm reader at a county fair: entertaining, not clinical.

Remember that many common behaviors are not disorders. Plenty of people without ADHD run late, misplace items, or forget birthdays. Many people without autism find eye contact uncomfortable. Everyday traits don't equal diagnoses.

If you decide to see a therapist, pay attention to how they handle the first meeting. If they aren't asking probing questions or exploring why you feel the way you do, that's a red flag. A good therapist doesn't just listen; they help you define the problem and start solving it.

A results-oriented therapist will use evidence-based techniques (more on those later), provide direct and honest feedback, and guide you toward independence—not dependence on therapy. Be cautious of clinicians who lean on buzzwords like *trauma bonding* or *manifesting* without offering clinical depth, measurable progress, or a willingness to challenge you. Therapy isn't about pinning a lifelong label on normal struggles; it's about finding concrete strategies that help you move forward.

CHAPTER EIGHT

THE CULT OF TRAUMA

It was the fall of 2023, and I'd just finished cycling the six-mile loop around Central Park. As I pedaled back to my apartment through the heart of Manhattan, weaving through the usual chaos of cars, people, and vendors, I noticed an SUV parked in the bike lane. The driver opened the door slightly, saw me, and then closed it to allow me enough space to go by. I continued to pedal.

Just as I reached the SUV, the driver flung open the door. There was no time to react. I slammed into it, flew over the door, crashed into the side of a parked cab, and landed in the street. People crowded around, staring into my face and asking if I was okay. I was terrified, and I knew something was terribly wrong. It felt as if my leg might snap in half. The pain was excruciating. At the time, I didn't realize it, but I had fractured my leg just below the knee. The agony only intensified as people dragged me to the sidewalk, out of traffic, where I waited forty-five minutes for an ambulance.

The fracture required surgery: a metal plate and seven screws, each 2¾ inches long. I couldn't walk for ten weeks and spent six months in physical therapy. I was finally able to ride my bike again, but the injury wasn't finished with me. A year later, I needed a second surgery.

This experience could be considered a form of trauma, as

it met some of the criteria for Post-Traumatic Stress Disorder (PTSD). I had a close brush with death, and for several months, I experienced lingering distress. I avoided the street where the accident occurred, and whenever I saw a black SUV, I would tense up.

However, I didn't have nightmares, flashbacks, or obsessive thoughts about the event. Though I was certainly angry about what had happened, my anger didn't reach the level of significant distress. Over time, as I healed, I mostly stopped tensing up when I saw SUVs and eventually felt confident enough to get back on my bike. Still, when I see a car door opening ahead of me, I feel a brief surge of anxiety and a trace of the old anguish. The body and mind don't always heal on the same timeline.

Stressful events and our reactions to them exist along a continuum, and that continuum is different for everyone. Just because I recovered and returned to biking relatively quickly doesn't mean the same outcome will occur for everyone in every situation.

What concerns me as a therapist is that people seem to be increasingly losing sight of this continuum, instead labeling every stressful event as *trauma.* The term has broadened far beyond its original meaning. Social media influencers, without the proper mental health expertise, often toss it around carelessly, without recognizing the impact this language has on expectations about emotional recovery.

Here's how different stressors fall along that continuum:

On one end, you have life-altering, unexpected events like extreme violence. These are experiences that most people find overpowering—and they often trigger PTSD reactions in individuals who are particularly susceptible.

In the middle, you'll find distressing experiences like the accident I experienced on my bike. These often lead to lingering anxiety and physical or emotional unease, but they typically don't trigger a full-blown PTSD response.

At the other end of the spectrum are mild stressors, like being stood up for a date. We're all familiar with these types of events, which occur frequently in daily life. While uncomfortable and sometimes frustrating, they don't cause psychological damage. In fact, they can often lead to growth, providing valuable opportunities for resilience.

Extreme stressors	Medium stressors	Mild stressors
War	Messy divorce	Being stood up for a date
Terrorism	Some car accidents	Having a rash break out
Natural disasters	Losing your job	Getting passed over for a promotion at work
Violence	Miscarriage	Getting snubbed by a friend
Sexual assault	Identity theft	Having someone forget your birthday
Losing a parent at a young age	Getting scammed	Having someone make a passing negative comment on your appearance
Losing a child	Dealing with knee pain	Reading comments you don't agree with on the Internet
	Living through the COVID-19 pandemic	Talking to someone from the opposing political party

The pathologizing of normal

The word *trauma* was once obscure and rarely used among the general public. But something has shifted over the last decade. Today, thousands of podcasts feature "trauma" in their titles. It's the central theme of TV dramas. On YouTube, you'll find yoga routines aimed at helping with post-traumatic stress. And Instagram and TikTok, of course, are full of "signs you might have trauma." On Instagram, millions of posts are tagged with #trauma, and Google searches on the topic have surged over the years.

I'm willing to give the general public a pass on the overuse and misuse of the term *trauma*. The social media influencers who toss it around without any real mental health expertise are making the problem worse, but the unfortunate truth is that they might not fully understand the harm they're causing. However, my colleagues in the therapy profession should know better. They have no excuse.

Mental health professionals should understand the actual definition of *trauma* and how to apply it correctly. They shouldn't be using the term when it's not warranted.

In my experience with both patients and colleagues, I've noticed an alarming trend: More and more therapists are distorting the definition of trauma to include nearly any experience of discomfort. Whether in their clinical practices, on social media, or elsewhere, many therapists now label everyday stressors—like a rainy forecast, a critical remark, or a difficult work assignment—as "traumas." This troubling shift in thinking pathologizes normal human experiences. According to this warped perspective, even mild stressors can supposedly cause lasting changes to one's behavior and personality and require processing, therapy, self-care, and avoidance.

Do you find yourself overthinking a stressful situation at work? According to many therapists today, that's your trauma speaking.

Struggling with procrastination? Stop blaming yourself. In this new therapeutic narrative, it's a symptom of past trauma.

In addition, you'll find people on TikTok and other social media platforms who will blame your trauma for:

- Struggling with making small decisions
- People pleasing
- Doomscrolling
- Feeling defensive
- Perfectionism
- Your hatred of crowds
- Having a high pain threshold
- Feeling guilty about relaxing
- Overapologizing
- Fidgeting

By indulging patients who self-diagnose and validating watered-down definitions of trauma, these therapists are fostering avoidance—of personal growth, of emotional resilience—the very qualities therapy is meant to nurture. They apply this very serious term irresponsibly, leading people with uneventful childhoods and typical life experiences to use mild stressors as excuses to avoid personal growth, crucial conversations, relationship repair, and emotional resilience. This is a huge contributor to the decline of our nation's collective mental health.

For some people, trauma has become a shield to explain away anything. They can be confronted with any type of bad behavior: sexual infidelity, their constant stream of unwarranted criticism, their seeming inability to complete their fair share of household chores. The common response is that they blame their trauma for their actions (or inaction). A husband caught in an affair claims his childhood abandonment issues made him seek validation elsewhere. A boss who berates employees justifies it by saying he grew up in a hypercritical household. A roommate who never picks up after themselves insists that their executive dysfunction is rooted in past emotional distress. The self-help, social media, and mental health industries are squarely to blame for this reckless and irresponsible mislabeling of everyday life challenges as PTSD.

What is trauma?

The word *trauma* comes from the Greek term for *wound*. Serious therapists reserve this term for describing severe emotional and sometimes physical responses—including shock, denial, panic, sleep disturbances, and flashbacks—that can persist long after someone experiences an intensely stressful event such as an accident, rape, or natural disaster. Day after day, week after week, month after month, the pain and stress remain fresh, as if the event just happened. In this way, trauma can be likened to a wound that refuses to heal.

Even when an event is traumatic, not everyone develops psychological symptoms afterward. In fact, most people don't—a phenomenon I'll explore further in this chapter.

However, when these distressing symptoms persist, it's because the brain is trying to prevent the same situation from happening again. In other words, it's an adaptive response. Over the course of human evolution, remembering painful or frightening events increased the odds of survival. As a result, we're wired to remember negative events more vividly than positive ones. While many people wish they could avoid uncomfortable emotions like anxiety, panic, or anger, these negative states serve an important function: They're the brain's way of getting our attention.

To illustrate this, imagine you accidentally touch a hot burner on the stove. After the pain, you'd likely learn a critical lesson: Be more cautious around the stove. This memory helps protect you from harm moving forward.

Sometimes, an experience can be so intensely negative that it prevents someone from moving forward, causing them to endlessly replay the event in their mind. Scientists first observed this phenomenon in soldiers returning from war. After World War I, for example, some combat veterans came home forever changed. These "shell-shocked" veterans couldn't relax, couldn't sleep, lashed out in anger, isolated themselves, and seemed to undergo drastic personality changes.

Over time, psychologists discovered that combat was just one of many events capable of leading to this condition. The war-specific term *shell shock* was replaced with the more comprehensive diagnosis of Post-Traumatic Stress Disorder (PTSD). People can develop PTSD after being physically and violently attacked, surviving terrorism, or enduring a natural disaster. PTSD can also occur after witnessing danger, even if you weren't personally victimized. For instance, first responders to the Sandy Hook Elementary School mass shooting, where twenty children and six educators were murdered, reported suffering from intrusive memories and flashbacks of the horrific scene they witnessed that day.[1]

I mentioned the American Psychiatric Association's *Diagnostic and Statistical Manual of Mental Health Disorders* (DSM) in the previous chapter. According to the DSM's diagnostic criteria, for you to be diagnosed with PTSD, you must experience *all* of the following for a month or longer—and it must lead to significant distress:

- You experienced a direct or indirect exposure to death, threatened death, actual or serious injury, or actual or threatened sexual violence.
- You persistently re-experience the event through unwanted memories, nightmares, flashbacks, emotional distress, or physical reactivity.
- You avoid activities, places, emotions, and thoughts that remind you of the traumatic event.
- You experience at least two of the following: inability to recall some of the original trauma, overly negative thoughts about one's self or the world, exaggerated blame of one's self or others for causing the trauma, negative mood, decreased interest in activities, feeling isolated, difficulty feeling positive emotions.

- You experience at least two of the following: irritability and aggression, risky or destructive behavior, hypervigilance, heightened startle reactions, difficulty concentrating, or sleep disturbances.

Note that the very first qualification for trauma, facing "a direct or indirect exposure to death, threatened death, actual or serious injury, or actual or threatened sexual violence," sets quite a high bar. And it's miles away from what many mental health influencers, and even licensed therapists, refer to as "trauma." According to the DSM's diagnostic criteria, trauma is defined as extreme danger. These extreme, life-threatening events can lead to shock, hypervigilance, panic, and a sense of helplessness. The American Psychiatric Association estimates that 3.5% of U.S. adults have experienced these types of trauma.[2] Put another way, by this definition, most Americans (96.5%) are *not* traumatized.

However, over the years, some mental health professionals have pushed to expand the umbrella of trauma to include more people. These professionals argue that the DSM trauma definition describes big or capital *T* traumas. Little or lowercase *t* traumas, they say, include non–life-threatening stressors such as emotional abuse, bullying, infertility, discrimination, social exclusion, divorce, and *financial hardship.*[3] Though the impact of these stressors certainly pales in comparison to the so-called "big T" traumas, these professionals claim that "little t" traumas can accumulate over time—similar to the expression "death by one thousand paper cuts"—eventually leading to significant distress that proponents of the theory have labeled "complex PTSD."

The so-called "little t" traumas can certainly be painful, especially in the moment or shortly afterward. I wish we lived in a world free from bullying, discrimination, social exclusion, and other triggers of minor stress responses. But the reality is, we don't—and these experiences are an inevitable part of life.

Each time we encounter something like this, we face a choice.

We can dwell on the pain, replay the event, and allow it to take over. Or we can acknowledge what happened, extract what is useful, and move forward, stronger for having done so. My goal as a therapist is to guide patients toward that second path whenever possible: the path of mental resilience.

This isn't just a personal philosophy; it's a practical one. Patients who develop resilience recover faster and avoid getting trapped in cycles of negativity. Over time, they build the strength to handle more serious challenges should they arise. As a clinician, it's far more productive to help someone progress than to keep revisiting the same pain. And as a culture, we benefit when more people learn to meet adversity with perspective and courage rather than fragility and avoidance.

When people see typical life events and reactions as traumas, they create a world where all stress is harmful and must be avoided. But you can never avoid *all* of life's stressors. Even if you could, attempting to do so would unnecessarily limit your life, robbing you of a multitude of pleasurable, exciting, and worthwhile experiences.

It's been scientifically proven that mild stressors keep us engaged and make us stronger. Research done on rats at the University of California at Berkeley, for example, determined that brief stressors trigger the brain to make new nerve cells, helping to improve mental performance. After immobilizing the rats in cages for a few hours, researchers documented a doubling of new brain cells in the hippocampus, an area of the brain involved in memory.[4] Research on humans confirms these findings, showing that mild stressors can improve memory, whereas boredom and lack of stress can worsen cognitive health.[5,6] Other research indicates that mild, predictable stressors may help to protect against depression and anxiety.[7]

In this way, repeated mild stressors can work like the dumbbell rack at your gym. As you face down each one, you adapt and grow stronger and better able to tolerate bigger and bigger stressors.

Conversely, just as your muscles weaken when you don't use them to lift heavy objects, your mind can also weaken when you refuse to expose yourself to challenges. Sometimes, muscles even need to be broken down in order to be built back stronger. Physical workouts need to be varied to work different muscle groups. Similarly, if you don't present your mind with chances to solve a variety of challenges and deal with adversity, your mild interpersonal skills can erode, and the ability to tolerate uncomfortable emotions dissolves. Rather than find ways to overcome difficulties, people give up and hide behind the pseudo-safety of their self-labeled trauma. And they're even more likely to stay behind that shield, and less likely to address the root cause, if it's bolstered by a coddling therapist.

When we refer to nearly any negative experience as trauma, we also minimize the experiences of actual trauma survivors who are grappling with true PTSD. By expanding the definition of trauma to include anything and everyone, it makes it harder for people with true PTSD to find the understanding, help, and support they need and deserve.

Just as significantly, by referring to non-traumas as traumas, my therapy colleagues are creating a society of emotional weaklings.

Everyone's triggered, no one's happy

The term *triggered* is another casualty of linguistic drift. Originally, a *trigger* referred specifically to something that reactivated symptoms of post-traumatic stress disorder. For many veterans, for instance, the sound of fireworks can bring back the chaos of combat. I once worked with a veteran who became visibly agitated by the screech of car brakes or the blare of a horn outside my office—ordinary sounds that could instantly transport him back to the battlefield, making the past feel immediate and real.

In recent years, though, the word *trigger* has been stretched to cover nearly any experience that provokes discomfort—from feeling mildly offended to being surprised or annoyed. The popular assumption has become: If something causes distress, it must be a trigger.

This isn't just a harmless shift in language. By labeling every unpleasant feeling or event as a *trigger*, people unintentionally train themselves to see normal emotional reactions as danger. They become more reactive and less resilient. Instead of confronting emotions, they avoid them—hiding behind therapeutic language that excuses rather than empowers. Over time, that mindset erodes the ability to cope with difficulty, both large and small.

Growing in the wrong direction

As I mentioned, only some of the people who are confronted with a life-threatening situation go on to develop PTSD symptoms. For example, according to some estimates, only about 24% of earthquake survivors will develop PTSD.[8]

What happens to the remaining 76%? In short, they grow and persevere.

Since the word *trauma* even entered into our lexicon, experts have known that no two people respond in precisely the same ways to the same experiences. For example, in an essay for *The Yale Review*, Aminatta Forna described the fate of her cousin, Morlai, who attempted to cross a checkpoint in the war-torn Sierra Leone during the 1990s. A soldier mistook Morlai for a rebel and dragged him away for execution. Morlai, however, lived and escaped because a soldier ordered to shoot him happened to be one of his former students. Forna wrote:

> In Western societies, we have begun to conflate every difficult experience with trauma, such that the words *suffering* and *trauma* have become interchangeable. But here was someone I

> knew well, the cousin with whom I had grown up and who was and is immensely dear to me, who had gone through something terrible and yet was not traumatized by it—who, in fact, was able to reach a place where he could laugh about his experience.[9]

Similar to the experience Forna captured in her essay, many Holocaust survivors persevered in horrendous conditions and treatment. After being liberated, many went on to fight injustice, start movements, and become some of society's most significant figures. In 2002, after extensively interviewing 133 Holocaust survivors for a research review, Roberta R. Greene, PhD, formerly of the University of Texas at Austin, concluded that humans are capable of experiencing extraordinary horror and go on to live extraordinary lives. Most of the survivors she interviewed had abandoned resentment and, instead, had embraced an outlook of hope.[10]

Healing doesn't happen overnight, of course. After experiencing an extreme stressor, many people initially face shock, disbelief, anger, or depression. However, as the weeks pass, survivors begin to reevaluate their priorities. They start reconnecting with friends and family, leaning on them for support. Over time, they may develop a renewed appreciation for the small, pleasant moments in life. Ultimately, they may experience a sense of liberation and begin to embrace new possibilities.

This is called "post-traumatic growth." Unlike PTSD, it's a concept that is rarely talked about or mentioned online. However, it's *common.* When Chinese researchers dug into the data from twenty-six randomized controlled trials involving 10,181 people who'd experienced potentially traumatic events, the researchers determined that more than half of people who experienced highly challenging events went on to experience moderate to high post-traumatic growth.[11]

Put another way, when people are confronted with life-threatening experiences, they *might* emerge with PTSD. However, it's just as likely that they *won't* and may even become more resilient because of—and not despite—the experience.

Research into stress has shown that while the impact of difficult experiences is undeniable, how individuals respond to them can vary dramatically. The "trauma mindset," for example, can keep people stuck in their suffering, feeling trapped by past events. In contrast, a "resilience mindset" encourages adaptability and the ability to overcome adversity, turning challenges into opportunities for growth. This distinction isn't just theoretical—it's something I've witnessed firsthand, both in my patients and in my own life.

The resilience mindset

Your mindset is the lens through which you experience the world. It shapes your expectations, interpretations, evaluations, and goals. If you have an optimistic mindset, you might continually notice the upside or silver linings in world events—even though other people may see them as traumas.

For example, when my father was a junior in high school, he lost his mother. Then, fourteen months later, he lost his father. Despite those profound losses, my father went on to graduate from college, develop a career, get married, and start a family. Decades later, he dealt with significant health issues, being diagnosed with prostate cancer, lymphoma, and multiple sclerosis. In the face of these health setbacks and limitations, my father maintained an active lifestyle. He cycled and hiked. It seemed as if life's challenges never fazed him. No matter what was going on, his positive mindset and great sense of humor remained nearly contagious right up to the day he died.

The world itself doesn't change—but your mindset can dramatically influence what you notice, pay attention to, and act upon.

Alia Crum, PhD, an associate professor of psychology at Stanford University, has studied two opposite mindsets when it comes to stress:

- **"Stress is debilitating."** This is the trauma mindset—especially as *trauma* is misused today. It sees only the downsides of stress. People feel helpless in the face of stress. As a result, they seek to eliminate or avoid all sources of stress from their lives.
- **"Stress is enhancing."** This describes a resilience mindset. It sees stress as a plus. In this way people see stress as a problem or puzzle that they can solve as long as they gather the necessary resources, time, training, and practice.

For one of her many studies on the topic, Dr. Crum asked employees at a financial institution to watch videos about stress. One group of employees watched videos that depicted stress as harmful. The other group saw footage that described stress as a positive performance enhancer. A week later, all employees were asked to give a talk to their colleagues. The employees who watched the "stress is enhancing" videos had more favorable blood cortisol levels, indicating that they were less reactive to the stressor of public speaking. Employees with a "stress is enhancing" mindset were also more open to feedback on their performance.[12]

Through several studies, Dr. Crum's research has determined that people with "stress is enhancing" mindsets lead to improved mood, attention, and cognitive flexibility in the face of a range of challenges.[13, 14] By seeing stress as a necessary ingredient in life, they can harness it for growth. It's difficult to imagine a scenario where getting stuck in a feedback loop with a therapist or the internet and wallowing in stress sounds like a better option than persevering. Dwelling on stress or trauma (whatever label you put on it) is not going to help in the long run.

A growing number of lazy and ineffective therapists undermine resilience and post-traumatic growth by persistently steering clients toward the negative. I once treated a patient, whom I'll call Emily, who came to me after months with another therapist. When I asked why she left, Emily explained that she had initially sought help for a straightforward conflict with her roommate. Instead of addressing that issue, her therapist repeatedly redirected the sessions toward Emily's childhood, with particular emphasis on her adoption.

"I told him it wasn't a big deal," Emily said. "I love my parents. They've supported me all my life. Without them, I wouldn't be applying to medical school. But my therapist insisted that my issues with my roommate must be rooted in PTSD from my adoption."

I could see how frustrated Emily was. She felt her therapist was misinterpreting her situation. "I told him my stress was from studying for the MCAT and feeling excluded from social events. That's where my tension was coming from, not my childhood."

As we talked, it became clear that Emily didn't have any symptoms of PTSD—no panic attacks, no nightmares, and no history of emotional trauma. She was a well-adjusted, ambitious young woman who simply had a conflict with her roommate. But her previous therapist's insistence on labeling her as "traumatized" only hindered her ability to address the real issue.

A similar story unfolded with another patient, Jessica, who came to therapy after a heated argument with a coworker left her feeling anxious. Her therapist, however, also diagnosed her with PTSD, despite Jessica not exhibiting any symptoms. "That incident must have been traumatic for you," the therapist said, and from then on, every session focused on Jessica's supposed trauma.

The therapist's diagnosis became so entrenched that Jessica began to identify with it. She told her family, friends, and even shared it on social media. "It's like being told you have diabetes when you don't," Jessica later explained, "and then telling everyone you know about it."

But as the weeks went by, Jessica found herself stuck in a cycle of therapy that focused solely on trauma, while the argument with her coworker remained unresolved. Fortunately, a close friend urged her to seek a second opinion. Unlike her previous therapist, I focused on helping Jessica develop healthier ways to handle interpersonal conflicts, encouraging her to use new communication strategies in her daily life. Over time, she was able to reframe difficult conversations as an inevitable part of life and learned how to engage with them in a constructive way.

I wish I could say that the above stories are rare, but I can't. I've heard from patients about therapists who attempted to convince them all of their current problems had traced back to trauma due to things like:

- Not taking enough of the right kind of vacations as a child
- Being the only minority student in a classroom
- Sharing a bedroom with other siblings
- Not being encouraged to pursue a specific career
- Not being complimented enough by one's parents

Those events and situations may certainly be stressful, and they may bring up some negativity. However, they *aren't* traumas. As I've mentioned, PTSD typically involves exposure to severe events like combat, accidents, physical assault, or natural disasters. A difficult conversation, while emotionally taxing, doesn't meet the threshold for the kind of trauma required for a PTSD diagnosis.

The problem with adopting a false PTSD diagnosis runs deep, as Jessica's and Emily's stories illustrate. By pushing a trauma narrative, these therapists may unwittingly cause distress that wasn't there before the therapy session. Instead of viewing uncomfortable and stressful events as challenges, a false PTSD label leads patients to expect everyone around them to cater to their "trauma" rather than encouraging them to develop and practice the skills needed to resolve conflict and move forward.

These patients become trapped in an endless therapy loop. Seeing themselves as broken, they interpret typical everyday stressors—like being cut off in traffic—as catastrophic. Rather than learning from past experiences, growing from their mistakes, or developing the communication and relational skills that would help them succeed, their knee-jerk reaction becomes predictable: make an appointment with a therapist to vent about the discomfort they just experienced. They feel validated and better in the moment. But this nonconstructive venting leads to a therapy-induced negativity spiral that does real harm.

When every stressor, no matter how mild, is labeled a "trauma," attention shifts away from coping and toward fixation. Ordinary difficulties are replayed, analyzed, and magnified until they feel far more consequential than they are. This process feeds negativity, fear, anxiety, and anger. Over time, people begin to organize their identity around perceived damage, seeing themselves as broken rather than capable. In some cases, that brokenness even becomes a source of meaning or status. A person who once struggled in a relationship may come to believe they are inherently "bad at relationships" because of their "trauma." What began as a manageable challenge turns into a self-fulfilling prophecy. The result is that a non-trauma is converted into a durable pattern of poor mental health.

This is exactly what happened to Jessica. She got the wrong diagnosis and ran with it. This made her generally more anxious and less confident about handling work conflicts. Ultimately, I helped her to get past this misdiagnosis and change her mindset from one of victim and feeling stuck, to victor and feeling strong.

Going "no contact"

In addition to making people weaker, the over-traumatization of everyday life is breaking families apart. Increasingly, young adults with no history of serious trauma are blaming their parents for minor disappointments—not taking them on vacations, packing lunches instead of letting them buy food out, declining to fund their lifestyle or career choices—and then cutting off contact altogether.

Much of this behavior can be traced to bad therapeutic advice, especially from clinicians with large online followings. More and more, these "influencer therapists" tell young people that the mildest stressors qualify as trauma to be avoided. After the 2016 and 2024 elections, for instance, some counselors went so far as to call exposure to opposing political views a form of trauma—and urged patients to go *no contact*.

But severing ties rarely solves the problem. Family relationships that could be repaired through conversation or genuine family therapy are instead abandoned, making reconciliation far more difficult.

Estrangement may be appropriate for a small minority who've endured true abuse. For most, however, it means losing crucial sources of emotional and financial support. America has always contained deep political and cultural divisions, but if "going no contact" becomes the default therapeutic prescription for disagreement, we risk a family crisis unlike any before.

When the very professionals meant to help us navigate conflict instead encourage avoidance, our divisions deepen. To reverse this trend, therapists must stop stretching the definition of *trauma* beyond recognition. It dishonors those who have survived genuine trauma and does nothing to build strength in those who haven't.

The solution isn't to pathologize ordinary stress and conflict but to cultivate resilience—to reframe challenges as opportunities for growth rather than proof of damage. Therapists should focus on helping people address the real causes of distress, not amplifying helplessness. Patients, too, should seek out professionals who foster self-reliance, not dependency.

By confronting adversity with courage and clarity, we reclaim personal strength and begin to shift the national narrative—from fragility to fortitude, from avoidance to accountability.

Therapy, at its best, helps us move forward, not remain trapped in past wounds or false identities. If we want to rebuild the fabric of society, we must stop treating everyone as perpetually damaged—and instead nurture a culture that values resilience, responsibility, and meaningful connection.

CHAPTER NINE

A NATION OF EMOTIONAL LIGHTWEIGHTS

Not long ago, I found myself in line at a food truck in New York City where I overheard a conversation that perfectly encapsulates the shift in how people approach ordinary distress today. One woman said, "Can you believe how cold it's been this winter?"

"I know! It's been terrible. It's been so bad that I had to increase my antidepressants," the friend replied.

"I think I'm going to have to do that, too," the other woman added.

I stood there in silence, eyes on the menu, but inside my head, professional alarm bells were going off. I figured the conversation would be about typical annoyances like dry skin or feeling chilled and how they were looking forward to spring. I didn't expect such a severe turn.

I've treated plenty of people with Seasonal Affective Disorder (SAD), a type of depression that seems to be triggered by lack of sunlight. When days are shorter and darker, our circadian rhythm changes. The brain makes more melatonin, a hormone that induces drowsiness. Too much of it at the wrong times can bring on fatigue, lack of motivation, and other symptoms.

That didn't seem like what was happening with the two women outside getting lunch. For one, the most effective treatments for SAD are often behavioral and involve spending more time outdoors, near windows, or in front of a light source. More importantly, SAD is triggered by shorter days, *not* colder ones. Increasing an antidepressant dosage because of colder weather wasn't just clinically dubious, it was absurd.

And it's not just the weather that's provoking heightened emotional reactions. More and more, patients tell me they can't tolerate what, until recently, would have been considered minor setbacks or everyday frustrations. One single patient, for instance, insists she "could never survive" being ghosted after a date. Others describe becoming enraged or inconsolable over a disappointing restaurant meal, missing the release of a limited-edition sneaker, or standing too long in line for a slice of pizza at the city's newest hot spot. In years past, these responses would have been viewed as disproportionate—far exceeding the situation at hand.

One striking shift in recent years is that many patients no longer view their emotional reactions as the problem. Instead, they attribute distress to their surroundings—their environment, circumstances, or the people around them. The word *toxic* has become a catch-all for anything unpleasant, especially in conversations about relationships and boundaries. What once described genuinely harmful situations is now applied to nearly anything that causes frustration or friction.

As a result, relationships are increasingly reduced to labels rather than explored for their complexity. Instead of working through conflict, many people cut ties or dismiss opportunities for growth. I've heard grievances about *toxic* bosses, coworkers, exes, neighbors, and even politicians or commutes. In this worldview, if something feels uncomfortable, it must be eradicated.

The term *toxic* has become part of everyday vocabulary—popularized by influencers and, regrettably, by some therapists as well. But in the process, its original meaning has been lost, and with it, our tolerance for the normal friction of human relationships.

It's human instinct to move away from pain and danger; it's wired into our survival system. In life-threatening situations, we're programmed to fight or flee. What's striking today, however, is how many modern Americans—especially those living in comfort and privilege—struggle to distinguish between genuine danger and mere inconvenience.

For most of us, the day's greatest stressor isn't a matter of life and death. It's something that simply makes us uncomfortable. Calling these situations—or the people involved—*toxic* may sound harmless, but the word often serves as an escape hatch from accountability. Instead of confronting their own anger or anxiety, many people externalize it, blaming others for their emotions. And once a situation is labeled *toxic*, avoidance becomes the preferred solution. But avoidance doesn't solve problems, repair relationships, or build emotional skill.

This mindset lies at the heart of *Therapy Nation*. Today's self-absorbed therapy culture teaches people to mistake ordinary discomfort for harm, validation for healing, and emotional dependency for emotional strength.

It's understandable when individuals fall into this pattern unknowingly. What's far more troubling is when licensed therapists—who should recognize and correct these tendencies—reinforce them instead, turning their patients into emotional lightweights rather than resilient adults.

The grit you need

Psychologist Angela Duckworth's research on success reveals a lesson today's therapists—and patients—desperately need to hear. After leaving a job in consulting, Duckworth began teaching math to seventh graders in a New York City public school. She quickly noticed that intelligence alone wasn't what separated the best students from the worst—it was perseverance.

That insight led her to pivot careers and spend the next two decades studying what predicts success. Across groups as different as West Point cadets, National Spelling Bee contestants, rookie teachers, and corporate sales teams, one trait consistently emerged: grit—the passion and perseverance to pursue long-term goals.

In a popular TED Talk, Duckworth explained that grit—not intelligence, background, or privilege—was the best predictor of success.[1] Gritty individuals were more likely to graduate, excel, and advance, no matter the environment. Grit is what emotional heavyweights use to get ahead—and it's the very quality today's therapy culture risks undermining.

Inventor James Dyson persisted through 5,127 prototypes before creating one of the most successful vacuums on the market. Then there's one of my favorite artists, Stefani Germanotta—better known to the world as Lady Gaga—who was dropped by her record label after only three months. Refusing to quit, she transformed rejection into fuel, building a career defined by reinvention and fearlessness. Today, she's one of the most acclaimed performers of her generation, with Grammy and Academy Awards to her name and an unmatched ability to connect through raw emotion and authenticity. These are examples of grit—the very qualities therapy should be nurturing, not avoiding.

Duckworth's research, reinforced by real-world experience, shows that grit is a critical ingredient of personal growth. When therapists encourage clients to label even mild discomfort as something to be avoided, they are not helping them succeed. They are not building grit. They are cultivating fragility. Instead of fostering resilience, this approach reinforces a victimhood mindset that has become increasingly common in contemporary culture. By validating every emotion without challenging it, therapy can trap people in passivity—leaving them stuck in treatment, or increasingly reliant on medication, simply to manage the ordinary stresses of daily life.

Helicopter parents and a new generation of lightweights

During the COVID-19 pandemic, it was estimated that more than 20% of youth worldwide had been diagnosed with clinically significant anxiety.[2] That's nearly double the rate of anxiety in children in 2012. While some experts attribute the rise in youth anxiety to the pandemic's direct effects, a deeper factor may lie in how parenting styles have evolved. Overprotective "helicopter" parenting, once rare, is now common, and its unintended consequences—limiting resilience and independence in children—are more evident than ever.

It's normal for young children to experience some fear in novel situations. After all, they don't yet have the life experience to understand what's truly dangerous versus what's merely different than what they are used to. These children might experience anxiety when, for example, their parents aren't around despite them being in safe surroundings at grandma's house.

In the past, children overcame these typical fears through exploration and new experiences. The rise of overprotective "helicopter" parenting has created a generation struggling with self-reliance and emotional strength. Parents, with the best intentions, hover over their children, shielding them from adversity and preventing them from learning how to navigate life's challenges. This overbearing protection, rather than fostering safety, limits the child's ability to build resilience and decision-making skills. Today, parents increasingly accommodate their children's fears and coddle them. They sleep with children who are afraid of the dark and hover over children during playdates.

Of course, it's natural to want to help your children if they're uncomfortable. But by not giving them the opportunity to face fear, these parents turn mildly anxious children into severely anxious teens and young adults.[3] When a parent continually speaks up for a shy child, the child eventually learns to rely on other people to do the talking. When a parent fills out the paperwork to exempt a child from standardized tests, the student with test anxiety learns how to avoid tests—not how to take them. These actions also teach children that things like tests, the dark, and speaking up for yourself are okay to fear, rather than to conquer.

What anxious children need is the opposite of this overly accommodating parenting. While I don't work with children, I've counseled many people who have carried these anxiety issues into adulthood. The right approach is to help them face what they fear in small, manageable doses. Each success adds confidence, which serves as an antidote to fear. We've discussed earlier the idea that small doses of anxiety can make us stronger. That's true for adults and kids. Indeed, when parents were taught how and why to stop accommodating their children, 87% of their children reported less severe symptoms of anxiety.[4] In shielding children from anxiety, we inadvertently create a generation ill-prepared for life's inevitable struggles, leaving them more fragile and less capable of facing challenges head-on.

The numbing of America

It's never been easier to avoid the slightest discomfort.

With the latest technology at our fingertips, you can distract yourself from any unpleasant feeling for hours, even days. If you're stressed or feeling down, you can binge-watch an entire season of the latest hit show, gamble away your savings on an app, or lose yourself in video games for hours on end. And if those distractions aren't enough, there's always a range of substances—some legal, others far from it—to help numb the feeling.

Between 2016 and 2022, the rate of antidepressant prescriptions rose 66%.[5] Despite their name, these medicines are often prescribed to treat anxiety in addition to depression. For the people who need them, antidepressants can help them feel calm enough to tackle therapeutic goals, such as holding down a job. They can also be life changers when prescribed appropriately.

But like the women in the food truck line who apparently needed drugs to handle weather changes, more Americans are increasingly prescribed antidepressants for the wrong reasons and rely on them for situations that do not call for them.

Interestingly, in the 1950s, when it was discovered that a drug called meprobamate, branded as "Miltown," could relax people without putting them to sleep, the medicine almost didn't make it to market. The drug company that owned the patent assumed that few consumers would be willing to pay for a substance just to feel less stressed and more tranquil.[6] Initially, when the drug was released, sales were slow. After several months, however, Hollywood celebrities discovered it. People began passing Miltown around at parties. By the end of the first year, sales had hit $2 million. Other calming medicines soon followed, including chlordiazepoxide (Librium), diazepam (Valium), alprazolam (Xanax), clonazepam (Klonopin), and lorazepam (Ativan).

Today, most of us know someone who's been prescribed medication for a situation that doesn't truly warrant it—or who uses these drugs without a prescription. Maybe you've even been there yourself. Many people, for instance, take medications to help them sleep, even though these drugs were never approved for that purpose and can be habit-forming.

Medications once reserved for serious anxiety or panic disorders are now routinely prescribed by primary care physicians. While such drugs certainly have their place, Americans are increasingly turning to them for the wrong reasons. I often remind patients that medication can't reveal what's driving their distress, nor can it teach the tools or skills needed to address the underlying cause.

And prescription pills aren't the only way to blunt anxiety. People turn to nicotine, cannabis, and alcohol as well—substances that may temporarily soothe but ultimately create their own problems. All are habit-forming; all carry health risks. Nicotine, in particular, is so dangerous it comes with a warning label.

Likewise, many people falsely assume that alcohol is either harmless or health promoting. However, according to decades of research, alcohol is a carcinogen that has been linked to increased rates of mouth, throat, colon, rectal, liver, and breast cancer. It can also harm the brain, liver, pancreas, lungs, and heart.[7] Similarly, cannabis has been linked to cancer and respiratory problems.[8] I've also seen in patients just how harmful marijuana can be in other ways—how it contributes to their depression, motivation issues, and anxiety. Also, despite common misperceptions, marijuana dependence is very real. Once those who are dependent are able to quit it, they feel much better.

Then there's the growing problem of contamination, especially of street drugs. Not long ago, for example, I counseled an attorney who was grieving the death of his friend who had overdosed and died after taking a fentanyl-laced club drug. Upon learning of this story, I suggested that he might want to cut out his own drug use, especially given what he'd just experienced. I even suggested that his getting clean could serve as a way to honor his late friend.

A few weeks later, I received an email from the patient, explaining his reasons for no longer seeing me. "My last therapist never told me to stop! She said it was fine as long as I used a test kit for fentanyl!"

Alas, the man told me he would seek out help from another therapist instead. While I was perfectly happy to help him process his grief, I felt duty bound to help him take real steps to avoid the dangerous, potentially deadly behavior that had already claimed his friend. There are many different ways that humans grieve, but numbing the pain by continuing to indulge in activities whose murderous potential has recently been brought home to you is not a healthy way to do it.

I know that many therapists disagree with me on this. I have heard from patients who were told that using dangerous drugs is acceptable as long as minimal precautions are taken, such as home testing before use. I don't agree with that approach. It does a disservice to patients and to society. It reflects a broader pattern of therapeutic indulgence, where harm is softened rather than confronted and the underlying problem is left unaddressed. As a therapist, I see it as my responsibility to be honest about how these substances undermine psychological health, not to normalize their use.

Sadness, fear, and anger, though difficult, can be helpful emotions. When you pay attention to their underlying message, they can guide you in evaluating your life and making important decisions. But when you turn to a drug to numb these emotions, you miss out on what they're trying to tell you. Instead of addressing the root of the issue, you deepen the problem and further entrench your reliance on the medication.

On numbness and dumbness

In addition to turning to drugs, many people try to avoid the sting of uncomfortable emotions by suppressing them. For instance, at a funeral, instead of allowing themselves to cry, they stiffen up, blink rapidly, and try to appear strong and unaffected.

Occasionally, this type of emotional suppression can be useful. If you're enraged by something your boss said in a meeting, you likely don't want to act on the impulse to punch your boss in the face.

However, when emotional suppression becomes a habit, it can backfire. The emotion doesn't go away—it intensifies, often manifesting in physical problems.

The director of Stanford's Psychophysiology Lab, James Gross, PhD, has spent decades studying what happens when people attempt to suppress—and not feel—their emotions.

In a series of experiments, he and a team of researchers asked study participants to watch films designed to elicit feelings of disgust. Some participants were told to behave "in such a way that a person watching you would not know you were feeling anything." Others simply watched the film and reacted normally. The result: People who tried to suppress feelings of disgust became more stressed physiologically. Though their facial expressions appeared neutral, sensations of fight-or-flight—a pounding heart, tense muscles, increased blood pressure—worsened.[9] In another study with a similar setup, researchers tested people to see how many details they could remember about the film they'd just watched. People who'd tried to suppress their emotions remembered less of the movie than people who hadn't tried to suppress.[10]

Other research has linked the habitual use of emotional suppression with increased aggression, worsened mood, increased negativity, and lower levels of well-being.[11] Not surprisingly, it's also associated with fewer close relationships and increased levels of heart disease and poor health.[12, 13]

While suppression may seem like a way to control emotions, it often drives people toward other unhelpful coping mechanisms. Whether we bury our feelings or vent about them endlessly, the result is the same: we avoid the hard but necessary work of sitting with discomfort long enough to learn from it. Venting may feel like release, but it often backfires, leaving us more agitated than before.

Venting in circles

Sigmund Freud and other early mental health pioneers believed that unexpressed negativity could build up in the body like hydraulic pressure in a closed system. If not periodically released, it would eventually explode in the form of hysteria, a term used in the late 1800s and early 1900s to describe extreme emotional outbursts.

To help people release these pent-up emotions, Freud recommended catharsis—activities like screaming, crying, punching objects, or even taking revenge as a way to release negativity in small doses. Cathartic relief is also behind the collective screaming sessions some people participated in during the pandemic. In 2022, a group of twenty Boston mothers gathered on the fifty-yard line of a local football field and screamed for twenty minutes to release the stress of balancing remote work and homeschooling young children. "It's just amazing how light you can feel after you do that," one mother said after her primal scream session.

Catharsis also underlies the experience of ranting about the frustrations of the day. While there's a benefit to getting things off your chest, there's a key difference between using this approach for minor everyday stressors and for more deeply rooted, pathological issues. The problem is that modern therapists often miss this distinction, encouraging endless venting from patients, which—without constructive growth—only contributes to the cycle of emotional lightness and avoidance.

The concept of catharsis sounds reasonable in theory. By talking or ranting (or screaming) about a negative experience or emotion, you release energy and consequently feel better. But in reality, all that venting can make you feel worse in the long run. It's like continually adding fuel to a fire. Whenever you talk about a frustrating event, you amplify the feelings related to it. This explains why research has linked venting to *increased* aggression.

In one study, researchers criticized essays written by six hundred students. Some students then took the sting of criticism out on a punching bag. Later, all study participants were allowed to blast the person who'd criticized their writing with a loud noise. The students who'd wailed on punching bags were more likely to blast loud noises than the students who hadn't vented.[14] Many other studies have led to similar results. It didn't matter how people vented. In each study, venting worsened the negativity rather than releasing it. [15, 16, 17, 18, 19]

Sadly, some therapists have built entire practices around the idea of catharsis. Session after session, they sit quietly as patients vent about the injustices of the day—rarely interjecting, challenging, or offering a plan for change. I know this because many of my patients come to me after that kind of experience, often surprised by how different my approach feels.

One man, for example, sought me out after his previous therapist retired. When I asked about his goals, he said he wanted to manage stress more effectively and strengthen his relationships. Yet instead of working toward those goals, he spent our sessions unloading a long list of grievances. After two meetings, I gently interrupted to explain that my style was more active—I ask questions, share observations, and help develop strategies for improvement. He agreed to try this, but by the next session, he had returned to his familiar cycle of complaint. When I reminded him again of my role, he stopped coming. I can only assume he found another therapist willing to let him keep talking instead of helping him move forward.

What emotional heavyweights do

Truly resilient individuals—what you might call emotional heavyweights—understand that all emotions come in waves.

When emotional heavyweights experience discomfort—whether sadness, frustration, or anxiety—they don't push it away. They sit with it, trusting their ability to handle it. Instead of avoiding or suppressing pain, they use it as fuel for learning, growth, and resilience.

Emotional heavyweights don't chase constant happiness or comfort. They recognize that anger, frustration, stress, boredom, and sadness are natural parts of life. When things get tough, they don't give up—they persevere. They allow themselves to feel fully, not to wallow, but to move forward with clarity and strength.

Most importantly, emotional heavyweights act. They think differently, challenge their assumptions, and face uncertainty head-on. They question their own stories, consider other perspectives, and grow through what they experience.

Unfortunately, our culture doesn't reward this kind of strength. If anything, it encourages emotional lightweight behavior—avoidance, self-absorption, and endless validation. That's why therapy must serve as a counterweight, not a mirror.

When therapists prioritize validation over growth, therapy becomes an echo chamber instead of a catalyst for change. If a patient—let's call her Julie—complains that her boss is a "threat to her inner peace" and her friends are "unsupportive," a therapist focused on comfort will reassure her that she deserves to cut people off, set "hard boundaries," and avoid anything unpleasant.

The result? Julie doesn't grow stronger; she becomes more fragile. She quits her job impulsively, ghosts longtime friends, and ends up lonelier and more anxious than before. Instead of learning to navigate emotional strain, she runs from it. And the very person meant to guide her toward resilience—her therapist—has reinforced her avoidance.

This is the therapy trap in action. Too often, therapy coddles instead of challenges, validates instead of strengthens. But life doesn't get easier when we dodge discomfort—it gets harder.

True emotional strength is built by confronting difficulty, questioning our own narratives, and tolerating pain in the service of growth. That is what real therapy demands. Anything less fails the patient at the very moment strength is supposed to be built. Therapy should forge emotional heavyweights—people capable of carrying responsibility and discomfort—not produce emotional lightweights who collapse under ordinary strain.

CHAPTER TEN

THE PROBLEM WITH VALIDATION CULTURE

At a Fort Wayne youth basketball game during the spring of 2023, a spectator didn't like the referee's call. Enraged by this perceived injustice, reportedly, the man quickly descended the bleachers, stormed onto the court, and got in the ref's face. When the man didn't get the desired reaction, he allegedly started throwing punches.[1, 2, 3]

The man who stormed the court was the father of one of the players, all of whom happened to be in eighth grade. Incredibly, as the man kept swinging, several eighth-grade players tried to pull him off and shield the referee.

These disgusting displays of parental aggression have been unfolding during every type of youth sport—hockey, basketball, soccer, baseball, and more. No town nor city is immune.[4, 5, 6] During these encounters, adult spectators attack one another, coaches, referees, and even, in some cases, the children on the field. Just after a sixth grade basketball game, one parent bit off the ear of the opposing team's coach.[7] At a different game, another spectator shot and killed the coach of an opposing team.[8]

I've described only a few of the sickening encounters, but there are many, many more. If you've ever been a spectator on the sidelines of a youth sports game, you've likely witnessed this behavior for yourself. These altercations are *that* common. In a survey of 17,000 referees by the National Association of Sports Officials, respondents identified parents as the most frequent aggressors during these events.[9] The increasing prevalence of this disgusting behavior led *USA TODAY* to proclaim: "Sports parents are out of control."[10]

These reckless displays aren't just examples of poor sportsmanship; they are symptoms of a broader validation culture that rewards self-absorption at everyone else's expense. This mindset now permeates nearly every corner of society, where expressing outrage or hurt feelings is treated as justification for any behavior.

It shows blatant disrespect for authority figures like referees and coaches. More troubling still, it disregards the children playing and models that disrespect for them. In doing so, it teaches kids that respect is optional and that their emotions should always come first.

When I was growing up, adults were expected to set the tone. Kids might have mouthed off, but parents and coaches modeled restraint. Today, that standard has flipped. Parents who lash out from the sidelines may not realize they're teaching entitlement—showing their children that self-expression trumps self-control and that validation is more important than values.

While examples of reckless parents in youth sports are troubling, they are merely symptoms of a deeper societal issue—one that permeates every aspect of life, including therapy. What was once a tool for personal growth and resilience has now become yet another platform for reinforcing self-absorption and victimhood. As we look at the behaviors that highlight this trend, it becomes clear that the landscape of therapy is not immune to these societal forces.

This obsession with self-centeredness isn't confined to the sidelines of a basketball game. It's evident in the digital world and in our everyday interactions.

Social media, as usual, amplifies these tendencies. A popular Instagram account devoted to "parking spot shaming," for instance, posts photos of cars taking up multiple spaces or blocking handicapped spots. What was once simple frustration has turned into public performance—a way to feel morally superior by exposing someone else's flaws. And as that impulse spreads, the same self-absorption shows up offline. Small acts of courtesy, like holding the door or offering a seat to an elderly person, are giving way to self-righteous outrage over minor offenses.

The hunger for attention doesn't stop there. Some people take selfies in dangerous places—close to erupting volcanoes, on the edges of tall buildings and cliffs, or near sharks and other wild animals. In their pursuit of an impressive post, hundreds have died—tumbling from waterfalls, falling into the path of oncoming trains, plunging off cliffs, being gored by bison and elephants, or being electrocuted after touching live wires.[11]

This near-total self-absorption does more than harm the individuals involved. It's ripping society apart. Consider "swatting," a modern phenomenon when people call the police, not to report others for their infractions, but often because of some argument or difference of opinion. These typically anonymous callers claim a dangerous activity is being planned at the address of their target, and the local police arrive in full force, terrifying anyone at home.[12]

The signs are everywhere—in both the real world and the digital one. Instead of considering the needs or views of others, it seems as though we are living in the age of "me, myself, and I."

We have many expressions that are supposed to warn against this kind of behavior: Before you criticize someone, walk a mile in their shoes. Treat others the way you'd like them to treat you.

These and other such words of advice seem to have fallen by the wayside. Instead, the more common mantra seems to be "my way or the highway." Rather than walk a mile in someone else's shoes, people seem hell-bent on obliterating all traces of any human who looks or thinks differently than they do.

Therapists are further exacerbating this problem by encouraging a generation of patients to seek validation for their false beliefs and bad behavior. This only deepens their entrapment in endless therapy that gets them nowhere—in fact, it makes them sicker.

Affirming victimhood

One of my patients, Gabrielle, once shared with me what happened when she started seeing her previous therapist.

The therapist had asked, "What brings you in today?" Without hesitation, Gabrielle dove straight into her complaint about Sabrina, a coworker—a topic that had become all too familiar in Gabrielle's sessions.

"You won't believe what she did this time! She barged into my office and asked me all these questions, pretending she wanted to learn from my expertise. Of course, like an idiot, I answered her, thinking she genuinely wanted to know how I solve some pretty complex problems at work. Then, during a staff meeting later that day, she parroted everything I just taught her—without giving me any credit, of course! She's such an intellectual mooch and a bully. She's only out for herself! I feel uncomfortable whenever she's around. I can't stand going to work and seeing her. She's such a phony."

"So, you referred to her as a bully?" the therapist asked tentatively.

"Yes! She's cold and calculated—one hundred percent. It's all about her. She's always backstabbing me. She sees me as a roadblock to her promotion, not a colleague."

"This sounds like a toxic situation for you," the therapist said, nodding sympathetically. "You're right. She does sound like a workplace bully."

"Thank you! That's exactly what I was thinking!"

These types of therapists are common, as I've learned not only from treating their unsatisfied patients but also from conversations with friends and acquaintances in therapy. In these overly affirming sessions, if the patient thinks someone is a narcissist, the therapist agrees. If the patient believes their workplace is toxic, the therapist nods in support. If the patient claims they had an abusive childhood, the therapist buys into the narrative, hook, line, and sinker. If the patient adopts a victim mentality, the therapist reinforces it, fueling the victim narrative that has come to define much of modern therapy culture.

In Gabrielle's case, the way to approach it was to ask questions that help her see the situation more clearly and fairly. Is it possible that Sabrina wasn't intentionally trying to backstab her? Could Sabrina have spoken up in the meeting for other reasons? Does Sabrina have any positive traits that don't seem toxic or bully-like? Is she ever kind or generous to others at work? How do Gabrielle's other coworkers view Sabrina?

Most importantly, I'd press Gabrielle to consider: What can you do to prevent feeling taken advantage of again? In other words, I'd work to get Gabrielle out of the "victim mindset" that so many therapists are inadvertently reinforcing, and that the industry at large is perpetuating.

This line of questioning is essential because people seek therapy for a reason—and it's rarely because they already see the world clearly. Unfortunately, most therapists don't challenge their patients. Instead, they placate them, often reinforcing a narrative of blame and victimhood. This misguided therapeutic approach doesn't help patients, nor does it serve society as a whole.

The vast majority of people struggling with their mental health don't assess situations or others with accuracy. Instead, they tend to misinterpret the actions of those around them, reading nefarious intentions where there may be none. No one can read minds; we can only infer what others think or want based on their words or actions. But those inferences are often way off the mark and biased by how we're feeling in the moment—especially among people dealing with depression, anxiety, or other mental health challenges.

For example, when a friend forgets to wish someone a happy birthday, a mentally healthy person might feel bad at first, but would likely assume their friend was busy or simply forgot. Eventually, they would move on with their day, letting the slight go. But someone struggling with depression might falsely conclude that their friend no longer cares about them and maybe others feel the same, or that this person intentionally left them out to hurt their feelings. Similarly, someone with anxiety might notice two coworkers speaking in hushed tones and immediately assume they're gossiping about them. A mentally healthy person, however, might wonder this, but would probably come up with a much more neutral explanation in the end.

Remember that confirmation bias causes people to pay attention to details that confirm their opinions. Because of this mental filter, Gabrielle likely only told her therapist details about Sabrina that aligned with her own assessment of Sabrina as an "intellectual mooch and bully." Without prompting, Gabrielle may have kept any details supporting a more balanced view to herself. She was then left clinging to her victim label and wearing it like a badge of honor.

Other common cognitive biases that might be coloring Gabrielle's assessment of her work situation:

- **The actor-observer bias**: Gabrielle may attribute her own success to hard work and talent. Conversely, she may falsely believe that the success of others—and especially Sabrina—comes from luck, favoritism, grift, or backstabbing.
- **Anchoring bias**: Gabrielle's first impression of Sabrina may have gone badly. Now, she may interpret all other information through that negative lens, refusing to see any evidence contradicting it.

- **False consensus bias**: Gabrielle may assume other coworkers share her opinion about Sabrina, even though she hasn't asked them.
- **The hostile attribution bias**: Gabrielle has assumed Sabrina's intentions are hostile or threatening, but she doesn't honestly know that.

Entire books have been written about cognitive biases, and these are just a few examples. My point is to illustrate how these mental filters shape how we perceive the world. As therapists, it's our job to help patients recognize their biases for what they are—unrealistic and often outright incorrect ways of interpreting situations. When a therapist accepts a patient's view without challenging it, without probing for underlying biases, the entire therapy process becomes a waste of both the patient's and therapist's time.

Gabrielle's therapist did her no favors by labeling the work situation as "toxic" and Sabrina as a "bully." Gabrielle might have felt validated during the session and perhaps even for a few hours afterward. But that sense of affirmation wouldn't have lasted. By the time Gabrielle walked back into her office the next day, she'd find herself no better off than before the session. After all, her therapist had given her no new behavioral tools or strategies to navigate her work situation.

Even worse, Gabrielle was now more entrenched in her false beliefs. With the stamp of approval from her therapist, Gabrielle saw herself as the "victim" and Sabrina as the "villain." Rather than understanding her own role in the situation or looking inward, Gabrielle's victim mindset allowed her to place all the blame on external forces beyond her control. This left her with nothing productive to do to improve her work environment. Instead, she wallowed in negativity, injustice, and self-inflicted pain—reinforced and further ingrained in the next therapy session.

Gabrielle's story mirrors what I've heard from countless patients about their experiences with previous therapists. I can't emphasize this enough: Affirming a patient's false sense of injustice has no real benefits. Instead, it cultivates learned helplessness, keeping patients dependent on their therapists for brief moments of vindication, which usually dissipate hours after the session ends.

A culture of complaint

Some people are, without question, true victims—those who've been injured, harmed, or violated. That's not what I'm describing here. Gabrielle isn't a victim; she's caught in a frustrating situation that, after being repeatedly validated by others, has snowballed into a victim mentality rooted in self-absorption. She now sees herself as uniquely wronged, even when the evidence doesn't support it. And unfortunately, her therapist was only reinforcing the problem.

People with a victim mentality view the world as fundamentally unfair. In their eyes, everyone is out to get them, the system is rigged against them, and change feels impossible. They rarely look inward for solutions; instead, they project blame outward—onto others, institutions, or circumstance.

This mindset is notoriously hard to break because it feels so justified. It also comes with seductive short-term rewards: moral innocence, a sense of righteousness, and the attention, sympathy, and approval of others—including therapists all too eager to validate the story.

But over time, this path leads straight to misery. It breeds bitterness, resentment, and anxiety. Minor slights become major offenses. Petty grievances dominate conversation. I've seen people berate waitstaff for a delayed drink, demand to see a manager over a perceived slight, or even accuse a child's lemonade stand of breaking the law. The underlying impulse is the same: to secure the upper hand by claiming the mantle of the aggrieved.

A now famous example of this self-entitled behavior unfolded in 2020, when Christian Cooper, a Manhattan-based bird watcher, was in Central Park searching for a rare mourning warbler. That's when he noticed an unleashed dog in an area with clear signage indicating that leashes were required. He asked the dog's owner to leash her dog. Rather than own up to her own wrongdoing, the dog owner responded by calling the police—on *Cooper.*[13]

People with a victim mindset tend to use weaponized therapy-speak to denigrate the people around them. Everyone they dislike or who fails to affirm them is a psychopath. Interestingly, people who continually signal their victimhood are *more* likely to have the psychological traits they accuse others of having. They tend to score high in Machiavellianism, narcissism, or psychopathy.[14]

When left unchecked, this mentality can turn into an identity characterized by grievance—an integral ingredient in the recipe for violence.[15] Take a close look at the beliefs of many mass killers: Robert Bowers, who attacked the Tree of Life synagogue in Pittsburgh and was later convicted; Dylann Roof, who murdered nine parishioners in Charleston, South Carolina, and sits on federal death row; Elliot Rodger, who carried out the 2014 Isla Vista killings before taking his own life; the Columbine High School shooters, who also died at the scene; and Timothy McVeigh, the Oklahoma City bomber who was convicted and executed. A common thread runs through their stories. They saw themselves as victims. In some cases, grievance may have begun with a real slight or disappointment, a moment when they felt ignored, rejected, or powerless. But by fixating on that sense of injustice, they inflated it into identity. They came to believe they had nothing left to lose and that violence would even the score.

One particularly jarring example came in 2024, when Luigi Mangione was charged with shooting and killing UnitedHealthcare CEO Brian Thompson. Prosecutors allege that Mangione had written the words *Deny*, *Depose*, and *Delay* on the bullets, which they said referenced tactics used by insurers to contest patient claims. Mangione has pleaded not guilty, and at the time of this writing, his case has not yet gone to trial.

Later, when police arrested him, they found a manifesto. In it, Mangione allegedly wrote that he'd targeted UnitedHealthcare not because they were his insurer but rather because they were the largest insurance company in the U.S. He allegedly wrote, "Frankly, these parasites simply had it coming. A reminder: the U.S. has the #1 most expensive health care system in the world, yet we rank #42 in life expectancy . . . they continue to abuse our country for immense profit because the American public has allowed them to get away with it."[16]

Regardless of Mangione's *beliefs* behind his alleged actions, one might expect that the public would view Mangione's alleged *behavior* in the same way they see the actions of Timothy McVeigh and other murderers. That's not what transpired. Instead, Mangione's victim mentality went viral. There was an outpouring of grievance, vitriol, and rage—on Mangione's side. On social media, people posted tirades about the times insurance companies had denied their claims. In these warped takes, insurance customers are always the victims, company CEOs like Thompson are always the villains, and an accused killer like Mangione is automatically a hero. So many people were infected by this victim virus that many corporations beefed up CEO security for fear of copycat killings.[17]

For these reasons, one of a therapist's primary roles should be to help patients uproot the victim mentality and keep their thinking in check. Unfortunately, rather than challenging this narrative, many therapists inadvertently affirm and reinforce it. And as these newly validated patients leave their sessions, they carry that mindset into their daily lives—spreading it through their relationships and across social media.

To be clear, most therapists don't harm their patients intentionally. Many simply lack the training or experience to counter this powerful way of thinking. Inexperienced clinicians often make the mistake of believing every word their patients say. In the television series *House*, Dr. Gregory House, played by Hugh Laurie, reminds his medical team that "everybody lies." His point: Doctors can't rely solely on what patients report—they must verify the facts.

The same principle applies to psychotherapy. Patients often exaggerate, omit, or reinterpret details. You're only hearing one side of the story. A patient might call a spouse a "narcissistic piece of garbage" in one session and a "total sweetheart" in the next.

A skilled therapist distinguishes between validating emotions and validating perceptions. They might say, "It sounds like you're frustrated," or "It sounds like you're hurt." What they won't say is, "He sounds like a real jerk," or "Of course you're miserable—your boss is impossible." The first approach acknowledges feelings; the second affirms unverified beliefs. The difference can determine whether a patient grows stronger or stays stuck.

Other therapists have been tricked into believing that endless validation and affirmation are the only tools in their therapeutic arsenal. Consider the growing number of professionals graduating from the social justice–themed therapy programs that I mentioned in Chapter Six. It can be argued that by encouraging patients to see themselves in binary terms—such as privileged or underprivileged—these therapists end up leading many people to view themselves as powerless victims in a society stacked against them.

Finally, it takes significant effort to help patients recognize how their biases are harming them. After hours upon hours of listening to patients, some therapists likely overaffirm due to burnout or sheer laziness. That shouldn't happen, but it does—and I can understand why. If therapists took more control of their sessions, challenging their patients' rambling and working toward concrete solutions, they would break the monotony and avoid burnout on their end as well. Therapy could become more effective, not just for the patients but for the therapists themselves.

Over-affirmed, under-challenged

By this point, we've seen that many people enter therapy for the wrong reasons. They expect therapists to affirm every opinion, validate every grievance, and give their sense of persecution a professional seal of approval. For them, moral judgments about others often begin with the phrase "My therapist said . . ."

What they want is the opposite of what they need.

Patients need therapists who are willing to challenge them. That work is rarely comfortable. As I've written earlier, when I've encouraged patients to question their assumptions or think differently, some have left therapy or responded with anger. I have no regrets. My responsibility is to offer the therapy people need, not the comfort they may prefer.

Good therapists help patients separate legitimate, fact-based problems from imagined or exaggerated ones. When they notice signs of grievance, they slow down and ask questions that prompt reflection: "What evidence supports your belief that your spouse is a narcissist?"

Bad therapists don't ask those questions. They overvalidate. They reinforce the notion that feelings should always take precedence over facts, that disagreement is danger, and that discomfort equals harm. And this mentality doesn't stay in the therapy room—it spills into the culture. If someone dislikes a book, they demand it be banned. If a politician votes the wrong way, they don't debate; they threaten. On social media, they block and unfriend anyone who dares to challenge them.

People who think differently are labeled *toxic*, their ideas unworthy of discussion. Outrage replaces dialogue. Vilification replaces understanding.

Therapists must stop reinforcing the belief that every individual is the center of their own universe, entitled to perpetual validation. Real happiness doesn't come from obsessing over yourself—

it comes from engaging with the world, building genuine relationships, and learning to tolerate discomfort.

Self-care vs. self-indulgence

Self-care has become yet another buzzword, often used as an excuse for selfish, antisocial behavior. It's a prime example of therapy-speak being weaponized, turned into a tool for individuals to justify their actions against one another.

Originally, the concept of self-care was a treatment for depression. People struggling with severe depression sometimes find themselves so overwhelmed that they can't perform basic daily tasks like brushing their teeth, showering, or eating. In these cases, establishing a routine to manage these simple activities helped them regain structure and the ability to participate in life again.

Later on, the concept of self-care was extended to professionals like physicians, teachers, and others in helping professions. By tending to their own basic needs—eating a healthy diet, exercising, and getting enough sleep—people in these fields were less likely to experience burnout. It was similar to the well-known advice to "put on your oxygen mask before helping others" in an airplane. By prioritizing their own well-being, helping professionals could recharge and have the energy and capacity to better care for those they serve.

For decades, outside of the settings I just mentioned, the phrase "self-care" was obscure. Then, around 2016, right after Donald Trump won his first presidential election, the phrase flooded into the mainstream with the force of a Category 5 hurricane. All over the internet, Hillary Clinton supporters encouraged one another to practice "self-care," seemingly using the phrase interchangeably with "stress management" and "self-pampering." The website Quartz published an article with the headline "The

Rise of Donald Trump Demands We Embrace a Harder Kind of Self-Care."[18] Another site posted, "A Self-Care Guide of TV to Watch to Forget About Donald Trump."[19]

It was likely around this time that self-care stopped being about recharging so we could show up for others and started being all about the self. As validation culture grew, self-care was reframed as a moral right. The idea took hold that putting your own comfort first, even at the expense of others, was not just acceptable but something to be celebrated. The result is a version of self-care that often blurs the line between healthy restoration and outright indulgence, where every boundary or inconvenience is treated like an absolute.

According to Google Trends, searches for "self-care" have surged in recent years—especially since 2016. On social media, #SelfCareSunday has become a weekly ritual, though most of what's shared bears little resemblance to the original idea. On platforms like TikTok, self-care has become shorthand for indulgence and beauty. Scroll through the videos under #selfcare and you'll find influencers detailing 10-step bath routines that require buying a small fortune in products. Yes, you read that right: a 10-step bath routine. Apparently, none of the steps involve simply turning on the water, getting in, and relaxing.

Beyond these elaborate bathing rituals are endless clips of young women applying cleansers, toners, mud masks, and moisturizers, or showcasing their nail care regimens. Some even argue that Botox qualifies as "self-care"—including twentysomethings who don't yet have wrinkles. "Preventative Botox," as it's called, promises to stop them before they start. Other so-called preventative treatments—eyebrow tinting, spray tans, lash lifts—claim to save time on beauty routines but only add more to the list of things to manage.

While this sort of excess may not be psychologically dangerous, the trend takes a darker turn inside therapy offices. Increasingly, therapists endorse these indulgent routines by prescribing "self-care" without defining what it truly means. With professional approval, the term has become interchangeable with *protecting my peace.*

That misinterpretation gives patients permission to avoid discomfort rather than confront it. Instead of addressing problems directly, they "protect their peace" by quitting jobs, ghosting friends, or withdrawing from challenges. In this way, self-care becomes a euphemism for avoidance.

True self-care builds strength, not fragility. Taking care of oneself is essential—but constantly cutting out anything that disrupts comfort, relaxation, or "me time" doesn't heal. It stunts growth, weakens resilience, and ultimately creates more problems than it solves.

The real path to healthy relationships

To thrive, relationships require compromise. If everyone in every relationship adopts a "my way or the highway" stance, it won't be long before people are at each other's throats. When individuals refuse to bend, conflicts escalate, resentment festers, and relationships break down. If we take the notion of "protecting our peace" to its extreme, there will be no peace left to protect.

The healthiest, most enduring relationships aren't built on a winner-takes-all mentality. Instead, they are grounded in a willingness to listen, adapt, and meet each other halfway. Compromise doesn't mean sacrificing core needs or values; it's about recognizing that no two people are identical and that navigating differences is essential for coexistence.

As discussed earlier, many therapists discourage compromise, instead promoting a version of self-care and boundary setting that fuels selfishness. Patients are often advised to prioritize their own feelings above all else, to cut ties rather than work through conflicts, and to view any discomfort as a sign that a relationship is toxic.

This mindset doesn't foster stronger, more resilient individuals. Instead, it breeds isolation, intolerance, self-absorption, and an inability to form meaningful connections. Ultimately, people become lonelier and more disconnected than before.

I once worked with a couple married for six years, standing on the brink of divorce. The husband, Michael, felt his wife, Lori, never made time for him, always prioritizing her routines—yoga, work, time with friends, solo vacations—over their relationship. Lori, on the other hand, had been seeing a therapist who reinforced the idea that her needs should always come first, and any request from Michael to adjust her schedule was seen as an infringement on her boundaries.

Lori's therapist had encouraged her to set rigid boundaries without considering Michael's needs. She was told that if Michael truly loved her, he would accept her as she was, without expecting any compromise. But Michael wasn't asking Lori to abandon her self-care; he simply wanted a more balanced relationship where both partners made room for each other.

When Lori and Michael came to me for counseling, I helped them understand that relationships require reciprocity and flexibility, not unilateral demands. I encouraged Lori to challenge the extreme version of self-care she had adopted and helped her see that making time for her husband wasn't a betrayal of herself—it was an investment in their marriage. At the same time, I worked with Michael to express his needs in a constructive way, rather than with resentment.

Over time, they found a middle ground. Lori continued her self-care routines, but she also made a conscious effort to prioritize quality time with Michael. He, in turn, learned to appreciate Lori's need for personal space while also feeling valued in the relationship.

Had Lori stuck with the advice of her previous therapist—one that equated compromise with self-sacrifice—her marriage likely would have ended. But by embracing the idea that relationships require flexibility and mutual effort, Lori and Michael strengthened their bond rather than walking away from it.

Selfishness never serves a relationship. Over the years I've seen many different versions of this, from "golf widows" to (more recently) "yoga widowers" like Michael. He and Lori were fortunate. In many relationships, one or both partners struggle to find a healthy compromise.

This dynamic is something I see frequently in my practice. What I emphasize in these situations is that true growth isn't about rigidly protecting your own feelings at the expense of connection. It's about learning how to engage with others in a way that respects both individual needs and the relationship itself.

Therapy should be about developing strength, not indulging weakness. It should focus on accountability, not endless validation. When we shift away from excessive self-centeredness and prioritize resilience, responsibility, and genuine connection, we begin to address the deeper issues in society. Until then, we risk being surrounded by people who believe the world revolves around them—a recipe for disaster.

If therapy fails to challenge individuals and foster emotional resilience, our society will grow increasingly unable to navigate life's complexities—leading to deeper isolation, greater intolerance, and a breakdown of meaningful connection.

CHAPTER ELEVEN

THE WEAPONIZATION OF PSYCHOLOGY

Have you ever been on the receiving end of any of these phrases?

"You sure do like to argue."

"Why are you always overreacting?"

"This conversation is over."

"Say what you want. I don't care."

"Why is everything such a big deal to you?"

"You're crazy."

If so, a "self-aware narcissist" influencer on TikTok would like you to know that you likely were in a relationship with a narcissist.

Those statements are from one of *many* social media videos that spread confusing, inaccurate, and often downright misleading mental health advice. Along with these tips, you can also learn how to identify a psychopath, toxic person, abusive partner, love bomber, or emotionally unavailable individual, among other psychological traits and conditions. While some of this social media content comes from licensed therapists, the vast majority of these videos are produced by people with no mental health qualifications whatsoever.

This behavior isn't limited to TikTok—it's all over social media, in popular song lyrics, and even in sitcoms. The normalization of therapy culture in entertainment has made therapy-speak not just acceptable, but fashionable. Unfortunately, overzealous, social media–driven therapists are only fueling the problem, lending false legitimacy to the flood of "How to spot a . . ." videos that spread dangerous misinformation.

This *therapy-speak*—the use of therapeutic terminology outside of sessions—has become increasingly widespread, and just as increasingly misleading. An analysis of five hundred TikTok videos with the hashtags "mental health" or "mental health tips" found that 31% misused or inaccurately presented psychological terms. Despite this, only 9% of the TikTok creators had any relevant qualifications to offer mental health advice, and a mere 1% included a disclaimer about their lack of credentials.[1]

Whether intentional or not, mental health influencers are diluting and stretching the definitions of countless conditions, creating the false impression that far more people suffer from them than actually do. And it does more than create confusion. As this book has shown, the misuse of psychological language encourages self-diagnosis, pathologizes ordinary discomforts, and, as discussed in the previous chapter, turns self-care into self-obsession.

Now we'll explore another serious consequence: how this watering down of mental health language is making real suffering harder to recognize and address.

When psychological terms lose their true meaning, they stop being tools for self-understanding and become, instead, weapons of insult. During a disagreement, one friend may ask another "Why are you so sensitive?" The other friend might lash out with a remark like, "That's something a narcissist would say." In these moments, using such terms often feels like a "trump card"—they're deployed with a sense of superiority, as if they've just triumphed over a less evolved opponent.

Yet it's *not* a win.

Rather than fostering consensus or understanding, psychological warfare simply shuts down debate and deepens divisions. People attack with incorrect jargon, but no one listens. Minds close instead of opening.

The rise of therapy-speak

When actress Gwyneth Paltrow and Coldplay lead singer Chris Martin ended their marriage in 2014, Paltrow published a statement that, in part, read:

"We have always conducted our relationship privately, and we hope that as we consciously uncouple and co-parent, we will be able to continue in the same manner."[2]

Paltrow had seemingly picked up on the "consciously uncouple" concept from Katherine Woodward Thomas, a marriage and family therapist, who has written books and taught seminars on this idea. Back in 2014, therapy-speak was much less pervasive, and people all over the internet got a laugh out of Paltrow's awkward use of the phrase "consciously uncouple." Why not just call it a divorce?

Now, more than a decade later—with therapy-speak infiltrating every corner of society—I wonder if Paltrow's "conscious uncoupling" announcement would still be met with the same ridicule. Unlike in 2014, today you can find countless videos online promoting the supposed benefits of "conscious uncoupling." In other words, what was once fringe has gone mainstream.

The same can be said for many other therapy terms, which I'll explore more deeply in the following pages.

When celebrities speak openly about depression, anxiety, or

suicidal thoughts, it can reduce stigma—a positive development. But celebrities also set trends. When they begin using psychological language, their followers often follow suit, adopting the terminology without understanding it. As a result, people start diagnosing themselves or others based on what they've heard rather than consulting a qualified professional.

A trained therapist uses "therapy-speak" in its proper context, clarifying what terms mean and what they don't. Outside the therapy room, however, the public's casual use of psychological jargon is only deepening our confusion—and, ultimately, our division and distress.

Dropping diagnostic daggers

Humans have likely been using words to vilify one another since the dawn of language. Insults, in other words, are nothing new.

What's different now is that our insults increasingly take the form of psychological diagnoses. This doesn't just malign someone—it pathologizes them.

Consider what happens when a spouse repeatedly calls their partner "abusive" to win arguments over housework, childcare, or sex. The word is loaded, and it's often used to silence. At first, the partner may back down out of guilt or confusion. But over time, they may start to internalize the label—thinking, *Fine. If you see me as abusive, then I'll act that way.* Ironically, this can create more of the behavior the accusation was meant to stop.

When we pathologize someone, we take a complex, often solvable issue and inflate it into something much bigger. If you view someone as inconsiderate, you might believe an honest conversation could resolve the problem. But if you label them as disordered, you may conclude they're beyond help—and the relationship beyond repair. That shift in perception can lead you to end friendships or partnerships prematurely, then wonder, *Why can't I find anyone who truly understands me?*

In the following pages, I'll explore how this dynamic plays out through four of the most popular "diagnostic daggers" in our cultural lexicon: *toxicity*, *emotional labor*, *boundaries*, and *narcissism*.

The toxicity is in the dose

Hundreds of years ago, the Swiss physician and chemist Paracelsus observed, "All things are poison, and nothing is poison; only the dose makes a thing not a poison." Today, this idea is often shortened to "the dose makes the poison," and it remains a foundational concept in toxicology—the science of poisons.

The principle is simple: Too much of anything, even water or oxygen, can cause harm. Conversely, even known poisons can be harmless—or beneficial—in small doses. Many cancer medicines, for example, are lifesaving at carefully measured increments, but deadly if too much is given. Similarly, apple seeds contain trace amounts of amygdalin. When digested, amygdalin breaks down into cyanide, a poison. But the amount in a typical apple seed is so tiny that accidentally swallowing one poses no danger.

Studying "toxicity" has long been a legitimate part of scientific inquiry. But today, the word has escaped the laboratory and migrated into the therapist's office. From there, new variants have incubated and spread, first through indulgent therapists, then through their many patients, and finally into the popular lexicon. We've moved beyond the reasonable concept of "the dose makes the poison" to recklessly labeling people, situations, and events as simply "toxic." Today, this word has become one of the most overused catch-all terms in pop psychology, and one of the most weaponized cudgels of therapy-speak.

Another example of how toxicity is in the dose is emotional criticism. There's a difference between a partner who occasionally snaps out of frustration or offers constructive feedback with love, and one who constantly berates you, undermines your confidence, and turns every disagreement into a character attack. In the first case, these moments, though unpleasant, can often be resolved through honest communication and mutual effort. In the second, the pattern is corrosive and requires a different level of intervention. But when all forms of criticism are labeled as "toxic" or "abusive," it becomes harder to distinguish between normal relational friction and truly harmful behavior.

But much of what people call "toxic" today *isn't* dangerous at all.

For example, when a coworker suggests you "stop interrupting" them during a meeting, it's not toxic. It's an attempt to help you understand how your actions affect them.

Similarly, when a friend disagrees with you about religion and politics, it's not toxic. It's simply a difference of opinion.

When a roommate confronts you about eating their stash of chips, they're being assertive, not toxic.

When your parents stop handing over money every time you ask, they're not toxic. They're being responsible.

When your boss pressures you to meet a deadline, it's not toxic. It's expected—part of being a paid employee.

When therapists and influencers lean into this lazy labeling of common problems as "toxic," it lowers the threshold of what's considered normal. Some degree of hardship was, until recently, expected as part of life. When something didn't go your way, you might not have liked it, but you didn't immediately see it as a sign that another person needs therapy or an antidepressant. In most cases, such experiences can be taken as part of the human experience and a way to build character.

Freely tossing around the "toxic" label can also shape your

decisions and actions in harmful ways. If you convince yourself that a coworker is toxic, you may avoid them, gossip about them, or even try to undermine them. In doing so, you could end up sabotaging your own career, not theirs.

The truth is, many of life's uncomfortable moments and emotions serve an essential purpose. They push us to pay attention, work harder, solve problems, change direction, learn lessons, reassess priorities, repair relationships, and, ultimately, grow into stronger, more capable people.

Sometimes, the toxicity is in us

I once counseled a lawyer named Jim who came to see me for social anxiety. He explained that he often felt anxious around his boss, who happened to be the CEO of the firm.

"Why do you think that happens?" I asked.

"I think it's because he's so imposing," Jim said. "He's a former professional athlete. The man is huge. It's intimidating to be around him."

"Has your boss ever done anything to make you uncomfortable?" I asked.

"No," Jim said. "It's just how I feel."

"Has he ever singled you out or made you feel like you didn't measure up?"

"No, not at all. I just don't like being around him. I hate to admit it, but he scares me."

As we spoke, it became clear: Jim's anxiety wasn't based in fact, which is often the case with anxiety. The brain can conjure up untrue thoughts and beliefs—like "no one likes me" or "everyone thinks I look stupid"—which trigger uncomfortable bodily sensations, such as a pounding heart or tense muscles.

In therapy, we uncovered that Jim was a competent attorney

who consistently met deadlines and received positive reviews. Still, despite a complete lack of evidence, he felt certain his boss was judging him negatively. This false belief caused him to get flustered whenever his boss was around. He stumbled over his words and worried it would eventually cost him a good performance review.

If I were to take my cues from modern therapy practices, I might have encouraged Jim to explore why everyone else is at fault for him feeling this way, or dig into his childhood to uncover traumatic experiences. Maybe I'd learn that Jim's boss reminded him of his father, and that could have led to endless sessions examining how his upbringing was responsible for his adult anxiety. It could have led to me suggesting Jim leave his "toxic" workplace for one where he felt more comfortable.

That wasn't my approach. Based on what Jim shared with me, I knew the "toxicity" was in his mind, not his workplace. If Jim didn't change his habitual thinking patterns and behavior, his social anxiety would follow him wherever he went. So, I encouraged Jim to do what he feared most: be around his boss more often.

"Why don't you volunteer to give presentations instead of waiting to be called on?" I suggested. I also worked with Jim on his confidence, helping him focus on his many positive traits, including his sense of humor. Jim loved comedy, so I suggested he sign up for an open mic night to practice public speaking.

"No way," Jim said. "I could never do that. I'd choke."

"How about we work up to it?" I suggested. "Let's start with something slightly outside your comfort zone but that still feels doable."

Jim agreed to present a three-minute set in front of three people at a dive bar in the East Village. The experience was anxiety provoking, but he survived—and even made friends with other aspiring comedians. As his confidence grew, he took on bigger opportunities. Within months, he was performing in front of one hundred people. At work, Jim felt less intimidated by his boss. Stand-up comedy had given him a sense of confidence and control that he hadn't had before. He also felt more at ease with the spontaneity and unpredictability of the workplace.

Jim's transformation is impressive. It's a powerful example of the benefits that come from confronting uncomfortable experiences directly—rather than overtherapizing or overanalyzing them, relying on inaccurate labels, or avoiding them altogether.

"I'm not doing that emotional labor for you."

In a 1983 book, sociologist Arlie Hochschild coined the term *emotional labor* to describe the uniquely draining experiences of people who worked in the service industry. These workers spent many hours a day managing the emotions of others in order to provide service with a smile. Consider the call center employee who works for your health insurance company. Such a person likely answers complaints day in and day out from angry customers, yet has very little power to do anything to solve their problem. Mostly, they listen as someone rants, interjecting with platitudes like "I'm sorry you feel this way" and "This sounds very frustrating for you." As the call center employee attempts to manage the caller's emotions, they also have to manage their own. At all times, they must sound unfrazzled.[3]

People in many professions—flight attendants, coffee baristas, even psychotherapists—practice emotional labor, as Hochschild described it, which often leads to burnout.

Like the term *privilege*, this concept of emotional labor remained obscure outside of the occasional sociology class. Then, around 2015, it exploded into the mainstream. That's when it became popular with social justice warriors, who used it to describe the free, invisible, and often thankless emotional work done by women and minorities.[4, 5] It was around this time that feminist thinkers, along with some therapists, began counseling women that they did not "owe emotional labor to anyone."

On the internet, the phrase soon evolved into the elitist refrain it is today: essentially code for, "I'm not making time for your BS." Person A would post a controversial viewpoint, and when Person B asked for clarification—an example, a study, evidence—instead of engaging, Person A would often reply, "I don't owe you my emotional labor." In other words: "Do your own research, moron." The phrase became a convenient way to shut down debate and avoid uncomfortable conversations.

To be fair, the original intent was understandable. It was meant to acknowledge that women, minorities, or marginalized groups should not be expected to shoulder the burden of constantly making their life experiences digestible and palatable for others. But over time, "I don't owe you my emotional labor" has expanded beyond that context and now excuses people from any effort to explain their stances at all. It has shifted from protecting emotional energy to rejecting any responsibility to share ideas or participate in good faith discourse. The result is a culture where dialogue dies before it begins, replaced by mic drops and one-liners designed to shut people out rather than bring them in.

One of the biggest problems with this dynamic is that people on the receiving end often have no idea what the phrase even means. Instead of sparking reflection or inspiring someone to reconsider their position, it blocks any chance for productive conversation. Those using it often assume the other person will go off, do more research, and ultimately come back enlightened. In reality, most people simply roll their eyes, feel dismissed, and become even more entrenched in their own beliefs—or worse, assume the person wielding the phrase has nothing meaningful to say.

If your goal is for someone to understand what you're going through, then skip the buzzwords and focus on having a productive conversation instead.

"Stop crossing my boundaries."

Boundaries are essential for maintaining emotional well-being and personal space. They are particularly beneficial for people who dedicate their lives to helping others, often at their own expense. For instance, a stressed-out working parent of young children might set a boundary not to check email or answer the phone during the hour they get their children ready for bed. In other cases, strict boundaries are necessary to protect ourselves or our children. If one spouse is battling addiction, the other may need to limit the addicted partner's contact with the children—at least until the addict seeks help and achieves sobriety.

But boundaries aren't always clear-cut. Sometimes they're misused, particularly when they become tools for manipulation or control. Some therapists will suggest boundaries to people who don't need them or in situations where they aren't warranted. Because of this, the word *boundaries* is increasingly becoming synonymous with *take me or leave me.*

In Chapter Three, I described a woman who, during the 2024 election between Donald Trump and Kamala Harris, told her father that if he voted for Trump, he would never see his grandchildren again. Imposing this boundary demands political conformity as the price of interaction with family members. For example, one spouse might threaten, "If you divorce me, you will never see your children again."

Unfortunately, children are often caught in the crossfire of manipulative boundaries. These threats deprive them of the opportunity to maintain a relationship with someone they've come to love.

But that's not the kind of boundary I'm talking about here. True boundaries are about respecting both oneself and others. When therapists treat them as rigid lines in the sand that others must respect, they fail to acknowledge that real boundaries are flexible and open to negotiation. Authentic boundaries encourage growth, respect, and mutual understanding—not avoidance and exclusion.

Take Esther, a patient who began therapy after her adult daughter, Sophia, moved back home following a job loss. At first, Esther did what any loving mother would do. She welcomed Sophia with open arms, hoping that the time at home would help her financially recover and give her space to find a new job.

Esther didn't expect much in return. She simply asked of Sophia what she would expect from any other house dweller: clean up after herself, do her own laundry, and wash her own dishes. Unfortunately, these basic expectations were not met.

Sophia never replaced the toilet paper after using the last square. She didn't clean. She didn't cook. She didn't shop for groceries. In her room, trash piled up in the bin. Dirty clothes were left on the bathroom floor. Her socks were scattered across the den. Her dishes remained in the sink, untouched.

In our therapy sessions, I helped Esther explore ways to approach Sophia with understanding and compassion. But in real life, when Esther asked Sophia to help out, she received an unexpected response.

"My therapist said that, for my mental health, I don't have to bend to other people's rules. She encouraged me to practice self-care and protect my mental health by setting up boundaries. That's what I am doing. You need to accept me the way I am. I'm not going to change for you."

Esther was stunned, and frankly, so was I when she shared this during our session. If anyone needed to set a boundary, it was Esther—not Sophia. Yet somehow, Sophia had managed to twist the concept of a boundary into an excuse to avoid responsibility (and flaunt an alarming level of ungratefulness).

To be fair, I don't know exactly what Sophia discussed in her therapy sessions, nor can I say with certainty what her therapist advised. Still, it appears that, like many others, her therapist emphasized Sophia's comfort above nearly everything else. In this case, her "boundaries" functioned less as a tool for healthy self-protection and more as a wall, shutting out any request for change or growth.

Other manipulative boundaries might sound like the following:

- "If you keep dating people of the same sex, you're no longer welcome in this family."

  What this means: This boundary isn't about personal comfort. It's a demand for conformity, used to control the other person's life choices.

- "If you don't major in engineering, I'm cutting off your inheritance."

  What this means: This isn't setting a boundary for well-being—it's a financial manipulation aimed at forcing a decision under threat.

- "If you don't break up with your boyfriend, I'm not talking to you again."

  What this means: A demand for compliance with personal preferences, using the threat of severing a relationship to manipulate someone's romantic choices.

- "If you don't loan me the money, you're dead to me."

  What this means: This is a boundary disguised as a financial request, but it's really a way to impose guilt and force an obligation.

Unfortunately, some of my therapy colleagues are encouraging this manipulative behavior. One of my patients, Sarah, told me she had been looking forward to seeing her sister, Heather, who would be visiting from out of town. Like Sarah, Heather was also in therapy. But unlike Sarah, Heather was working with a therapist who validated her every whim, encouraging her to set unreasonable and manipulative boundaries.

For example, Heather disliked Sarah's boyfriend, Dave. The rift was mostly political, and Sarah was well aware of it. Heather seemed to bring it up during every text and phone call. Even so, Heather and Dave had remained cordial in person, agreeing to disagree and sticking to neutral topics whenever they were together.

Despite this, just before the trip, Heather contacted Sarah and said, "I'd love to see you, but not when Dave is around. If Dave has to be there, I don't want to see you."

Sarah was devastated.

"What changed?" I asked her.

"She's seeing a new therapist," Sarah told me. "The therapist said Heather needs to set boundaries to avoid any uncomfortable situation at all costs—that she shouldn't have to be around anyone who triggers her."

The above example illustrates therapy gone wrong, yet it has become the norm, not the exception, and it's making people sicker and dividing families.

When used effectively, boundaries are meant to focus on what you can control—your time, your energy, and your space. For example, if you're feeling overscheduled, you might set a boundary by limiting yourself from taking on new projects. Or, if close contact makes you uncomfortable, you could politely tell someone that you're more comfortable shaking hands than hugging.

Boundaries are about managing your own behavior—something that is entirely within your control. They are not about trying to control other people's behavior, which is mostly out of your hands.

Finally, boundaries can and should be flexible, because life is unpredictable. For instance, you might set a boundary by putting your phone on "do not disturb" mode between 11:00 p.m. and 7:00 a.m. to ensure you get uninterrupted sleep. That's a healthy boundary, and people will quickly learn that while they can still text or call during those hours, you won't respond. But if a friend or family member is in crisis, you might choose to adjust the boundary, allowing their calls to come through so you can be there when they truly need you.

"You're such a narcissist!"

People with narcissistic personality disorder are estimated to make up less than 6.2% of the population.[6] Based on how TikTok describes "ways to spot a narcissist," it's easy to fall into the trap of believing that the diagnostic label applies to a much larger portion of the world's population.

People often use the word *narcissist* as a catch-all for *selfish*. However, in psychology, narcissism has a very specific meaning. It's one of the ten recognized personality disorders, which are far more enduring and pervasive than temporary emotional disturbances like depression or anxiety. These disorders shape how someone thinks about themselves, how they respond emotionally, how they relate to others, and how they control their behavior.

Specifically, according to the latest criteria from the Diagnostic and Statistical Manual of Mental Health Disorders (DSM), someone with narcissistic personality disorder would exhibit the following personality traits and behaviors.

- Grandiosity (a sense of superiority or self-importance)
- A preoccupation with success, power, brilliance, beauty, or love
- A belief in their specialness and desire to associate with other "special" people
- A need for admiration and compliments
- An expectation of favorable treatment
- Behaviors that take advantage of others
- A lack of empathy
- Feelings of envy, or beliefs that others are envious of them
- Arrogant language and behaviors

If you're like many people, looking at the list above, you've probably thought of someone in your life who might be a narcissist. But it's crucial to remember that personality disorders are complex and challenging to diagnose. Even highly trained professionals don't always get it right—sometimes with serious consequences. So, what does that say about the ability of the average person—without formal training—to diagnose their friends, family, or acquaintances with this disorder? In my view, the odds are somewhere between 10% and zero.

The truth is, most people who are labeled as narcissists aren't clinical narcissists at all—at least not by the official diagnostic criteria. When most people accuse someone of being a narcissist, they're not referring to consistent traits. Instead, they're typically pointing to behavior that occurs only occasionally or in specific situations, which may be more about momentary frustration or conflict than a personality disorder.

Most people exhibit *some* of the traits associated with narcissism at different times. Maybe they push through a crowd without thinking, lose their temper, or try to cozy up to a higher-up in the hopes of getting ahead. Maybe someone acts arrogantly while driving, convinced that everyone else on the road should retake driver's ed. Yet, in other areas of their life, like at work and with their family, they might be genuinely humble, treating those beneath them in the corporate hierarchy with respect and recognizing their intelligence and talents.

The term is also often conflated with well-intentioned self-interest. For example, if a woman ends a relationship because of incompatibility or because she no longer feels in love, a heartbroken partner might label her "a narcissist" simply because her decision involves self-focus. In reality, that kind of self-awareness and autonomy is not the same as being clinically narcissistic—marked by grandiosity, a lack of empathy, or an obsession with one's specialness.

No matter how much we strive to be empathetic and kind, everyone has moments when they come across as selfish, rude, or even cruel. None of that makes them narcissists. It simply makes them human.

Perhaps nowhere is the "narcissist" label more overused—and more damaging—than in the world of dating. On social media, *love bombing* has become a buzzword, often described as a manipulation tactic used by narcissists. A love bomber showers their partner with affection, compliments, and promises—talking about marriage, kids, or saying "I love you" within days or weeks. The intent, supposedly, is to create an intense emotional bond so quickly that the other person feels invested and, eventually, trapped. The "bomb" isn't cruelty or criticism but an overwhelming rush of affection designed to gain control.

While love bombing is real, it's rare. What's far more common is that once the "honeymoon" phase fades, people stop performing their idealized selves and begin acting more authentically. When someone interprets that natural shift as a "red flag," they may end a promising relationship prematurely. The issue here isn't a personality disorder—it's unrealistic expectations.

Earlier, I noted that therapy-speak can sometimes help reduce stigma. In this case, it does the opposite. When people call anyone they dislike a "narcissist," they turn a clinical diagnosis into an insult. Narcissistic personality disorder doesn't make someone a terrible or unfixable person, and many who have it work hard to manage their tendencies. But in today's climate, wielding the label "narcissist" is essentially declaring someone morally defective.

The same misuse extends to other terms casually borrowed from the DSM. Calling someone "histrionic" references histrionic personality disorder. Referring to someone as "borderline" comes from borderline personality disorder. Words like *psychopath* and *sociopath* describe severe clinical conditions—typically associated with violent criminals or con artists—not annoying coworkers or exes. They were never meant to replace everyday words like *jerk*, *cheater*, or *creep*.

Tossing these diagnostic terms around so freely makes people see pathology where none exists—and unfairly harms those on the receiving end of the label, whether they have the diagnosis or not.

Say what you mean

This chapter has examined just a few of the most commonly weaponized therapy terms, but you've probably encountered many more—*gaslighting*, *projecting*, *bipolar*.

These words may sound authoritative, but they often lack real substance. They're used to belittle others or shut down conversation. More often than not, they serve as a crutch for people who feel insecure or lack the vocabulary to express themselves clearly.

As a therapist, I've helped countless individuals navigate difficult encounters with friends, family, romantic partners, and colleagues. There are healthy ways to handle conflict—but hiding behind clinical jargon isn't one of them. After all, no one wants to be pathologized unless they've sought mental health care themselves.

It's bad enough that terms meant to diagnose serious conditions have devolved into casual slang. But anyone familiar with social history knows that slang comes and goes. We now look back and cringe at words like *groovy*, *dope*, or *beast*. The sooner we start being more discerning about using psychological language as casual insult, the better off we'll be as a society.

CHAPTER TWELVE

THE ELEMENTS OF BAD THERAPY

Throughout this book, I examine how certain dynamics within the therapist–patient relationship have come to damage the profession itself, leave patients feeling worse rather than better, and quietly erode our nation's mental health and emotional resilience.

I firmly believe that when psychotherapy is practiced by an experienced professional using proven, evidence-based methods, it can—and often does—lead to meaningful change. Yet today's challenges are so complex that it's worth stepping back to examine the larger, systemic forces that have prevented psychotherapy from realizing its full potential. These forces include therapists clinging to outdated or unproven techniques, insurance systems that reward pathology over progress, and patients who, often unknowingly, sabotage their own growth.

Each of these factors has helped create a system that keeps far too many people stuck—an endless cycle of therapy that leaves them weaker, more self-involved, and no closer to genuine resilience.

Ineffective therapy

The term *psychotherapy* is an umbrella that encompasses dozens of therapy styles and schools, some far more evidence-based than others. I won't attempt to catalog every ineffective or dubious approach here—there are simply too many to summarize succinctly, which is itself a problem. Instead, I focus on three of the most common and most damaging.

Psychoanalysis

If you asked a random person to name a famous figure in the history of psychology, they'd likely mention the Austrian neurologist Sigmund Freud. Freud's work, which began in the late 1800s and early 1900s, brought psychotherapy from the fringes into the mainstream.

Freud encouraged his patients to speak freely, allowing whatever came to mind without restriction. He believed that this "free association" technique helped patients uncover unconscious or repressed memories, thoughts, and motivations. Lying on a couch, patients were urged to speak with brutal honesty, sharing everything—no matter how unpleasant, embarrassing, or distressing. Through this verbal release, Freud argued, patients could uncover repressed memories of childhood trauma, "Mommy and Daddy" issues, and even events from infancy.

Freud is often revered as one of medicine's great pioneers. Yet not all his ideas have stood the test of time. Many are now considered outdated, and some even laughable. Few today would defend his Oedipus complex, which claimed that all children secretly wish to kill their same-sex parent to possess the opposite-sex parent. His theories on dream analysis have also largely been dismissed. And then there is "penis envy"—the notion that girls feel inferior because they lack a penis—a concept Freud presented with utter seriousness that has since become a cultural punchline.

Despite this, many practitioners still cling to Freud's outdated theories, including free association. Today, if you choose to work with a psychoanalyst, you might commit to two to five sessions a week, lying on a couch and talking endlessly—primarily about your childhood. This open-ended, unstructured talking can go on for years, often without measurable progress.

Some modern psychoanalysts claim that their approach has evolved to include more research-based techniques and shorter treatment plans. Yet even they admit that their patients frequently remain in therapy for years without significant change. This, in essence, is the therapy trap.

Given that psychoanalysis has been around for over a century, one would expect researchers to have documented its benefits. Unfortunately, that's not the case. Over the past two decades, numerous attempts have been made to review and analyze randomized controlled trials supporting the effectiveness of psychoanalysis. What researchers have found, however, is far from encouraging. Most of the available research consists of low-quality studies and anecdotal case reports, many of which lack control groups and rely on flawed data.[1, 2, 3, 4, 5]

This absence of robust data makes it difficult to know whether psychoanalysis offers any actual benefits. In an era when we demand more from therapy—accountable results, concrete progress—psychoanalysis remains an outlier, offering little more than an open-ended loop of self-exploration without any tangible resolution.

In contrast, another form of psychotherapy, Cognitive Behavioral Therapy (CBT), was developed more recently by Aaron Beck, the psychiatrist behind the widely used Beck Depression Inventory for diagnosing depression. I'll delve into the benefits of CBT later, but for now, consider this: psychoanalysts have often dismissed CBT as therapy for the budget-conscious, given its fewer sessions and faster results. However, unlike psychoanalysis, this "budget" therapy is backed by hundreds of well-designed studies supporting its effectiveness. So, ask yourself: Which type of therapy would you prefer to pay for? The budget-friendly option with proven results, or the more expensive, seemingly endless approach, often delivered by someone relying on outdated techniques?

I've articulated my opinions about endless psychoanalysis for years. After I published my *New York Times* op-ed in 2012, it was the Freudian psychoanalysts who came after me the hardest. Their rancor didn't make me reconsider my views—it cemented them. It confirmed what I already suspected: These practitioners, aside from clinging to outdated therapeutic techniques, often lacked even basic problem-solving and interpersonal skills. Their world is so peculiar that whenever I encountered psychoanalyst colleagues—whether at professional gatherings or even in the elevator of my office building—my attempts at light, casual conversation were often met with a robotic "How does that make you feel?" That alone was enough to be irritating. If patients take away anything from years of psychoanalysis, it might just be a stronger constitution—earned by enduring the terminal repetition of "How does that make you feel?" twice a week, year after year.

In sum, psychoanalysis is outdated, ineffective, and more likely to keep people stuck than help them move forward.

Whenever someone tries to convince me of its merits, I remind them of Woody Allen. The filmmaker, once romantically involved with actress Mia Farrow (who starred in more than a dozen of his films), was famously accused by Farrow in 1992 of sexually abusing one of their adopted daughters—a charge he denied. Not long after, he went on to marry another of Farrow's adopted daughters, Soon-Yi Previn, who was thirty-five years his junior.

Allen's fascination with psychoanalysis is well documented. He spoke openly about being in therapy for decades—sometimes attending sessions up to five times a week. His films, such as *Annie Hall*, *Manhattan*, and *Deconstructing Harry*, are filled with neurotic characters engaged in endless therapy, often to comedic effect. If psychoanalysis truly led to growth and resolution, Allen would have been its model patient. Instead, he became a caricature of everything that's wrong with it.

Allen seems to view psychoanalysis as both an intellectual pursuit and a futile, never-ending process. His work suggests that while he sees some value in therapy as a tool for self-awareness, he also recognizes its limitations. Allen has often joked about spending years in therapy without making meaningful progress, revealing a deep cynicism about its effectiveness even as he remains drawn to it. In many ways, Allen has become the ultimate poster child for psychoanalysis gone wrong—proof that the longer someone stays in therapy, particularly psychoanalysis, the more self-absorbed and neurotic they are likely to become.

The overriding problem with psychoanalysis is its fixation on the past and on patients' self-contained inner worlds. Too many psychoanalysts dwell on childhood experiences and unconscious motivations, encouraging patients to endlessly dissect what happened years ago rather than focus on what to do now and in the years ahead. While the past can offer insight, therapy should be about progress, not perpetual excavation or self-knowledge for its own sake.

When therapy devolves into talking in circles about one's upbringing, it stops being treatment and becomes storytelling—often with a price tag of thousands of dollars. This approach leaves patients more anxious, more self-absorbed, and more neurotic than when they began.

Then there is the sheer length of the process. Woody Allen famously joked about decades on the couch, but the reality is less amusing. Traditional psychoanalysis can stretch on for years, even decades, without producing tangible results. Meanwhile, patients remain stuck in the same cycles of unhappiness, paying enormous sums for sessions that fail to deliver meaningful change.

Therapy should be a strategic, time-limited tool—one that helps people identify concrete problems, take action, and move forward with their lives. It should not become a lifelong exercise in emotional archaeology that leaves them stuck rather than strengthened.

Finally, there is the issue of dependency in psychoanalysis, a dynamic often built into the model itself. Many psychoanalysts, whether intentionally or not, foster relationships where patients become reliant on them indefinitely. That is not just unhelpful; it is unethical. A good therapist's goal should be to make themselves unnecessary by equipping patients with the tools to manage life independently, not to keep them coming back week after week, year after year. If your therapist is more focused on why you feel a certain way than on what you can do about it, you are not getting real help. You are wasting time, money, and opportunities to actually get better.

Next, let's turn to humanistic therapy, which was introduced as a "new" approach but, like psychoanalysis, is not without its flaws.

Humanistic Therapy

By the 1950s, psychoanalysis had solidified its status as the gold standard for therapy, but cracks were beginning to show. Many began to question the validity of its underlying assumptions. In response, alternative forms of therapy began to emerge, with "humanistic therapy" standing out as a prominent challenger. Unlike psychoanalysis, which was fixated on exploring the past, humanistic therapists focused on the present. Drawing from the works of existential philosophers like Jean-Paul Sartre, Martin Buber, and Søren Kierkegaard, humanism championed the idea that individuals could find meaning and purpose in their lives by embracing the here and now.

If this approach sounds more like the syllabus of a college philosophy course than a practical solution to alleviate anxiety or depression, that was, in many ways, the point. Humanistic therapy sought to transcend the clinical and move into the realm of existential exploration, which, for some, created a rather strange divide between theory and therapy. And that's where things started to get weird.

Proponents of humanistic psychology argue that their "holistic" approach encourages clients to embrace a "process of becoming." Clients learn to become more present, which proponents say opens them up to more self-awareness and understanding of what truly matters. According to humanistic principles, humans should not be viewed merely as the sum of our parts, and we exist in a "cosmic ecology." By emphasizing a client's positive traits, humanistic therapists want to help people find increased wisdom, growth, and fulfillment.

While these lofty ideals might sound appealing in the theoretical world of humanistic therapy, they often fall short when faced with the messy realities of life.

In a profile of humanistic therapy featured by the American Psychological Association, a humanistic psychologist shared the example of a woman with a driving phobia. During their sessions, the psychologist helped her uncover that the root of the phobia lay in a deeper internal conflict: a tension between her desire for independence and her fear of jeopardizing her marriage. According to the psychologist, the woman feared that if she drove too far from home, she might never return. This, the psychologist suggested, was the emotional core of her phobia.[6]

If I were that woman, I probably would have overcome my driving phobia on the spot, just to speed away from that psychologist as fast as possible. Maybe, just maybe, this psychologist happened to find the one person on earth whose fear of driving was truly rooted in such a convoluted internal struggle. Still, I'm not buying it.

Humanistic therapists do offer specific tools—like spending time in nature—that have been shown to help people relax. But these strategies aren't unique to humanistic therapy. In fact, many therapists, regardless of their approach, recommend them at one point or another.

More importantly, this form of so-called therapy has even less empirical evidence than psychoanalysis.

While humanistic therapy offers support and affirmation, it often lacks the structure and direction necessary for real, lasting change. Rooted in broad, feel-good ideals like self-actualization, it prioritizes open-ended self-exploration over measurable progress.

Not surprisingly, this approach tends to attract those drawn to meditation, mindfulness, Tibetan singing bowls, yoga, and other mind-body practices centered on self-awareness and present-moment living. These activities can certainly help people relax, and relaxation has its place. But feeling better in the moment, or being encouraged to "find your own answers," is not the same as doing the hard work of therapy.

Comfort is not treatment. Without structure, goals, and accountability, humanistic therapy often fails to address the underlying problems that brought someone to treatment in the first place. Lacking clear strategies or evidence-based interventions, it can trap people in a cycle of endless self-reflection, much like psychoanalysis.

The core problem with humanistic therapy is that it does not provide the tools needed to overcome deeper emotional struggles. When it comes to conditions such as depression, anxiety, trauma, and phobias, it consistently falls short, offering reassurance instead of solutions. People in real distress need more than validation. They need structured guidance and actionable strategies that produce lasting change. While humanistic therapy is compassionate, it rarely delivers more than temporary relief.

Unproven Fringe Therapies

Next, let's address a disturbing trend gaining traction in the mental health world: the promotion of unproven fringe therapies. Therapists offer techniques like past life regression or Reiki, claiming to provide relief without scientific backing. It's staggering how many charlatans profit by peddling fake cures to people with real anxiety and depression.

You'll find individuals promoting:

- Red lights applied to the face or skull
- Sound baths that involve listening to the sound of Tibetan "singing bowls"
- Past life regression, which uses hypnosis to help patients uncover the details of their previous lives
- Reiki and other forms of "energy work" that use human touch to change or balance the body's so-called energy fields
- Re-parenting, which involves role-playing so a client can experience the empathetic parenting he or she feels was missing from their childhood
- *Forest bathing*, a fancy term for hanging out in the woods

Some of these methods are certainly relaxing. They may even be somewhat helpful for people with certain conditions. Similar to any other form of rest, they could help to relieve tension temporarily. They shouldn't, however, be seen as a stand-in for genuine psychotherapy when it comes to addressing specific mental health issues.

Dangerous therapies

Some of the most harmful therapists don't necessarily practice any formalized method they learned in graduate school. Instead, they seem to invent their own therapies, often with disastrous consequences. In addition to wasting their patients' time with endless treatment, these practitioners suggest their patients make dangerous life changes, all in the name of "therapy."

Nothing illustrates this more than the story of a young tech professional who came to see me after a devastating breakup.

He had been in a committed four-year relationship that he assumed was monogamous. His girlfriend had been seeing a therapist to discuss some issues she had with the relationship. Eventually, she started to question her sexuality and express some attraction to women. This is a serious, delicate sort of issue for someone already involved in a committed relationship, and one that a responsible therapist would have talked through very carefully. The girlfriend has the right to explore this side of herself, but honesty with her current partner should have been an essential part of the equation.

That's not what her therapist thought. Instead, the therapist suggested that she explore her attraction to women behind her current partner's back. "Try to see this as a healthy exploration. It will help you to grow as a person and better understand yourself and what you truly want in a partner," the therapist encouraged.

What followed was a predictable disaster.

The man noticed his girlfriend spending more and more time with someone he assumed was just a friend. Eventually, it came up in conversation, and she confessed the true nature of her relationship with the other woman. The news was devastating, but he loved her and wanted to make things work. At first, he tried to see her actions as a temporary detour, something she would move through during this phase of "self-exploration," before eventually returning to him. He held on to the hope that someday they would both look back on this period with understanding—and with each other.

But that's not what happened. After the initial period of hopefulness, the man grew increasingly anxious and resentful. Instead of feeling more connected, he felt as if he was losing his girlfriend. Their already fragile intimacy was now burdened by jealousy, insecurity, and emotional detachment. By the time he came to see me, the relationship was over, and he was looking for the courage to dip his toe back into the world of dating.

When he told me the story, I was floored. Granted, I always approach these situations with some caution. I never know for certain whether a client is giving me the full story. Maybe, if his girlfriend were in the room, I would have heard a very different version of events.

But even with that in mind, the therapist's role here seemed unmistakably reckless.

Still, the story tracked with a trend I'd been noticing for some time. Increasing numbers of therapists seemed to be sanitizing and giving their stamp of approval to once stigmatized romantic arrangements such as polyamory, polygamy, open marriage, the use of sexual surrogates, and orgies. The "find a therapist" tool for *Psychology Today* allows people to search specifically for "open relationship, non-monogamy" therapists.[7] Licensed marriage and family therapists Kate Loree and Rhea Orion have even penned whole books about the topic.[8, 9] As different types of romantic arrangements emerge, it makes sense for therapists to help their clients navigate that changing landscape in ways that keep them mentally and physically healthy.

But in my client's case, there was no mutual decision to "open" the relationship. The actions of his ex-girlfriend's therapist seemed like a huge betrayal of trust, as well as a reckless gamble with someone else's emotional and physical well-being. This wasn't just a failure in judgment. The therapist actively encouraged behavior that would be acknowledged by any serious practitioner—indeed, any sensible person—as selfish, deceitful, and cruel.

My patient was left emotionally shaken, questioning everything about the relationship and his own self-worth. Worse, his physical health had been put at risk, all because a therapist recommended his ex-girlfriend prioritized personal gratification over personal responsibility.

During our time together, I helped the young man rebuild his confidence, develop healthy boundaries, and embrace the idea that the collapse of one relationship didn't have to define his future. He was now better equipped to find a partner who shared his values, free from the shadow of manipulation and emotional betrayal. With time, he was able to reenter the dating world with a stronger sense of self and a clearer understanding of what he needed in a partner. He was upfront with anyone he dated that he was *not* into polyamory or open relationships.

As I considered his case, I tried to put myself in the other therapist's shoes. If someone came to me about struggles in their relationship, I cannot imagine recommending cheating as a solution. If a patient confessed to considering or engaging in infidelity, it is hard to see how any therapist could encourage it or frame it as a therapeutic "growth exercise." Nor would I tiptoe around the issue.

To the contrary, I would confront it head-on.

Over the years, I've challenged many patients about their destructive choices, whether it's cheating, dishonesty, or reckless behavior. Therapy isn't about validating poor decisions. It's about helping people take responsibility and make better ones.

For me, this is a no-brainer. High-risk, harmful actions demand accountability, not validation. Therapy should help people figure out what's best for them in an ethical, responsible way, not just give someone a green light to do whatever feels good in the moment.

A therapist's job isn't to endorse one partner's self-serving desires at the expense of the other. It's to help couples confront what's actually happening between them, rebuild trust, and work toward a solution that strengthens their relationship, not fractures it.

Anything less isn't just irresponsible. It's destructive to the patient, their partner, their community and, if therapists keep encouraging behavior that violates basic norms, it can harm society at large. This was not just about failed therapy; it was a clear violation of trust.

"Empowerment" therapy

Another harmful technique centers on self-empowerment. It's often suggested to young women who struggle with assertiveness. Learning how to speak up for oneself can certainly be life-changing, especially for someone who previously maintained relationships through people-pleasing. I'm all for that. However, without guardrails, assertiveness can border on dangerous, which is what happened with someone I treated several years ago. We'll call her Alice.

When Alice first showed up for therapy, she seemed humiliated and shaken. As I eventually drew out of her the reasons why, I almost couldn't believe her story.

Alice had been dating a guy for only a few weeks. Things seemed to be going well. Then her birthday came and went without a word from him. There was no call and no text—nothing. Understandably, she felt hurt and confused. For guidance and perspective, she made an appointment with her therapist.

This therapist gave Alice a stunning piece of advice. She encouraged her to go to the man's house, knock on his door, and demand to know why he hadn't contacted her.

The therapist framed the exercise as an act of empowerment. It would allow Alice to take control of the situation, assert herself, and get the answers she felt she deserved.

So, she took her therapist's advice. One evening, she showed up at the man's home uninvited, knocked, and waited. The result was a total disaster.

The young man was caught off guard and clearly uncomfortable. He barely let Alice inside, offered a half-hearted excuse about being busy, and made it obvious that he wasn't interested in seeing her again. She left feeling embarrassed, rejected, and regretting the entire situation. Instead of finding closure, she felt as if she had given away her dignity during a moment of desperation.

What the therapist overlooked was that empowerment doesn't come from forcing an uncomfortable confrontation. It comes from recognizing when your dignity is more valuable than a fleeting answer.

After that incident, Alice ended her work with that therapist. Soon after, she found her way into my office. She was mortified as she recounted what she had done that night. *What was I thinking?* she kept asking. The better question was one she hadn't yet considered: *What was her therapist thinking?*

What if the man had been with someone else? What if he had reacted angrily? What if he had simply seen her as desperate and needy, undoing whatever attraction had existed? Under the banner of "empowerment," the therapist had encouraged impulsive behavior without weighing the real-world consequences. True strength, however, doesn't come from forcing confrontation. It comes from knowing when to walk away.

I helped Alice reframe the experience. The real issue wasn't why this man had ignored her—it was why she felt the need to chase him down for an explanation. She was investing far more in him than he was in her, and the truth was simple. His silence *was* the answer. He wasn't interested. A good therapist would have helped her see that, process the rejection, and move on with her self-respect intact. Instead, she was pushed into a humiliating encounter that only deepened her pain.

This is what bad therapy looks like. It mistakes entitlement for empowerment. It encourages emotion-driven actions without considering the consequences. And worst of all, it can leave patients feeling worse than before they stepped into a therapist's office.

Coercive therapy

I've consistently argued that therapy is most effective when the patient and practitioner work together to set specific goals and develop a clear plan to achieve them. But it should go without saying: Except in extreme cases, therapy must be voluntary. Barring situations where involuntary commitment is necessary to prevent imminent harm, imposing therapeutic practices on someone against their will—or under coercion—is the height of unethical behavior. It is also one of the most dangerous forms of bad therapy that, sadly, still exists in the world.

The most glaring example of this is the range of long discredited—yet still shamefully practiced in some corners of the nation—techniques that attempt to "cure" or "convert" individuals from homosexuality.

In 1899, a German psychiatrist claimed that forty-five hypnosis sessions and a trip to a brothel had successfully turned one of his patients from gay to straight. Ever since, so-called "therapies" to change someone's sexual orientation have persisted. Based largely on the concept of Pavlovian conditioning, these techniques have included:[10, 11, 12, 13]

- Castrating and lobotomizing gay men in an effort to remove their sex drive.
- Applying painful electric shocks to men—sometimes to their genitals—to punish them for feeling excited when they viewed gay porn or photos of their lovers.
- Forcing men to take chemicals that made them vomit as they viewed images of gay porn.
- Sending teens to conversion camps where, according to survivor accounts, they were isolated from family and friends, told to pray away their "depravity," and mocked. If they failed to abandon their sexual orientation, some of these teens were punished. They were starved, beaten, and deprived of water.[14, 15]
- Encouraging patients to snap a rubber band on their child's wrist whenever they're aroused by a member of the same sex or feel an urge to wear clothing typical of the opposite sex.

For many years, the more violent forms of conversion therapy remained secret, with few survivors speaking up about the torture they'd experienced. To the public and even to the parents who sent their children to these camps, the violent techniques were conveniently omitted from marketing materials. Instead, for proof of concept, conversion therapy proponents presented case studies of "no longer gay" clients.

One famous example came in 2001, when Robert L. Spitzer, MD, presented a study of two hundred people who claimed to no longer be gay.[16] At the time, Spitzer reported that the two hundred people had gone from "predominantly or exclusively" gay to "predominantly or exclusively" straight. By 2012, however, Dr. Spitzer had repudiated his own findings and apologized to the gay community for his unproven claims, writing in a letter published by *The American Prospect* and later in *Archives of Sexual Behavior*:

> I also apologize to any gay person who wasted time and energy undergoing some form of reparative therapy because they believed that I had proven that reparative therapy works with some "highly motivated" individuals.[17]

To date, no research has proven that any of these coercive tactics do what they claim. On the contrary, research shows that they cause serious harm, leading to poor self-esteem, depression, social withdrawal, and sexual dysfunction.[18, 19, 20, 21, 22]

The American Psychological Association, American Psychiatric Association, American Medical Association, National Alliance on Mental Illness, and the American Academy of Pediatrics all oppose conversion therapy. I may not agree with all of my colleagues or all of our professional organizations about everything, but I feel confident in the knowledge that any serious therapist, whatever the school of thought in their practice, would immediately condemn this. More than half of American states have banned or limited its practice, but it can still be found in some parts of the country. The UCLA School of Law estimates that hundreds of thousands of LGBTQ people have been subjected to this form of "therapy," about half of them as teenagers.[23] A 2023 Trevor Project report estimated that 1,300 conversion therapists were still practicing in the U.S.[24]

In my practice, I've treated a handful of adults who shared that they were subjected to conversion therapy as teenagers. They're perfectly content with their sexuality, but the harmful effects of the treatment they endured in their youth still linger, even decades later.

I cringe whenever I hear the term *conversion therapy*. It's certainly not worthy of being called "therapy." While it's an extreme example, it serves as a stark warning about the danger that arises when therapists abuse their power or prioritize their own ideology over the well-being of their patients.

Though we've made progress in rejecting these practices, the scars they leave are often lifelong. Therapists who engage in such practices aren't just violating ethical codes, they're actively contributing to the suffering of vulnerable people, and their harm ripples through generations.

A field guide to bad therapists

Not all bad therapists fit neatly into the categories I've already discussed. Some have the training and credentials to help their patients—but for some reason they've abandoned everything they've learned. Some are simply burned-out, going through the motions. Others were never particularly effective to begin with. Like any profession, therapy has its share of underperformers.

It's not just certain schools of thought that produce bad therapists. Even if you avoid psychoanalysts, quacks, and humanists, you might still end up in a room with a therapist who lacks competence or is fiercely committed to a method that simply won't help their patients.

Here are some other general types they tend to fall into, with some even overlapping or bleeding into each other.

The Sounding Board

Bad therapists often act as sounding boards, passively listening without guiding their patients to think or behave differently. They encourage rumination—the endless replaying of problems—by continually asking how the patient feels rather than helping them find solutions.

A typical conversation with this type of therapist might sound like this:

> **Patient:** "My partner never listens to me."
>
> **Therapist:** "I'm hearing that this is difficult for you. Say more."
>
> **Patient:** "It's frustrating."
>
> **Therapist:** "I hear that this situation is upsetting for you. Let's explore that. Can you tell me more?"

And so it continues, with the therapist asking for details or simply echoing back the patient's words. The real problem remains unaddressed, and potential solutions never surface. These therapists often mistake validation for therapy, believing that if a patient feels "seen" or "heard," their work is done.

But therapy is not about endless listening—it's about change, growth, and progress. A good therapist challenges patients to confront their difficulties and think differently. If your sessions feel aimless, or if you keep revisiting the same issues without tangible improvement, that is a red flag. Therapy should be a strategic, goal-oriented process. Otherwise, it becomes little more than a paid venting session.

The Pathologist

I've mentioned this type of therapist elsewhere. These practitioners tend to label and diagnose all uncomfortable feelings and experiences as problems and symptoms. They encourage people to take antidepressants and anti-anxiety medications—which some people do need—but they fail to also help their patients change the basic facts of their lives necessary for progress, some of which cause them to need those medicines in the first place.

But it's worth noting that therapists don't always drift into pathologizing because they genuinely believe more drugs will solve everyone's problems. Much of its popularity among well-meaning therapists stems from the swamp of health care bureaucracy that we, as well as our patients, have to navigate.

Insurance and the CPT Trap

We know that it can often be difficult for patients to find mental health providers that are covered by their insurance network to begin with. And even when the provider is in-network, a patient's insurance won't cover an appointment unless a diagnosis is given.

Just like other medical visits, therapy requires a diagnosis and a CPT code ("current procedural terminology") so insurance companies know how to process the claim. These codes were meant to standardize billing and ensure coverage decisions are clear. Decades ago, insurers often capped mental health visits at around thirty sessions a year. Those caps disappeared long ago—but many therapists still act as if they're in place, limiting patients out of habit rather than necessity.

Unfortunately, therapist laziness can also play a role. Some therapists have learned that certain CPT codes and diagnoses, particularly major depression, are more likely to be approved and covered by insurance. Rather than spending time advocating with insurers on a patient's behalf, they take the path of least resistance.

To save time and ensure reimbursement, symptoms are exaggerated or framed to fit an easier, more reliably covered diagnosis. In the past, this practice was often rationalized as a necessary workaround in a difficult insurance environment. Today, however, with far broader mental health coverage, there is little justification for diagnosing a serious disorder that does not exist.

And yet, I still hear colleagues describe doing exactly this with unsettling regularity.

It may seem like some harmless back-end finagling, but patients are not well served by therapists who tweak diagnoses just to avoid the bureaucratic hassle. Some patients do warrant severe diagnoses like major depression and the like, but for other patients without those conditions, inflated diagnoses can be dangerous. If a diagnosis is absolutely necessary, something like "adjustment disorder"—used to cover stress from a new job, relationship changes and so on—would be more appropriate. If someone is erroneously given a major diagnosis, instead of learning how to adapt, they resign themselves to a lifetime of labels and prescriptions, maybe even believing they're permanently broken instead of capable of change.

The Codependent Therapist

This therapist makes the session about themselves rather than about the patient.

Rather than getting people better and sending them on their way, these therapists end up creating an unhealthy dependency, or keeping someone in therapy indefinitely to sustain their practice. Codependents exhibit one of the worst traits found among different kinds of bad therapists: As I've mentioned in earlier chapters, they warn patients that they need intense weekly sessions or they'll fall apart. They go on talking and talking for years and years, continually asking them about the same traumas, the same life situations, and the same problems, but never helping the patients get to a resolution.

The Friend

It's not uncommon for clients to see their therapist as a close friend—or even their favorite person. This makes sense. Good listening skills and a genuine desire for someone's well-being are hallmarks of any strong friendship, and skilled therapists are (or should be) trained in both. Like a friend, most therapists want what's best for their patients. The relationship also hinges on trust, creating a space where patients feel free to express themselves. That kind of connection can feel profoundly personal, and it's easy to start believing your therapist truly "gets" you. Unlike a true friend, though, a therapist will send you a bill. A therapist's role isn't to provide comfort for the sake of comfort. Their goal, if done right, is to facilitate real change.

A good therapist doesn't just listen passively; they actively challenge you, sometimes in ways that feel uncomfortable or even confrontational. While a friend offers a sympathetic ear, a good therapist confronts uncomfortable realities, identifies unhealthy patterns, and pushes you toward growth—often in unexpected directions. If you're hesitant, they'll help you find a pace that works. Their challenges might not always feel friendly, but they are essential to helping you break free from limiting behaviors and beliefs.

The difference between a friend and a good therapist is that the therapist is committed not just to understanding your emotions, but to helping you transform them. In the end, our role is not to be a surrogate companion, but to provide the professional insight and structured support necessary to help you navigate the complexities of life and relationships.

That said, some therapists, unfortunately, blur the lines between these roles. They may intentionally or unintentionally slip into a more friendly, almost familial dynamic with clients, seeking emotional closeness for personal gratification or a misguided sense of being "liked." This may feel comforting in the short term, but ultimately hampers real progress. This dynamic undermines the very purpose of therapy. Rather than provide an objective, professional perspective that challenges and helps clients grow, this overly warm approach seeks to maintain a "buddy-buddy" relationship at the expense of effective treatment.

The Validator

In Chapter Ten, we saw how overly affirming therapists keep patients stuck. Instead of challenging them or offering tools for change, they sympathize and encourage endless rehashing of grievances. I've seen firsthand the damage this kind of validation causes. Patients spend years in therapy, spinning in toxic patterns because no one ever told them: "You're the problem"—and then showed them how to fix it. The result? Blown-up marriages, friendships, and careers, with therapists cheerleading the wreckage as part of "finding yourself." That isn't therapy. It's self-destruction.

Instead of indulging self-pity, a good therapist calls out self-defeating narratives with questions like, "What evidence do you have for that belief?" Therapy isn't meant to coddle victimhood. It's meant to push clients to confront the realities of their lives and see where they still have agency and control.

While much of the responsibility lies with therapists, patients are not passive participants in their own treatment. Certain behaviors can sabotage progress and turn even good therapy bad.

How patients harm their own therapy

While therapists must hold themselves to high professional standards, patients also play a significant role in shaping their therapeutic journey. In my experience, there are several common missteps that can turn what could be productive therapy into a waste of time.

Coming into Sessions Convinced About a TikTok Diagnosis

One of the most common pitfalls occurs when patients arrive at therapy armed with self-diagnosed labels, often picked up from social media. They proudly proclaim that they have depression, ADHD, or something else, convinced they already know what's wrong. This immediately sets therapy on the wrong footing, especially when paired with a therapist who validates the label rather than interrogates it. The result is a stalled process that never digs deeper to identify the real drivers of the patient's distress.

Expecting a Therapist to Be a Magician

Therapy isn't magic. A therapist can offer insight and strategies, but without motivation to change, progress is unlikely. If you're waiting for a therapist to "fix" you without doing any work outside of sessions, you're wasting your time.

As I tell my patients, therapy is just one hour of your week. Real change happens in the other 167. What we discuss in session only matters if it's carried into daily life.

Being Dishonest or Holding Back

Some patients hold back in therapy, editing or censoring themselves. They may fear being judged or feel embarrassed about certain issues. But if you're not honest, your therapist isn't working with the real version of you. If you hold back, you're depriving your therapist of crucial information that could help them better understand the problem. Similarly, if you only discuss surface-level issues or avoid difficult topics, you block your own progress. Therapy is meant to challenge you, not just soothe you—and if it's only providing comfort, it's little more than an expensive chat.

Blaming Others

Some patients come to therapy looking for a sympathetic ear rather than actual help. They want to vent their frustrations, often blaming others—partners, bosses, parents—for their problems, session after session. When a therapist tries to redirect the conversation toward solutions, these patients become defensive, accusing the therapist of not listening or "taking sides."

But what they perceive as a lack of listening is a therapist's attempt to steer the conversation toward something more productive. Let's be clear: Challenging you is not the same as dismissing you. A therapist's job isn't to nod along and agree with everything you say—it's to help you see things from a new perspective.

If every session devolves into blaming others, you're avoiding accountability. Therapy should focus on what you can control—your actions, responses, and behaviors. A good therapist would get bored with endless blame-casting (trust me)—and would work diligently to make the conversation more productive. If your therapist continues to support the belief that everyone around you is the problem and you're just fine, it may be time to reassess your therapist.

Using Therapy as an Emotional Crutch

Therapy should help you become independent, not dependent on weekly sessions to function. When therapy starts to feel like a security blanket rather than a path to real change, something has gone wrong. Venting in session can feel cathartic, but without applying what you learn outside the office, you're just spinning your wheels. Growth happens in the real world, not in a therapist's office.

How to vet a therapist

As I've argued throughout this book, not all therapists are created equal. If you want therapy that works, you need someone who will challenge you, hold you accountable, and help you move forward. So how do you find that person? Start by paying close attention to a therapist's marketing materials and client reviews, with a few important caveats.

A therapist's website and bio can offer essential clues to their approach. Does the therapist focus on change and growth, or do they emphasize comfort? A good therapist will stress results, personal responsibility, accountability, and skill-building. Be cautious of therapists who overuse terms like *safe space*, *explore your feelings*, or *support you on your journey* without mentioning actionable steps toward progress.

Also, be wary of therapists who place too much emphasis on group identity. While it's natural to have preferences for the gender or background of your therapist, if a therapist approaches their practice through an identity lens (like Social Justice Counseling), you may end up focusing more on how your identity shapes your feelings than addressing your actual problems.

Above all, remember that therapy should be about change and self-improvement, not endless reflection on the past.

CHAPTER THIRTEEN

WHAT'S THE POINT OF THERAPY?

Every therapist gets fired by a patient now and then. I'm no exception. Sometimes it's a simple mismatch of goals or personalities. But more often, in my case, it's because I say something they don't want to hear. I mentioned earlier the patient mourning his friend's overdose who shut down when I suggested he look at his own drug use. Another couldn't tolerate being told that his literal murderous rage toward Donald Trump wasn't a healthy response to Kamala Harris's election loss. A third fixated on a single comment I made in our first session, refused to hear any clarification, and stormed out mid-session.

Each of them came to therapy looking for validation. What they got was the truth, and that was enough to send them running.

I've been critical of therapists, of indulgence, lack of direction, and a tendency to validate weakness instead of building strength. But my critiques come from frustration, not cynicism. If I didn't believe therapy could work, I wouldn't still be doing it.

I believe in counseling that is clear-eyed, structured, and focused on results. And while I've spent much of this book calling out the ways therapists and patients alike are failing, sometimes dangerously so, I also want to acknowledge that no one, myself included, is perfect.

Despite the problems plaguing the field, I remain confident that good therapy has the power to help individuals and, by extension, strengthen the nation.

When done effectively, therapy pushes patients to tolerate discomfort, regulate their emotions, and adopt new perspectives that drive personal growth. The hallmark of transformative therapy is when a patient says, "I've never thought of it that way." True, lasting change occurs in those moments when someone suddenly sees the world, or themselves, through a completely different lens. This is the kind of therapy the best in our profession deliver: direct, insightful, and aimed at real, lasting change.

But, as I've seen too often in the profession, and as I discuss in this book, I fear that such breakthroughs are becoming increasingly rare. Instead, patients are stuck on a mental treadmill, feeling stagnant while the real issues remain unresolved.

Now more than ever, people need good therapists. The societal problems I've discussed—social media inauthenticity, political polarization, and isolation—aren't just abstract. They drive real mental health struggles. Yet too often, my colleagues offer anything but the help patients truly need. It's critical to know which types of therapy work and what realistic expectations look like. The goal isn't to stay in therapy forever. It's to grow, heal, and move on. That's the difference between therapy as a tool and therapy as a trap.

Why get therapy?

The goal of mental health therapy is similar to the goal of physical or occupational therapy. It's about change and results.

A good therapist won't just sit there, nodding and validating every emotion. It would be akin to a physical therapist who never asks a patient to push past temporary pain or weakness.

Good mental health therapists challenge their patients—sometimes even making them uncomfortable. After all, change is *uncomfortable*. Growth happens when patients move beyond their excuses, stop blaming others and the past, and begin taking ownership of their lives.

Some people might be fine paying for an hour a week with someone who acts more like a friend or a validator. That's their right. But they shouldn't expect their mental health to improve if their sessions amount to little more than weekly affirmations, where they're told what they want to hear instead of being challenged to face hard truths. When therapy becomes a space for comfort rather than growth, it's no wonder so many patients fail to make real progress. Therapy should teach people how to navigate life's challenges. If someone is still in therapy years later, talking about the same issues, either the therapist isn't doing their job, or the patient isn't being held accountable to do theirs.

The real measure of success isn't how long someone stays in therapy, but how well they function without it.

Not everyone needs therapy

That's not something you'll hear often—especially from therapists. But it's the truth. Some people genuinely benefit from it. For others, it's a waste of time and money at best—and outright harmful at worst. Therapy isn't a universal solution, and not everyone needs to sit in a therapist's office to work through life's challenges.

Most people only need therapy when they're struggling and can't manage to find the right solutions on their own. It's especially helpful for those who:

- Struggle with emotions or behaviors that interfere with work, relationships, or daily functioning
- Feel stuck in patterns—like repeatedly being passed over for promotions—that suggest something deeper is at play

- Keep making the same mistakes despite wanting different outcomes
- Have experienced real trauma (as defined in Chapter Eight) that continues to affect their daily lives
- Feel overwhelmed by anxiety, depression, or chronic stress

Therapy can also be valuable for people who think they're doing fine but may be overlooking subtle signs of distress. Some only realize in therapy that what they've been experiencing—fatigue, irritability, lack of motivation—has been depression all along. In that sense, therapy can act as early intervention, helping people spot and address problems before they spiral. Beyond that, it is also useful for those who are doing well and want to perform at their peak. As discussed earlier, this is the kind of work the psychiatrist Wendy Rhoades, played by Maggie Siff on *Billions*, specializes in. It is designed to help high achievers such as executives, athletes, and entrepreneurs sharpen their mindset, improve focus, and optimize performance. Many Wall Street executives and CEOs come to me for this exact reason. They are not in crisis; they are looking for an edge. In these cases, therapy is not about fixing something broken. It is about maximizing potential.

What these two categories of patients share in common is a willingness to change, to confront uncomfortable truths, and to take responsibility for their growth. When those qualities meet the right therapist, the results can be life-changing.

Who doesn't need therapy?

Many of the people mired in endless therapy today fall into neither of the two categories for which therapy truly works. They're not seeking an edge. Nor are they in deep distress. What they want is an ally who will listen to their endless complaints about all the people and problems making them miserable.

Sometimes this happens because, deep down, they're unwilling to change. But just as often, it's because they don't know any better—they assume that's what therapy is supposed to look like. That's what countless patients, friends, and acquaintances have told me over the years. Challenging that misconception is one of the reasons I wrote this book.

Too many people have bought into today's backward therapy culture, which presents therapy as a self-care ritual rather than a tool for change. In this view, a session with a therapist functions much like a trip to a spa—it's something you do to unwind. But real mental health therapy is more like physical therapy than a massage. The goal isn't to ease tension for a day; it's to build long-term strength and flexibility. It's about truly getting and staying better, not just feeling better in the moment.

People don't need therapy if they're already meeting life's challenges and managing stress, setbacks, and emotions without getting stuck. Despite what therapy culture suggests, not every uncomfortable feeling calls for intervention. Sadness, stress, frustration, and anxiety are part of being human—not automatic signs of a deeper disorder.

Therapy also shouldn't replace real friendships or social connection. Those relationships are what sustain people in the long term; therapy should be reserved for addressing specific psychological or behavioral issues.

What most people need isn't therapy—they need better habits, a healthier lifestyle, stronger discipline, more time outside their own heads, and the willingness to step outside their comfort zones. They need to stop overthinking and start doing.

I've seen many clients come to me after years in therapy elsewhere, saying they feel worse, not better. When therapy is misused, it doesn't merely fail; it breeds helplessness instead of resilience. The wrong approach keeps people stuck, fostering dependence rather than self-sufficiency.

If therapy isn't pushing you forward, it's holding you back. It should be a tool for growth and change, not a lifelong crutch.

What good therapists do

Good therapists function more like coaches, helping clients build resilience and strength. Anyone who has competed in sports or academic settings knows that the best coaches are relentless. In practice, they push their teams past fatigue and physical strain. When players think they have nothing left, a great coach asks for just a little more. That is how people move from good to better, and sometimes from good to great.

I was never a star athlete, but I remember my track and cross-country coach pushing me to give a little more each time I competed. The same was true for my baseball coach. I never excelled, but he helped me refine my skills so I could step into the batter's box with confidence. I didn't need a scholarship or a professional career. That confidence carried far beyond the field.

Mental health therapy should be no different. Therapists should emulate the greats—the Vince Lombardis, Phil Jacksons, and Pat Rileys of the world. The best mental health professionals don't just listen; they hold clients accountable, challenge limiting beliefs, and push them beyond what feels familiar and safe. They don't just talk about change—they create a plan for it and ensure their action is taken.

One of the biggest differences between effective and ineffective therapy is the presence (or absence) of clear goals. Think of these goals as metrics—they describe what the patient wants to improve and provide a roadmap for progress.

To understand the importance of goal setting, consider a patient of mine, Jennifer, who came to therapy because of social anxiety. She told me she avoided social events, including meeting up with friends and especially gatherings where she didn't know many people. Just imagining walking into a party made her feel paralyzed.

Jennifer explained that walking into a room of unfamiliar people triggered her the most. She feared being judged or saying something embarrassing. To explore this, I asked her a few targeted questions:

"What parts of social events make you the most anxious?"

"What's within your control in those situations?"

"What's one small step you can take this week to face that fear?"

As we explored her answers, we were able to craft a simple plan. She would organize a coffee meetup with two friends. Before going, she'd practice grounding techniques—like deep breathing or noticing her feet on the floor. Her only objective during the meetup was to stay for at least thirty minutes and ask one person a basic question.

At our next session, I asked how it went. "I felt nervous," she said, "but I stayed and even asked someone about their weekend." That was a win. Though she was nervous, we agreed she could try stretching a little further. Her next goal was to attend a group dinner and speak at least once—maybe offer a compliment or ask someone about their hobby.

Over the following weeks, we built on these experiences. She experimented with different coping techniques—some worked, some didn't. We adjusted along the way. The point wasn't perfection—it was progress.

Several months later, Jennifer was attending social events regularly. Her anxiety hadn't disappeared entirely, but it no longer controlled her. She had tools, strategies, and the confidence to push through discomfort—and she was using them. At that point, I discharged her from therapy. Not because she was perfect, but because she no longer needed weekly sessions to function. That's what good therapy should do: help people face their problems, gain real skills, and move on with their lives.

How good therapy feels

Imagine what would happen if, every time you went to the gym, you lifted the same weight and did the same number of reps and sets. You wouldn't see results—any exercise physiologist or personal trainer could tell you that. To build strength, you need progressive overload: gradually increasing the intensity, duration, or volume of your workouts. Real growth only comes from doing what feels uncomfortable.

Effective psychotherapy works the same way. If your sessions always feel soothing and easy, they're probably not working. Mental and emotional growth requires learning to sit with discomfort rather than avoiding it. Too many therapists skip this hard work, leaving patients stuck in cycles of self-absorption instead of progress. Good therapists push their patients to think differently and challenge the self-defeating narratives that hold them back.

Because of this, it's not uncommon for patients to feel frustrated by something their therapist says or encourages. That frustration often means the therapist is challenging them in ways that lead to real growth—the kind of work too many in the profession avoid. Without that tension, people stay stuck instead of moving forward. If a patient feels annoyed because their therapist is confronting what they'd rather not face, that's not a red flag—it's a sign they're in good hands.

Therapy should feel like work—but it should also feel worthwhile. Patients should leave sessions with a clearer sense of personal responsibility and concrete steps to improve their lives, not just a temporary sense of relief.

How long should therapy last?

Earlier, I discussed the many problems associated with endless therapy. This perspective traces back, in part, to the early days of psychotherapy. When Sigmund Freud practiced more than a century ago, patients often visited their analysts several times a week, sometimes for years, with no clear end in sight—and we all know how that turned out.

That same open-ended approach seems to be what many of today's celebrities and influencers expect. In 2022, actor and filmmaker Jonah Hill spoke publicly about his decades in therapy, describing it as an essential part of his life and identity. Yet despite years of treatment, his anxiety appeared unresolved. Rather than helping Hill overcome it, therapy seemed to mire him in it. After nearly twenty years of anxiety attacks, Hill announced that he would stop doing media appearances altogether. "If I made myself sicker by going out there and promoting [the film], I wouldn't be acting true to myself or to the film," he said in a prepared statement.

While Hill's openness about mental health is valuable, it also risks normalizing the idea that therapy should be a lifelong endeavor rather than a process aimed at change and independence. Once someone has made meaningful progress and built self-sufficient coping skills, ongoing therapy shouldn't be mandatory. Many of my patients, for example, benefit from quarterly or annual check-ins—wellness visits, much like medical checkups. But that's very different from seeing a therapist week after week when there's no clear need.

Hill's prolonged therapy journey isn't unique. It reflects a broader cultural trend, especially among public figures, of treating therapy as a permanent lifestyle rather than a temporary tool. That raises a larger question: What does it say about our society when therapy becomes the goal instead of the means to one? Rather than fostering resilience, this approach keeps people tethered to therapists indefinitely, delaying the development of autonomy, confidence, and the ability to navigate life on their own.

The slow, sinking swamp of endless therapy is one of the biggest problems in the mental health industry today. In my view, Jonah Hill has been poorly served by his therapists. I feel for him—and for the countless others who spend years, even decades, in therapy without making meaningful progress. When therapists expect patients to show up indefinitely, they perpetuate dependence, cultivating the belief that people need therapy simply to function. This mindset reinforces the self-absorption already pervasive in our culture. The longer therapy drags on, the more clients grow accustomed to centering every narrative around themselves, venting about minor inconveniences, and mistaking self-focus for self-awareness. Over time, they lose confidence in their own ability to handle life's inevitable challenges.

That's the dilemma—and the danger—of therapy today.

Types of good therapy

Not all therapy is created equal. Some approaches drive real change, while others trap people in a cycle of endless talking with no progress. The key is to choose a method that challenges you, holds you accountable, and pushes you toward results.

The most evidence-based forms of therapy include the following:

Cognitive Behavioral Therapy (CBT)

This approach is one I commonly use, and clients have found it to be most effective.

CBT focuses on identifying negative thought patterns and replacing them with healthier, more productive ways of thinking and behaving. It's action-oriented, making it a strong choice for people who want to see real change.

The psychiatrist Aaron Beck developed this form of therapy in the 1960s after noticing that his patients with depression often held beliefs that weren't true. These inaccurate, irrational thought patterns kept them trapped. He called these false thoughts "cognitive distortions." For example, someone with depression might engage in "catastrophizing." This is when a person assumes the worst possible outcome will happen, no matter how unlikely. They might think, "If I make one mistake at work, I'll get fired and never find another job." This exaggerated belief fuels anxiety and keeps them feeling hopeless.

Unlike the untested approaches I critiqued earlier, CBT is evidence-based. Decades of research and hundreds of studies support its effectiveness across a wide range of conditions, including depression, anxiety disorders, addiction, marital problems, eating disorders, and personality disorders.[1] For depression, research suggests CBT is more effective than some antidepressant medications.[2, 3]

Dialectical Behavior Therapy (DBT)

This spinoff of CBT was originally developed in the early 1990s by Marsha M. Lineham, PhD, a psychology researcher and professor, for patients with borderline personality disorder. Since then, dozens of research papers have been published, supporting the use of DBT to treat a range of other conditions, including suicidal ideation, anger and aggression, bipolar disorder, eating disorders, anxiety, and many other mental health conditions.[4, 5, 6, 7, 8] It's now widely used for anyone who wants help keeping emotions in check. DBT teaches specific skills like distress tolerance, mindfulness, and interpersonal effectiveness. DBT and CBT both focus on changing negative thought patterns, but DBT goes further by emphasizing emotional regulation, distress tolerance, and mindfulness. While CBT helps patients identify and challenge irrational thoughts, DBT teaches them how to accept difficult feelings and develop coping skills. DBT is often used for people with intense emotions, such as those with borderline personality disorder, whereas CBT is more commonly applied to anxiety and depression.

Eye Movement Desensitization and Reprocessing (EMDR)

Primarily used for people with PTSD, EMDR helps reprocess distressing memories so they lose their emotional charge.

During a typical session, a patient imagines a traumatic memory while moving their eyes in specific directions. It's thought that this can help people to reprocess traumatic memories so they can stop reliving them over and over. The therapy is typically delivered once or twice a week for six to twelve sessions.

Granted, there's less research to support the effectiveness of EMDR than for CBT or DBT. Still, the research done, at least so far, is promising.[9, 10, 11] While I don't offer EMDR, I have known colleagues who have had good results with it. Many clients report significant improvements in processing traumatic experiences.

How to be a good patient

It's essential to understand that therapy is an active, collaborative process. No matter how effective the therapeutic approach may be, it can fall short if the patient isn't fully invested in their progress.

The more effort, engagement, and accountability a patient brings to each session, the better the outcomes. To make therapy as effective as possible, consider these guidelines:

1. Come Prepared: Therapy isn't just a casual conversation. Before each session, reflect on what you want to discuss, what progress you've made, and areas where you're struggling. I appreciate it when patients bring notes—so don't be shy to do so.
2. Apply What You Learn: Therapy only works if you take the insights from each session and put them into practice in your life. If your therapist suggests a strategy, give it a try.

If you gain an understanding of a particular behavior, act on it. If you're struggling to apply what you've learned, share that with your therapist. The more information they have, the better they can adjust their approach to help you. Real change happens between sessions, not just during them.

3. Stay Open to Being Challenged: A good therapist will challenge your thinking. Instead of resisting, try to stay curious. Growth often starts with discomfort. Ask yourself: *What if they have a point? What if I try seeing this from another perspective?*
4. Be Honest—Especially When You Disagree: If something your therapist says doesn't sit well with you, speak up. Productive therapy involves honest dialogue, not just passive agreement. A good therapist won't be offended if you express your thoughts. If they seem defensive or upset by your honesty, it's a sign you may need to reconsider your therapist.
5. Set Clear Goals: Therapy should have a purpose. What are you hoping to change? What would success look like for you? If you and your therapist aren't working toward specific goals, sessions may become unfocused, leading to wasted time and money.

Putting therapy to the test

Most people wouldn't continue seeing a hairstylist who consistently gave them bad cuts. And if a restaurant repeatedly served tasteless meals, they'd stop going. If a personal trainer didn't help them improve, they'd find someone new.

For reasons that are hard to explain, patients rarely hold therapists to the same standards they expect of other professionals. Even when they see little or no improvement after weeks or months of therapy, many continue showing up out of habit. That needs to change.

To help patients evaluate whether their therapy is effective, I recommend using the following checklist. If you answer "no" to any of these questions, it might be time to consider finding a new therapist.

- Are you working toward your objectives? Therapy isn't about talking in circles. It's about addressing specific issues and making real progress. If you're beginning to see improvements in the areas you came to therapy to address, then therapy is likely working.
- Do you feel increasingly self-reliant? A sign of effective therapy is that you gradually need less support from your therapist. Instead of constantly seeking reassurance or answers, you'll begin to feel confident about yourself and using the tools you've developed, such as stress management, problem-solving, or decision-making. Therapy is meant to equip you to handle life's challenges independently.
- Are you noticing tangible changes outside of the therapy office? You'll notice the result of good therapy in how you interact with others, handle stress, and make decisions. Are you communicating more clearly? Are you handling conflict in a healthier way? Are you noticing that you have a more positive mindset? These changes indicate that therapy is leading to real-life changes.

If you're not seeing real progress in these areas, it's time to question whether you're getting your money's worth out of therapy. Therapy should be a catalyst for tangible, measurable change, not a never-ending cycle of frustration. Just as you wouldn't tolerate poor service in any other part of your life, don't settle for a therapist who isn't helping you move forward.

It's time to hold your therapist accountable. If they're not actively helping you make real progress, it's time to seek someone who will. Therapy should equip you to face life's challenges with confidence and independence. Don't waste your time or energy on therapy that doesn't deliver. Take charge, demand the results you deserve, and refuse to settle for anything less.

CHAPTER FOURTEEN

THE CULT OF THERAPY

Spend enough time listening to people whose friends, partners, or family members are in therapy, and you'll start to hear the same troubling pattern.

Spouses say their once-loving, supportive partners have grown distant, angry, hypercritical, or even unfaithful.

Parents describe adult children who sought therapy for everyday struggles—work stress, mild anxiety, dating nerves—only to come back convinced their families are "toxic" or "abusive." They rewrite personal histories, cut ties, and leave loved ones blindsided and broken.

Today's therapy is fluent in a new language—one filled with buzzwords, diagnoses, and mantras that excuse responsibility and shut down dissent. What was once meant to clarify now muddies reality. It's not healing—it's hypnotic. Therapy-speak has become a conversation killer, a verbal shield that shuts down discussion. Challenge the logic or offer a different perspective, and you risk being dismissed—or cut off entirely.

Therapy hasn't helped these patients grow; it's turned them into entitled bullies, armed with the gospel of their therapists. They parrot their therapist's words as if they were sacred truth, shutting down anyone who dares to challenge them.

These transformations are typical of patients ensnared in what I call the Cult of Therapy. It seeps into their thoughts, words, and actions. They become fluent in weaponized therapy-speak, deflecting responsibility for their unhappiness onto "dysfunctional" childhoods, "toxic" coworkers, and "narcissistic" spouses or friends who "don't get it" and "refuse to do the work." For all their supposed growth, they end up bitter, withdrawn, isolated, and visibly miserable.

I once counseled parents whose adult daughter was so enamored with her therapist that she flew cross-country just to attend sessions. Her dependence grew so intense the parents felt they were losing their own child.

For anyone who cares about someone caught in the Cult of Therapy, these changes are heartbreaking to witness. Loved ones watch helplessly as patients abandon supportive families, promising careers, and meaningful relationships—all under the illusion of "healing."

What defines a "cult"?

When people think of cults, they often picture figures like Reverend Jim Jones, who led the Peoples Temple to Jonestown, where hundreds drank cyanide-laced punch, including parents who gave fatal doses to their children.[1]

Other cult leaders inspired similar acts of blind devotion. In 1997, thirty-nine members of the Heaven's Gate cult took barbiturates mixed with alcohol under their leader's direction.[2] Charles Manson's followers committed nine murders at his command. David Koresh led the Branch Davidians to their deaths in 1993. And a 2023 HBO docuseries profiled Amy Carlson, who claimed to be the reincarnation of Jesus and convinced followers she could heal them with love.[3]

These infamous groups encouraged intense, religious-like devotion, manipulating followers with promises of salvation and purpose. Their notoriety has led many to equate cults with religion or spirituality, but that's a misconception. Many modern cults don't rely on faith at all. Rather, they weaponize psychology as their primary tool of manipulation.

Consider the case of the Sullivan Institute for Research and Psychoanalysis, founded by Saul Newton and Jane Pearce on Manhattan's Upper West Side in the 1950s.[4, 5, 6]

The Sullivan Institute lured followers—who became known as "Sullivanians"—with a distorted version of Freudian psychoanalysis. While traditional Freudian analysis has its own flaws, the Sullivan therapists introduced a dangerous twist. Newton and Pearce encouraged followers to break free from societal and familial constraints, promoting total liberation from their families of origin. Followers were urged to reject the expectations of their parents and society, instead forming new bonds, specifically with fellow members of the cult.[7, 8, 9]

Under Newton and Pearce's direction, followers were ordered to sever ties with their families, often through cold, impersonal letters. Parents were pressured to send their children to boarding schools, promising never to visit again.[10] The control was so absolute that one mother lost a custody battle after the judge ruled, "The patient spends more time with her therapist than with her son."[11, 12]

Once ties were cut, patients were absorbed into so-called "housing families" within the institute. Inside these insular units, they were coerced into sexual relationships with multiple members—including the leaders—under the guise that such "exploration" would foster emotional growth. Any hint of doubt or desire to leave was swiftly crushed. Followers were told that without the Sullivan Institute, they were doomed to ruin, institutionalization, or even death.[13]

Biographers have noted that the Sullivan Institute's influence reached into artistic and literary circles. For example, *Jackson Pollock: An American Saga* describes Pollock undergoing therapy with Jane Pearce and Paul Goodman, who later became central figures in the Sullivanian orbit.[14] Singer Judy Collins wrote about receiving psychotherapy informed by these ideas during the 1960s.[15] And novelist Richard Price described it as "add water and it's instant friends . . . it's instant sex life . . . it's like somebody opened the gates of heaven."[16] Their degree of involvement varied, but these accounts show how the group's ideas circulated among creative communities of the time.

The Sullivan Institute remains one of the most literal examples of a therapy cult. But it's far from the only one. In Los Angeles, the Center for Feeling Therapy marketed itself as the "new Freuds."[17]

More recently, therapy practices have taken on cultish elements by merging psychedelic use with dubious techniques like tapping into the body's "inner healing intelligence."[18] Some of these psychedelic-assisted therapies have drawn criticism, with accusations of sexual abuse by those involved.[19]

Today's Cult of Therapy

The Cult of Therapy today doesn't involve robes or rituals. It's built on dependence, isolation, and blind allegiance. A modern-day cult with the same kinds of promises—playing out one patient at a time.

When people first hear about groups like the Sullivan Institute, they're often shocked: *How could so many intelligent, capable people fall for something so clearly harmful?* But the same question could be asked of the millions of patients trapped in endless, ineffective therapy across America.

Most patients don't walk into a full-blown therapy cult like the Sullivan Institute. The modern Cult of Therapy has no headquarters, no grand master plan. There's no sinister cabal of therapists trying to take over the world. Most bad therapists we've discussed in this book are not malicious, but untrained and likely ignorant of the harm they're doing.

Instead, they're drawn into something quieter, more subtle, but no less damaging.

Yet the repercussions remain. In many cases, the cult consists of just two people: one leader and one follower—the therapist and the patient. I wish this weren't true. But cult-like dynamics play out every day, both in therapists' offices and online.

If this sounds far-fetched, consider how cults typically operate and what their appeal is. People are vulnerable to charismatic voices and promises of healing, from someone who the patient believes holds the sole cure for suffering: loneliness, anxiety, rage, depression, even existential despair.[20, 21] Their ideal recruits feel abandoned by family, by society, or both. They're lost, aimless, insecure, disconnected. What they crave is direction, purpose, belonging—and a sense that they matter. When someone finally sees them, hears them, affirms them, it feels transcendent. For those already struggling with fragile mental health, that feeling becomes addictive. It offers a euphoric reprieve from pain, not a way through it.

Slowly, patients find themselves giving more to therapy—more loyalty, more sacrifice, more dependence. They're privy to cult-specific language that allows them to feel "insider" identity and deepen the bond. To tighten control, followers become isolated from family, friends, and the outside world. Often, this happens through blame. Followers are led to believe their loved ones are the source of their pain—especially childhood trauma. And if you see your family as the root of all your problems, why wouldn't you cut them off?

With the outside world erased, the Cult of Therapy cultivates total dependence—financial, emotional, psychological. Fear becomes the key mechanism of control. Followers are warned that if they leave, their life will unravel. The threat of collapse is constant, keeping them tethered.

Sound familiar? This book is full of stories: therapists urging patients to cut off family and friends; patients parroting "My therapist says . . ." like gospel; therapists warning that terrible things will happen if treatment stops.

This dynamic—just patient and therapist—feeds into a basic human instinct: We like talking about ourselves. And in therapy, you're paying someone to listen, to focus solely on you for an hour or more each week. With that kind of attention, everyday experiences begin to take on exaggerated importance. A bad day becomes "clinical depression." A minor disagreement at work turns into a psychological case study. Everything becomes material. Everything becomes therapy.

And just like cult members, patients can become eager evangelists. As therapy has gone mainstream, a clinical tool has hardened into a social identity, drawing in people not because they're in crisis, but because participation signals insight, virtue, or belonging. A therapist on retainer has become the latest status symbol in urban and suburban America—on par with luxury gym memberships and exclusive preschools.

What makes the Cult of Therapy especially dangerous is how well it flatters the follower. The patient feels in control, convinced they're boldly steering their own journey toward self-betterment. In reality, many are simply intoxicated by self-fixation.

That intoxicating sense that it's you and your therapist against the world? That isn't empowerment. It's entrapment.

And it can quietly corrode a life. Friendships thin out. Marriages strain or end. Jobs suffer. The spiral is gradual, almost invisible at first, but the fallout is real.

In relationships and marriages, it can sometimes feel like a third party has entered the picture when one partner is in therapy and the other isn't. I've worked with many couples who've had to rebuild trust after one became overly reliant on a therapist who claimed to know what the other partner was thinking, feeling, or doing, only for those assumptions to be completely untrue.

This slow isolation is perhaps the most dangerous part of the Cult of Therapy. Boundaries are rigidly applied, with no room for nuance or repair. Patients are urged to distance themselves from anyone or anything that causes even mild discomfort. What starts as a conversation about hurt feelings with a parent can fester into hatred. Instead of guiding patients toward difficult but healing conversations, some therapists offer a simpler message: "Your parents were toxic. Your trauma is their fault. Cut them off. Protect your peace."

Eventually, some patients might begin to sense that something's off. The endless cycle of self-analysis and blaming others isn't helping. They start to wonder if the therapy is working. That's when the therapist makes the message clear: If you leave now, you'll backslide. You'll sabotage your growth. You'll never thrive in relationships. You won't achieve success. And worst of all, you'll end up right back where you started—reliant on the same toxic people you've been taught to cut off.

Even in the best circumstances, this borders on exploitation. Patients keep paying for sessions that go in circles—never addressing core issues, only reinforcing their dependence on more therapy. Over time, decisions big and small get filtered through the therapist's lens. The therapist, once a guide, becomes the gatekeeper to emotional stability—and even to identity.

This kind of dependency is both powerful and dangerous. It's what keeps patients trapped in the cycle—week after week, month after month, year after year—even when it becomes painfully obvious that the therapist's advice is doing more harm than good.

I might have thought all of this sounded bizarre if I hadn't worked with so many patients like Victoria.

In her late twenties, Victoria was a talented but struggling musician, lost in her career and seeking clarity and confidence through therapy. She started seeing a therapist her friends raved about. At first, Victoria was equally impressed. But over time, instead of sticking to practical guidance, the therapist drew her deeper into a rigid belief system. Therapy wasn't just a tool for growth, the therapist insisted—it was a way of life.

The therapist positioned herself as the ultimate authority on Victoria's emotional health. When Victoria voiced doubts, the therapist framed them as "resistance" to be overcome. "It sounds like you're not fully committed to the process," she would say, subtly turning any hesitation into a flaw. Gradually, Victoria stopped questioning the methods and surrendered to the therapist's control.

When Victoria eventually expressed a desire to move on, the therapist told her she wasn't ready. "You still have deep work to do," she insisted. The message was clear: Therapy wasn't about progress, it was about staying. Permanently.

Like any devoted cult member, Victoria grew increasingly dependent. She stopped making decisions without her therapist's approval. The more she dissected her past, the more fragile she became in the present. Her therapist urged her to cut ties with anyone who didn't "support her growth"—especially friends and family who questioned therapy's effectiveness. When Victoria thought about leaving, the therapist warned it would be an act of "self-betrayal" and claimed she would spiral without continued treatment.

Years passed. Then one day, an old friend bluntly asked her, "Has this actually helped you?" And just like that, the fog began to lift. For the first time, Victoria took a hard look at her situation. She realized she was no better off than when she had started: still struggling in her career, still lacking confidence, still uncertain about her future. She hadn't made progress; she'd been stuck in an endless loop of self-analysis.

That's when she found my services and I heard her story. I made it clear to her that I didn't demand allegiance. I didn't encourage her to "process" forever. Instead, we focused on concrete action. Within weeks, Victoria understood what had happened. She hadn't been healed, she'd been trapped. And like anyone leaving a cult, the hardest part wasn't walking away. It was unlearning the belief that she ever needed to stay.

The art of deprogramming

As I've made clear elsewhere, while I disagree with many of my colleagues in the therapy profession, I don't believe most of them set out to run their practices like cults.

Most likely, they believe they're doing the right thing for the right reasons. But that's the danger—the cult-like nature of modern therapy is so pervasive that even without a manipulative leader these dynamics can emerge quickly and dangerously. They seep into the patient-therapist relationship, and from there, into the patient's other relationships. Therapists, patients, and those in their lives need to recognize the warning signs, and ignore them at their peril.

I've worked with people on all sides of this issue, including family members watching loved ones get pulled into the Cult of Therapy. For them, it's terrifying. Their loved one visits the therapist frequently and comes home acting distant, asking odd questions, or parroting the therapist's words. Anything they say might get reported back—accurately or not. They can't tell if the therapist sees them as an ally or an enemy, though the patient's behavior often provides the answer. It feels invasive and unsettling because the therapist holds a "full picture" of them—but it's a picture filtered through one person's perspective. This often leads to the therapist advising the patient on how to "deal with" their family, based on a distorted view.

This dynamic is one reason why couples therapy can be so essential—yet many relationships unravel before they ever get there. Sometimes, it's therapy itself that sparks the breakdown.

As mentioned earlier, this often stems from one partner's therapist. The dynamics shift when a therapist shapes how someone navigates their relationship, relying solely on one side of the story. The non-therapized partner can start to feel isolated in their own home, even ganged up on by someone now armed with the phrase "My therapist says . . ." That kind of imbalance breeds resentment quickly, and sometimes irrevocably.

As Victoria's story illustrates, deprogramming someone from the Cult of Therapy is incredibly difficult. If family members approach too aggressively, the patient may feel belittled or shamed, which only pushes them deeper into their cult-like mentality. People have been conditioned to view any discomfort as toxic, any disagreement as abusive, and all family relationships as obstacles to their emotional salvation. By bluntly stating, "Your therapist is brainwashing you," loved ones risk playing right into the therapist's hands, further entrenching the cult mentality.

Instead, warmth, empathy, and curiosity are essential. So is clarity in communication. Family members have the best chance of success if they ask questions that prompt critical thinking. For example: "How does the price for this weekend intensive compare to what other therapists charge?" or "How much do you think is reasonable to invest in your emotional health?"

When clients tell me they've been stuck in a long-term therapeutic relationship, I ask straightforward, yet powerful, questions: How has your time with this therapist benefited you? Is your life objectively better because of this therapy? How is continuing down this path serving your growth or well-being?

It's crucial to frame these questions carefully, ensuring there's no ambiguity in what you're asking. This minimizes the risk of misinterpretation by the patient or therapist. Remember, you might be viewed as the source of the problem in their eyes.

Even when family members or friends approach the situation with care and patience, some patients remain resolute, unwilling to consider alternative perspectives. In such cases, the family's role is to wait and continue offering love. If the patient enforces a "boundary" and cuts ties, a respectful response might be: "I wish this weren't your decision, but I respect your right to make it. If you ever change your mind, I will always be here." Occasionally, perhaps on birthdays or holidays, a simple card or invitation can be sent, just to remind them that the door is always open.

By offering steady, unconditional support, family members can serve as the antidote to the cult-like narratives patients are fed behind closed doors. They don't enable delusion; they provide clarity. And when patients finally see through the haze and recognize the harm the therapy has caused, they'll know they have a place to return to—home. A place where love isn't conditional, and truth isn't filtered through buzzwords. It's in that unvarnished space that the real work of reclaiming a life can begin.

CHAPTER FIFTEEN

BACK TO SANITY

When I began writing this book, I thought I was writing about therapy, a profession that had lost its way and too often left people weaker instead of stronger. I wanted to expose its flaws, push therapists to do better, and help patients break free from the cycles of dependence and self-pity that modern therapy can feed.

But as I reflected on my two decades as a therapist, particularly during the turbulent 2020s when unrest and polarization peaked, I realized the problem was far bigger than my field. Therapy, having run amok, is shaping a nation that fears discomfort, clings to grievance, and is weighed down by emotionalism and division. What began in the therapy room now reaches far beyond it, remaking our entire culture.

Somewhere along the way, we forgot how to disagree without tearing each other apart, how to endure hardship without letting it define us, and how to grow stronger from pain rather than flee from it. We have mistaken validation for healing, grievance for growth, and comfort for strength. What therapists say in session now ripples far beyond the office or screen, shaping not only the patient's life but the world around them.

I often think back to Valerie, a patient who came to me after years in therapy with someone else. She could dissect her childhood from every angle, name each trigger, and map out her patterns with precision. Her journals were full of insights about why she hurt, yet none of it brought her closer to the life she wanted. Early on she told me, "I'm just learning how broken I am. But I don't feel like I'm getting stronger." That line stayed with me. Years of therapy had taught Valerie to understand her pain, but not to rise above it. She had been conditioned to believe that progress meant endlessly unpacking her wounds, circling the same traumas week after week, and sometimes even creating new ones.

We took a different approach. Instead of endlessly analyzing her past, we focused on her present and the future she wanted to build. Together we rebuilt relationships, challenged her thinking, and took concrete steps forward. There was no room for rumination because change required action. The work was hard, but through it, her strength returned. Little by little, she stopped asking, "Why am I this way?" and started asking, "What can I do now?" That shift changed everything.

Valerie didn't leave therapy with another label or sob story. She left with resolve, confidence, and a renewed sense of agency. Therapy became an occasional check-in, not a crutch. For the first time in years, she trusted herself, and more importantly, she moved on. Her story is not only about what therapy can do when it works. It is about what happens when someone stops letting pain control their life and starts moving forward.

Valerie's turnaround was not magic. It reflected what therapy was always meant to do: challenge as much as comfort, and push people to grow rather than keep them dwelling on their pain. The best therapists do not simply listen. They help patients see themselves clearly, set goals, and walk with them through discomfort until they come out stronger.

The state of Valerie's struggle when I first met her is far from unique. It has become the norm. Across the country, people are trapped in the same loop, believing they must completely heal before they can truly live. Relationships stall. Careers drift. Momentum dies. This isn't weakness. It is the product of a cultural script that tells us to circle our pain until it somehow disappears. But pain doesn't vanish. It changes only when we do.

I know because I have been there. Early in my career, I worked with a young woman who had endured more than her share of hardship: abuse, loss, and years of feeling powerless. I wanted her to feel heard, so I relied on what I had been taught: open-ended questions, empathy, and quiet nods for every hard feeling. Week after week, she poured out her suffering. I listened. I validated. I left each session believing I was helping until one day she asked, "Do you think I'm ever going to get better?"

Her question stopped me cold. I realized I hadn't challenged her or offered a way forward. I had mistaken sitting with her pain for helping her rise out of it. That moment reshaped my approach and strengthened my confidence as a therapist. I began asking harder questions, setting clear goals, and pushing patients to face what they were avoiding rather than run from it. Over time, I saw more patients transform by facing their pain and working through it. I came to see that the same principle applies far beyond the therapy room: real growth, personal or cultural, begins only when we step into what's hard.

When fragility defines us

These individual transformations stand in stark contrast to what is happening across the nation. Over the past two decades, therapy culture has seeped into nearly every corner of American life. It has taught us to see discomfort as trauma, disagreement as harm, and resilience as optional. The effects are everywhere: in schools where academic standards collapse under emotional accommodation, in workplaces where demands for "psychological safety" silence honest feedback, and in families where minor conflicts harden into lasting estrangements. Even politics has absorbed the therapy mindset. Grievance has become power, and victimhood the quickest path to moral authority. Public discourse is no longer about solving problems; it is about broadcasting wounds and competing to weaponize them.

We have trained individuals to avoid what's hard, and our institutions—schools, corporations, and even governments—have followed suit. This leads to more than personal weakness; it breeds institutional paralysis. Organizations freeze at the first hint of conflict. Leaders back away from enforcing standards. Communities forget how to argue, forgive, and move on. Weakness may become a habit we share, but progress does not stop because problems are too big. It stops because no one is willing to tolerate the discomfort required to solve them. If we cannot face the challenges needed to move forward together as a society, we will continue to unravel.

A rotten therapy culture is putting us at risk of societal decay. It erodes the qualities every society needs to endure: grit, tolerance, and the ability to live with opposing views. We can already see the cracks forming. On college campuses, debates that once sharpened minds now spark demands for silence. In workplaces, fear of offense stifles honest feedback. Even in our politics, disagreement increasingly ends not with compromise but with cancellation. These patterns are symptoms of a culture that no longer knows how to bear discomfort. It trades reason for reactivity and disagreement for public shaming. What began as a tool for healing has become a mindset that keeps people small, avoids challenge, and blames others for their pain.

This cultural slide will not reverse on its own. Therapists have a major role to play. In our uncertain world, anxious patients will understandably keep seeking treatment. For a good therapist, every session must be an opportunity to model resilience, help patients face what is difficult, and reject the false comfort of endless validation. Real cultural change can begin in the therapy room—with one patient, one challenge, one act of courage at a time. If more Americans emerged from therapy stronger and more resilient, rather than remaining trapped, the positive effects would be felt throughout society.

The grand sweep of human history reminds us that resilience is not a rare trait reserved for superhumans. It is woven into who we are. Our ancestors endured famine, war, and loss not because they were numb to suffering but because they understood something we have forgotten: Discomfort is not fatal. It is where strength is born.

During the Great Depression, generations stretched every resource, pushed through uncertainty, and rebuilt from nothing. There was no room for endless self-analysis; they had crops to plant, families to protect, and a nation to save. During the Civil Rights Movement, progress came not from dwelling on pain but from action, courage, and a shared purpose.

Other cultures remind us of this truth. In Japan, *gaman* means quietly enduring the unbearable with patience and dignity. In Scandinavia, *lagom* reflects a mindset of balance and restraint. These philosophies do not dramatize hardship; they expect it and embrace it as the process that shapes stronger individuals and more resilient societies.

The choice ahead

None of this is inevitable. The grit that carried past generations through hardship still lives in us. The question is whether we will call on it before weakness becomes our default.

I remember September 11, 2001. Office workers, covered in ash, walked silently across the Brooklyn Bridge as sirens wailed behind them. Strangers offered water, shoes, and shoulders to cry on. Shopkeepers swept debris from their storefronts while smoke still curled over Lower Manhattan. No one waited for perfect conditions to move forward. There was fear, and there was unspeakable loss, but there was also resolve. In the days that followed, New Yorkers lined up to give blood, draped banners from fire escapes, and stood shoulder to shoulder at candlelight vigils. The city did not collapse into panic. There was grief, but not grievance. Strength came from action, connection, and the quiet understanding that rebuilding does not begin with comfort. It begins with courage.

Reversing this cultural slide starts small. Therapists can lead by refusing to coddle and by restoring challenge as a core part of healing. Schools can stop treating challenge as harm and instead teach students to work through it. Leaders in every sphere, from business to government, can model grit by making tough decisions and standing by them. And each of us, in our own lives, can practice choosing action over avoidance, no matter how small the step. That might mean having a hard conversation instead of avoiding it, taking a risk you've been putting off, or facing a fear you've long sidestepped. Small acts of courage, repeated daily, are what strengthen both individuals and the culture they create. These shifts, repeated across millions of lives, can rebuild the resilience that hardship once forged.

We can build that kind of culture again, one that faces uncomfortable realities, teaches our children to embrace struggle, and reminds us that pain is not a life sentence but a catalyst for change. This is about more than therapy. It is about the country we want to be. If we continue to trade courage for comfort, we risk raising a generation unprepared for hardship and a society too brittle to survive real crises. But if therapists reclaim their mission to strengthen rather than soothe, they can help restore the resilience our nation so desperately needs. When parents, teachers, and leaders join in, that effort can spread beyond the therapy room and into a culture that rises to meet its challenges instead of crumbling under them.

History is watching, and so is the next generation. The future will not wait. The choice is ours: keep soothing ourselves into weakness, or face what is hard and grow stronger. If we choose courage now, we will not only recover, but will build a stronger nation ready for whatever comes next.

ACKNOWLEDGMENTS

This book took shape over more than two years, through many conversations and countless revisions. It reflects the influence of more people than I can fully name.

First and foremost, I want to thank my agent, Matt Latimer of Javelin, who helped shape the original idea for *Therapy Nation* and believed in it long before it had a title or clear structure. After reading an early opinion piece that hinted at what this book might become, Matt encouraged me to expand those ideas into something larger. He has a rare instinct for recognizing ideas that matter, along with the judgment to know when they are worth pursuing. His confidence in this project gave me the conviction to see it through.

I'm grateful to the entire team at Javelin for their support and professionalism throughout this process.

I owe particular thanks to Javelin's Dylan Colligan, whose steady guidance carried this book through every stage of its development. From early conception through final revisions, Dylan was present for the long stretches of uncertainty and refinement that writing a book like this demands. He brought consistency, clarity, and calm to a process that is often anything but, and helped keep the focus on what mattered most in the ideas and structure of the book.

I'm also thankful to Peter Joseph at Hanover Square Press, who first championed *Therapy Nation*. His early belief in the project was essential in bringing it to life. Thank you as well to Grace Towery and the team at Hanover Square Press for their work in seeing this book through to publication.

My sincere thanks to Alisa Bowman, whose collaboration was essential to this book. Her skill, patience, and generosity with her time helped expand the research, refine the ideas, sharpen the narrative, and bring coherence to a complex argument.

I'm also grateful to Rachael Nedrow, whose design insight and hard work helped shape the cover of *Therapy Nation*.

I owe a particular debt to the many patients I have worked with over the years. While confidentiality prevents me from naming individuals, their honesty, struggles, contradictions, and persistence shaped my understanding of both human psychology and the limits of modern therapeutic thinking. Listening to patients navigate confusion, distress, and cultural pressure did more than inspire this book. It made me a better therapist, and ultimately made this work possible.

I am deeply grateful to my mother, whose unwavering support sustained me throughout this process and who took a genuine interest in this work, proudly watching every television appearance along the way. Thank you as well to my brother, Matthew, and my sister, Susan, for their support.

Finally, I am especially grateful to Grace Samiee, whose support, patience, and steadiness carried me through every stage of this book. Her sharp ear for real-world stories sparked many of the ideas here, and the countless hours she spent reading and improving early drafts were invaluable.

Therapy Nation is the result of careful listening over many years. I am grateful to everyone who helped bring it into the world.

ENDNOTES

INTRODUCTION

1. Witters, Dan. "U.S. Depression Rates Reach New Highs." Gallup. May 17, 2023. https://news.gallup.com/poll/505745/depression-rates-reach-new-highs.aspx.
2. Clifton, Jon, and Julie Ray. "What's the Happiest Country on Earth?" Gallup. March 20, 2024. https://news.gallup.com/poll/612125/happiest-country-earth.aspx.
3. Alpert, Jonathan. "In Therapy Forever? Enough Already." April 21, 2012. "Opinion." *The New York Times*. https://www.nytimes.com/2012/04/22/opinion/sunday/in-therapy-forever-enough-already.html.
4. Burns. "373: Why Therapy Fails." Feeling Good. December 4, 2023. https://feelinggood.com/2023/12/04/373-why-therapy-fails.
5. LeJeune, C. "When Therapy Feels Like an Infinite Loop." New Harbinger Publications, Inc. April 25, 2023. https://www.newharbinger.com/blog/quick-tips-therapists/when-therapy-feels-like-an-infinite-loop.
6. Ma, Nicole Cain Nd. "Feeling Stuck in Endless Therapy Cycles?" YouTube. January 28, 2025. https://www.youtube.com/watch?v=FCxhcW1OyNQ.
7. Harris, Destiny S. "The Problem With Long-Term Therapy: Let's Talk About It." *Medium*. May 6, 2021. https://medium.com/age-of-awareness/the-problem-with-long-term-therapy-4333ea938cd1.
8. Cummins, Eleanor. "Why Therapy Is Broken." WIRED. September 26, 2022. https://www.wired.com/story/therapy-broken-mental-health-challenges.
9. Ducharme, Jamie. "America Has Reached Peak Therapy. Why Is Our Mental Health Getting Worse?" *Time*. August 28, 2023. https://time.com/6308096/therapy-mental-health-worse-us.
10. Ohlheiser, A. W. "Teletherapy Can Really Help, and Really Hurt." Vox. May 16, 2024. https://www.vox.com/technology/24158103/betterhelp-online-therapy-privacy-issues.
11. "Joe Rogan Experience #2109 - Abigail Shrier." June 27, 2024. https://www.youtube.com/watch?v=WTNjc8HyOaE.

12. Witters, Dan. "U.S. Depression Rates Reach New Highs." Gallup. May 17, 2023. https://news.gallup.com/poll/505745/depression-rates-reach-new-highs.aspx.
13. National Institute on Drug Abuse. "Drug Overdose Deaths: Facts and Figures." National Institute on Drug Abuse. August 21, 2024. https://nida.nih.gov/research-topics/trends-statistics/overdose-death-rates.
14. Cox, Daniel A. "The State of American Friendship: Change, Challenges, and Loss." The Survey Center on American Life. June 8, 2021. https://www.americansurveycenter.org/research/the-state-of-american-friendship-change-challenges-and-loss.
15. "New APA Poll: One in Three Americans Feels Lonely Every Week." n.d. Accessed February 14, 2025. https://www.psychiatry.org:443/news-room/news-releases/new-apa-poll-one-in-three-americans-feels-lonely-e.
16. CDC. "Suicide Data and Statistics." Suicide Prevention. January 30, 2025. https://www.cdc.gov/suicide/facts/data.html.
17. Geiger, Abigail. "Political Polarization in the American Public." Pew Research Center. June 12, 2014. https://www.pewresearch.org/politics/2014/06/12/political-polarization-in-the-american-public.
18. Boxell, Levi, Matthew Gentzkow, and Jesse M. Shapiro. 2020. "Cross-Country Trends in Affective Polarization." *Social Science Research Network*. https://papers.ssrn.com/abstract=3522318.

CHAPTER ONE

1. "Mental Health Treatment or Therapy among U.S. Adults 2023." n.d. Statista. Accessed March 14, 2025. https://www.statista.com/statistics/794027/mental-health-treatment-counseling-past-year-us-adults.
2. Brenan, Megan. "Americans' Reported Mental Health at New Low; More Seek Help." Gallup. December 21, 2022. https://news.gallup.com/poll/467303/americans-reported-mental-health-new-low-seek-help.aspx.
3. "Mental Health Treatment Among Adults: United States, 2019." September 29, 2020. https://www.cdc.gov/nchs/products/databriefs/db380.htm.
4. "Psychologists Struggle to Meet Demand amid Mental Health Crisis." 2022. https://www.apa.org/pubs/reports/practitioner/2022-covid-psychologist-workload.
5. Brenan, Megan. "Americans' Reported Mental Health at New Low; More Seek Help." Gallup. December 21, 2022. https://news.gallup.com/poll/467303/americans-reported-mental-health-new-low-seek-help.aspx.
6. "WISQARS Leading Causes of Death Visualization Tool." n.d. Centers for Disease Control and Prevention. Accessed March 14, 2025. https://wisqars.cdc.gov/lcd.
7. Cui, Lulu, Shu Li, Siman Wang, Xiafang Wu, Yingyu Liu, Weiyang Yu, Yijun Wang, Yong Tang, Maosheng Xia, and Baoman Li. 2024. "Major Depressive Disorder: Hypothesis, Mechanism, Prevention and Treatment." *Signal Transduction and Targeted Therapy* 9 (1): 30.
8. "Anxiety and Depression: Household Pulse Survey." CDC. National Center for Health Statistics. February 7, 2025. https://www.cdc.gov/nchs/covid19/pulse/mental-health.htm.

9. Fang, David, Yiran Eileen Zhang, and Sam J. Maglio. 2024. "Shortcuts to insincerity: Texting abbreviations seem insincere and not worth answering." *Journal of Experimental Psychology: General*, November. https://doi.org/10.1037/xge0001684.
10. "New APA Poll: One in Three Americans Feels Lonely Every Week." n.d. Accessed February 14, 2025. https://www.psychiatry.org:443/news-room/news-releases/new-apa-poll-one-in-three-americans-feels-lonely-e.
11. Jones, Jeffrey M. "Church Attendance Has Declined in Most U.S. Religious Groups." Gallup. March 25, 2024. https://news.gallup.com/poll/642548/church-attendance-declined-religious-groups.aspx.
12. "Service Organizations, Seeing Drops in Membership, Try to Find New Members." n.d. *Observer-Reporter.* Accessed February 14, 2025. https://www.observer-reporter.com/editors_pick/2024/aug/26/service-organizations-seeing-drops-in-membership-try-to-find-new-members.
13. Engle, Jeremy. "Are Youth Sports Too Competitive?" *The New York Times.* May 1, 2019. https://www.nytimes.com/2019/05/01/learning/are-youth-sports-too-competitive.html.
14. Geiger, Abigail. "A Half-Century after 'Mister Rogers' Debut, 5 Facts about Neighbors in U.S." Pew Research Center. August 15, 2019. https://www.pewresearch.org/short-reads/2019/08/15/facts-about-neighbors-in-u-s.
15. Lopez, German. "A Shooting over a Cheeseburger Tells Us a Lot about America's Gun Problem." Vox. June 2, 2016. https://www.vox.com/2016/6/2/11841554/gun-violence-cheesburger.
16. Crawford, Mike J., Lavanya Thana, Lorna Farquharson, Lucy Palmer, Elizabeth Hancock, Paul Bassett, Jeremy Clarke, and Glenys D. Parry. 2016. "Patient Experience of Negative Effects of Psychological Treatment: Results of a National Survey." *The British Journal of Psychiatry: The Journal of Mental Science* 208 (3): 260–65.
17. Lewis, Cara C., Meredith Boyd, Ajeng Puspitasari, Elena Navarro, Jacqueline Howard, Hannah Kassab, Mira Hoffman, et al. 2019. "Implementing Measurement-Based Care in Behavioral Health: A Review." *JAMA Psychiatry* (Chicago, Ill.) 76 (3): 324–35.

CHAPTER TWO

1. Neophytou, E., Manwell, L.A. & Eikelboom, R. "Effects of Excessive Screen Time on Neurodevelopment, Learning, Memory, Mental Health, and Neurodegeneration: A Scoping Review." *International Journal of Mental Health and Addiction* **19**, 724–744 (2021). https://link.springer.com/article/10.1007/s11469-019-00182-2.
2. Belsie, Laurent, and Scott Armstrong. "High Hopes and Hype Blaze Path For Information Superhighway." *The Christian Science Monitor*, January 13, 1994. https://www.csmonitor.com/1994/0113/13021.html.
3. Clary, Susan. "Willie King Said: 'Doctor, That's the Wrong Leg.'" *Tampa Bay Times.* October 3, 2005. https://www.tampabay.com/archive/1995/03/10/willie-king-said-doctor-that-s-the-wrong-leg.

4. Jenkins, Colleen. "Friday, a Jury Awarded Allan Navarro and His Family 116.7-Million for the Pain and Loss of His Crippling, Misdiagnosed Stroke. Tuesday Came the Verdict to Punish the Doctors: 100,100,000." *Tampa Bay Times*. October 4, 2006. https://www.tampabay.com/archive/2006/10/04/friday-a-jury-awarded-allan-navarro-and-his-family-116-7-million-for-the-pain-and-loss-of-his-crippling-misdiagnosed-stroke-tuesday-came-the-verdict-to-punish-the-doctors-100100000.
5. "Gwyneth Paltrow's Goop to pay $145,000 over claims its vaginal eggs have health perks." *CBS News*. September 6, 2018. https://www.cbsnews.com/news/goop-settlement-false-advertising-vaginal-eggs-gwyneth-paltrow.
6. Godoy, Maria. "Is The Food Babe A Fearmonger? Scientists Are Speaking Out." *NPR*. December 4, 2014. https://www.npr.org/sections/thesalt/2014/12/04/364745790/food-babe-or-fear-babe-as-activist-s-profile-grows-so-do-her-critics.
7. Adams, Matt. "Please Don't Cook Chicken in NyQuil, the FDA Asks TikTok Users." *NPR*. September 22, 2022. https://www.npr.org/2022/09/22/1124252556/nyquil-chicken-challenge-fda-warning.
8. Ohlheiser, A. W. "Why TikTokers Are Drinking Laundry Detergent." Vox. July 29, 2023. https://www.vox.com/technology/2023/7/29/23811639/tiktok-borax-challenge-dangerous-laundry-detergent.
9. Khong, Louise. "People Are Faking Travel Using Random Objects And It's So Ridiculous It's Kinda Funny." BuzzFeed. February 27, 2019. https://www.buzzfeed.com/louisekhong/fake-travel-tiktok-plane-challenge.
10. Sharkey, Patrick. 2024. "Homebound: The Long-Term Rise in Time Spent at Home among U.S. Adults." *Sociological Science* 11 (August): 553–78.
11. Martino, Jessica, Jennifer Pegg, and Elizabeth Pegg Frates. 2017. "The Connection Prescription: Using the Power of Social Interactions and the Deep Desire for Connectedness to Empower Health and Wellness." *American Journal of Lifestyle Medicine* 11 (6): 466–75.
12. Trachtenberg, Estherina. 2024. "The Beneficial Effects of Social Support and Prosocial Behavior on Immunity and Health: A Psychoneuroimmunology Perspective." *Brain, Behavior, & Immunity - Health* 37 (May): 100758.
13. Smith, Andrew P., and Hasah Alheneidi. 2023. "The Internet and Loneliness." *AMA Journal of Ethics* 25 (11): E833–838.
14. Bonsaksen, Tore, Mary Ruffolo, Daicia Price, Janni Leung, Hilde Thygesen, Gary Lamph, Isaac Kabelenga, and Amy Østertun Geirdal. 2023. "Associations between Social Media Use and Loneliness in a Cross-National Population: Do Motives for Social Media Use Matter?" *Health Psychology and Behavioral Medicine* 11 (1): 2158089.
15. "It's Time to Harness the Power of Connection for Our Health and Well-Being." n.d. Accessed November 10, 2024. https://www.who.int/news-room/commentaries/detail/it-s-time-to-harness-the-power-of-connection-for-our-health-and-well-being.
16. Hajek, André, and Hans-Helmut König. 2021. "Do Loneliness and Perceived Social Isolation Reduce Expected Longevity and Increase the Frequency of

Dealing with Death and Dying? Longitudinal Findings Based on a Nationally Representative Sample." *Journal of the American Medical Directors Association* 22 (8): 1720–1725.e5.

17. Ruggeri, Amanda. "People Have Always Whinged about Young Adults. Here's Proof." BBC. October 3, 2017. https://www.bbc.com/worklife/article/20171003-proof-that-people-have-always-complained-about-young-adults.
18. "What Gen Z Thinks about Its Social Media and Smartphone Usage." Harris Poll. September 10, 2024. https://theharrispoll.com/briefs/gen-z-social-media-smart-phones.
19. "Call Me Maybe (Not): A Quarter of Young People Never Answer the Phone." n.d. *Uswitch*. Accessed November 12, 2024. https://www.uswitch.com/media-centre/2024/04/Call-me-maybe-quarter-young-people-never-answer-phone.
20. Kessler, Ronald C., Patricia Berglund, Olga Demler, Robert Jin, Kathleen R. Merikangas, and Ellen E. Walters. 2005. "Lifetime Prevalence and Age-of-Onset Distributions of DSM-IV Disorders in the National Comorbidity Survey Replication." *Archives of General Psychiatry* 62 (6): 593–602.
21. Jefferies, Philip, and Michael Ungar. 2020. "Social Anxiety in Young People: A Prevalence Study in Seven Countries." *PloS One* 15 (9): e0239133.
22. Koo, Hoon Jung, Sungbum Woo, Eunjoo Yang, and Jung Hye Kwon. 2015. "The Double Meaning of Online Social Space: Three-Way Interactions among Social Anxiety, Online Social Behavior, and Offline Social Behavior." *Cyberpsychology, Behavior and Social Networking* 18 (9): 514–20.
23. Molloy, Mark. "Online Shaming: The Dangerous Rise of the Internet Pitchfork Mob." *The Sunday Telegraph*. June 25, 2018. https://www.telegraph.co.uk/news/2018/06/25/online-shaming-dangerous-rise-internet-pitchfork-mob.
24. "Internet Shaming: When Mob Justice Goes Virtual." CBS News. August 20, 2017. https://www.cbsnews.com/news/internet-shaming-when-mob-justice-goes-virtual.
25. Cinelli, Matteo, Gianmarco De Francisci Morales, Alessandro Galeazzi, Walter Quattrociocchi, and Michele Starnini. 2021. "The Echo Chamber Effect on Social Media." *Proceedings of the National Academy of Sciences of the United States of America* 118 (9): e2023301118.
26. Chester, David S., and C. Nathan DeWall. 2016. "The Pleasure of Revenge: Retaliatory Aggression Arises from a Neural Imbalance toward Reward." *Social Cognitive and Affective Neuroscience* 11 (7): 1173–82.
27. Mochon, Daniel, and Janet Schwartz. 2024. "The Confrontation Effect: When Users Engage More with Ideology-Inconsistent Content Online." *Organizational Behavior and Human Decision Processes* 185 (104366): 104366.
28. Martingano, Alison Jane, Sara Konrath, Sasha Zarins, and Anastesia A. Okaomee. 2022. "Empathy, Narcissism, Alexithymia, and Social Media Use." *Psychology of Popular Media* 11 (4): 413–22.
29. Pera, Anna. "Social Media and Empathy Around the Globe." *Psychology Today*. May 17, 2023. https://www.psychologytoday.com/us/blog/what-do-you-mean/202305/social-media-and-empathy-around-the-globe.

ENDNOTES

CHAPTER THREE

1. Guadagno, Rosanna E., Daniel M. Rempala, Shannon Murphy, and Bradley M. Okdie. 2013. "What Makes a Video Go Viral? An Analysis of Emotional Contagion and Internet Memes." *Computers in Human Behavior* 29 (6): 2312–19.
2. "GOP Official Quits After Charges She Used Racist Obama Meme." AP News. July 3, 2016. https://apnews.com/general-news-2dd2d2dd54094261b6a148da62d7c6e6.
3. Gabbatt, Adam. "Golden Escalator Ride: The Surreal Day Trump Kicked off His Bid for President." *The Guardian*. June 14, 2019. https://www.theguardian.com/us-news/2019/jun/13/donald-trump-presidential-campaign-speech-eyewitness-memories.
4. Borchers, Callum. "Why a YMCA in a key battleground state banished CNN and Fox News from its TVs." *The Washington Post*. March 5, 2017. https://www.washingtonpost.com/news/the-fix/wp/2017/03/05/why-a-ymca-in-a-key-battleground-state-banished-cnn-and-fox-news-from-its-tvs.
5. "John Hinckley Jr." Biography. April 2, 2014. https://www.biography.com/crime/john-hinckley-jr.
6. Wilber, Del Quentin. "Reagan Survived an Assassination Attempt and His Response Changed the Trajectory of His Presidency." AP News. July 14, 2024. https://apnews.com/article/reagan-assassination-attempt-trump-butler-gunman-bd3c038d706de55a64727f7d15dffbc8.
7. Associated Press. "McCain Counters Obama 'Arab' Question." YouTube. October 11, 2008. https://www.youtube.com/watch?v=jrnRU3ocIH4.
8. Hong, Sounman, and Sun Hyoung Kim. 2016. "Political Polarization on Twitter: Implications for the Use of Social Media in Digital Governments." *Government Information Quarterly* 33 (4): 777–82.
9. Sims, Grant, Justin Hendrix, and Paul Barrett. "How Tech Platforms Fuel U.S. Political Polarization and What Government Can Do about It." Brookings. September 27, 2021. https://www.brookings.edu/articles/how-tech-platforms-fuel-u-s-political-polarization-and-what-government-can-do-about-it.
10. Wintemute, Garen J., Sonia L. Robinson, Andrew Crawford, Daniel Tancredi, Julia P. Schleimer, Elizabeth A. Tomsich, Paul M. Reeping, Aaron B. Shev, and Veronica A. Pear. 2023. "Views of Democracy and Society and Support for Political Violence in the USA: Findings from a Nationally Representative Survey." *Injury Epidemiology* 10 (1): 45.
11. "Dueling Realities: Amid Multiple Crises, Trump and Biden Supporters See Different Priorities and Futures for the Nation." PRRI. October 19, 2020. https://www.prri.org/research/amid-multiple-crises-trump-and-biden-supporters-see-different-realities-and-futures-for-the-nation.
12. Opzoomer, India. "America Speaks: What Do They Think about Cross-Party Marriages?" YouGov. September 24, 2020. https://today.yougov.com/society/articles/32171-america-speaks-what-do-they-think-about-cross-part.
13. "If You Were Single and Dating, How Willing, If at All, Would You Be to Date Someone with Political Views That Are Different from Your Own?" n.d.

Accessed November 22, 2024. https://today.yougov.com/topics/politics/survey-results/daily/2020/08/11/eacef/3.

14. "Have You Ever Had a Friendship End Because of Disagreement over Politics?" n.d. Accessed November 22, 2024. https://today.yougov.com/topics/politics/survey-results/daily/2024/08/16/4aa50/2.
15. Van Bavel, Jay J., Shana Kushner Gadarian, Eric Knowles, and Kai Ruggeri. 2024. "Political Polarization and Health." *Nature Medicine* 30 (11): 3085–93.
16. Boxell, Levi, Matthew Gentzkow, and Jesse M. Shapiro. 2017. "Greater Internet Use Is Not Associated with Faster Growth in Political Polarization among US Demographic Groups." *Proceedings of the National Academy of Sciences of the United States of America* 114 (40): 10612–17.
17. P. Barrett, J. Hendrix, and J. G. Sims. "Fueling the Fire: How Social Media Intensifies U.S. Political Polarization—and What Can be Done About It." NYU Stern Center for Business and Human Rights. September 2021.
18. Boxell, Levi, Matthew Gentzkow, and Jesse M. Shapiro. 2020. "Cross-Country Trends in Affective Polarization." *Social Science Research Network*. https://papers.ssrn.com/abstract=3522318.
19. NYU Web Communications. "Political Polarization Poses Health Risks, New Analysis Concludes." Accessed November 22, 2024. https://www.publichealth.columbia.edu/news/political-polarization-poses-health-risks-new-analysis-concludes.
20. Berger, Miriam. 2021. "U.S. Listed as a 'Backsliding' Democracy for First Time in Report by European Think Tank." *The Washington Post*. November 22, 2021. https://www.washingtonpost.com/world/2021/11/22/united-states-backsliding-democracies-list-first-time.
21. France-Presse, Agence. "US Added to List of 'Backsliding' Democracies for First Time." *The Guardian*. November 22, 2021. https://www.theguardian.com/us-news/2021/nov/22/us-list-backsliding-democracies-civil-liberties-international.
22. Parker, Ned, and Peter Eisler. "New Cases of Political Violence Roil US Ahead of Contentious Election." *Reuters*. October 21, 2024. https://www.reuters.com/world/us/new-cases-political-violence-roil-us-ahead-contentious-election-2024–10–21.
23. Parker, Ned, and Peter Eisler. *Reuters*. "Political Violence in Polarized U.S. at Its Worst since 1970s," August 9, 2023. https://www.reuters.com/investigates/special-report/usa-politics-violence.
24. Alter, Charlotte. "Why So Many Mass Shooters Have Domestic Violence in Their Past." *Time*. June 14, 2017. https://time.com/4818506/james-hodgkinson-virginia-shooting-steve-scalise.
25. Shapiro, Emily, and Mark Osborne. "Wife of alleged Virginia shooter: 'I can't believe he did this.'" ABC News. June 15, 2017. https://abcnews.go.com/US/wife-alleged-virginia-shooter/story?id=48071222.
26. "Virginia shooting: suspect identified as James T. Hodgkinson." *The Guardian*. June 14, 2017. https://www.theguardian.com/us-news/2017/jun/14/virginia-shooting-suspect-james-t-hodgkinson-leftwing-activist.
27. Heinzmann, David. "Suspected Va. Gunman Identified as James T. Hodgkinson of Illinois." Chicagotribune.com. June 14, 2017. https://web.archive.org

/web/20170614180201/http://www.chicagotribune.com/news/local/breaking/ct-james-hodgkinson-shooter-20170614-story.html.

28. Wimmer, Danny. "Final Sentences Ordered in Whitmer Kidnap Plot." December 7, 2023. https://www.michigan.gov/ag/news/press-releases/2023/12/07/final-sentences-ordered-in-whitmer-kidnap-plot.
29. White, Ed, and Associated Press. "Man in Gov. Whitmer Kidnap Plot Says Group Was Ready to Use Grenade Launcher to Fight Security." PBS News. March 24, 2022. https://www.pbs.org/newshour/nation/man-in-gov-whitmer-kidnap-plot-says-group-was-ready-to-use-grenade-launcher-to-fight-security.
30. Smith, Allan. "Whitmer Says Trump 'complicit' after Feds Reveal Thwarted Plot to Kidnap Her." NBC News. October 8, 2020. https://www.nbcnews.com/politics/2020-election/whitmer-says-trump-complicit-after-feds-reveal-thwarted-plot-kidnap-n1242641.
31. Lobo, Arpan. "3 Years after Plot to Kidnap Gov. Gretchen Whitmer, Here Are the Trial Outcomes, Verdicts." *Detroit Free Press*. September 18, 2023. https://www.freep.com/story/news/local/michigan/2023/09/18/whitmer-kidnapping-trial-verdict-guilty-acquitted/70889492007.
32. Cameron, Chris. "These Are the People Who Died in Connection With the Capitol Riot." *The New York Times.* January 5, 2022. https://www.nytimes.com/2022/01/05/us/politics/jan-6-capitol-deaths.html.
33. ibid.
34. Har, Janie. "Man Serving 30 Years for Attacking Nancy Pelosi's Husband Gets a Life Term on State Charges." AP News. October 29, 2024. https://apnews.com/article/david-depape-nancy-pelosi-husband-paul-attacked-454cbde088fcae22a356f1f8dd0e9eba.
35. Dale, Daniel. "Fact Check: Six False Claims Fully Disproven by the Newly Released Paul Pelosi Evidence." CNN. February 2, 2023. https://www.cnn.com/2023/02/01/politics/fact-check-paul-pelosi-attack-evidence/index.html.
36. Weisman, Jonathan. "An Attempt to Kill an Ex-President, Caught in Real Time, Stuns the Country." *The New York Times.* July 14, 2024. https://www.nytimes.com/2024/07/14/us/politics/trump-shooting-social-media.html.
37. Ortiz, Erik. "Arson suspect was angry with Pennsylvania Gov. Josh Shapiro over Palestinian stance, search warrants say." NBC News. April 16, 2025. https://www.nbcnews.com/news/us-news/arson-suspect-angry-pennsylvania-gov-josh-shapiro-palestinian-stance-s-rcna200852.
38. Lavietes, Matt. "Man pleads guilty in arson attack on Pennsylvania Gov. Josh Shapiro's residence." NBC News. October 14, 2025. https://www.nbcnews.com/news/crime-courts/man-pleads-guilty-arson-attack-pennsylvania-gov-josh-shapiro-rcna237510.
39. Associated Press. "Man charged with killing a top Minnesota House Democrat pleads not guilty." CNN. August 7, 2025. https://www.cnn.com/2025/08/07/us/vance-boelter-minnesota-lawmakers-shot.
40. Associated Press. "What we've learned about the case against the man charged in Charlie Kirk's killing." September 17, 2025. https://apnews.com/article

/charlie-kirk-shooting-suspect-things-to-know-dcde3f792f4d6636d44fb9f4fa53569c.

41. Rhone, Kailyn. “What to Know About Jimmy Kimmel’s Show.” *The New York Times*. September 20, 2025. https://www.nytimes.com/2025/09/20/business/jimmy-kimmel-show-abc-kirk-fcc.html.
42. Alsharif, Mirna. “Charlie Kirk’s killing sparks firings and outrage as reactions expose deep divides.” NBC News. September 14, 2025. https://www.nbcnews.com/news/us-news/charlie-kirk-workplace-firings-disciplinary-action-rcna231131.
43. Doherty, Erin. “America is bracing for political violence—and a significant portion think it’s sometimes OK.” Politico. November 3, 2025. https://www.politico.com/news/2025/11/03/poll-americans-political-violence-00632864.
44. Iyer, Kaanita. “Swiping right ahead of the election: Popular dating apps have new features to show off political views.” CNN. October 17, 2024. https://www.cnn.com/2024/10/17/tech/dating-apps-politics-election/index.html.
45. Mulroy, Clare. “Done with X? How to Delete Your Twitter Account in a Few Easy Steps.” *USA TODAY*. November 20, 2024. https://www.usatoday.com/story/tech/2024/11/20/how-to-delete-twitter-x-account/76294560007.
46. Kan, Michael. “X Lost Record Number of Users After Election Day.” PCMag. November 13, 2024. https://www.pcmag.com/news/x-lost-record-number-of-users-after-election-day.
47. Fraser, Timothy, Daniel P. Aldrich, Costas Panagopoulos, David Hummel, and Daniel Kim. 2022. “The Harmful Effects of Partisan Polarization on Health.” *PNAS Nexus* 1 (1): gac011. https://pmc.ncbi.nlm.nih.gov/articles/PMC9802430.
48. Cacioppo, John T., and Stephanie Cacioppo. 2014. “Older Adults Reporting Social Isolation or Loneliness Show Poorer Cognitive Function 4 Years Later.” *Evidence-Based Nursing* 17 (2): 59–60.
49. Cole, Steven W., John P. Capitanio, Katie Chun, Jesusa M. G. Arevalo, Jeffrey Ma, and John T. Cacioppo. 2015. “Myeloid Differentiation Architecture of Leukocyte Transcriptome Dynamics in Perceived Social Isolation.” *Proceedings of the National Academy of Sciences of the United States of America* 112 (49): 15142–47.
50. Schleimer, Julia P., Paul M. Reeping, Sonia L. Robinson, and Garen J. Wintemute. 2024. “Social Network Size and Endorsement of Political Violence in the US.” *Injury Epidemiology* 11 (1): 56.
51. Tim Hains. “Yale Psychiatrist: If Family Members Or Close Friends Voted ‘Against You,’ It’s Fine To Not Be Around Those People,” RealClearPolitics. November 12, 2024. https://www.realclearpolitics.com/video/2024/11/12/yale_psychiatrist_if_family_members_or_close_friends_voted_against_you_its_fine_to_not_be_around_those_people.html.
52. Allcott, Hunt, Luca Braghieri, Sarah Eichmeyer, and Matthew Gentzkow. 2020. “The Welfare Effects of Social Media.” *American Economic Review* 110 (3): 629–76.
53. “The Hidden Tribes of America.” n.d. Accessed November 21, 2024. https://hiddentribes.us/#the-exhausted-majority.

ENDNOTES

CHAPTER FOUR

1. Nadeem, Reem. "In a Politically Polarized Era, Sharp Divides in Both Partisan Coalitions." Pew Research Center. December 17, 2019. https://www.pewresearch.org/politics/2019/12/17/in-a-politically-polarized-era-sharp-divides-in-both-partisan-coalitions.
2. Hegland, Austin, Annie Li Zhang, Brianna Zichettella, and Josh Pasek. 2022. "A Partisan Pandemic: How COVID-19 Was Primed for Polarization." May 5, 2022. *The Annals of the American Academy of Political and Social Science* 700 (1): 55–72.
3. ibid.
4. Martela, F., E. Laitinen, and C. Hakulinen. "Which predicts longevity better: Satisfaction with life or purpose in life?" *Psychology and Aging*. September, 2024. 39 (6): 589–98.
5. Williams-Farrelly, Monica M., Matthew W. Schroeder, Claudia Li, Anthony J. Perkins, Tamilyn Bakas, Katharine J. Head, Malaz Boustani, and Nicole R. Fowler. 2024. "Loneliness in Older Primary Care Patients and Its Relationship to Physical and Mental Health-Related Quality of Life." *Journal of the American Geriatrics Society* 72 (3): 811–21.
6. Alcaraz, Kassandra I., Katherine S. Eddens, Jennifer L. Blase, W. Ryan Diver, Alpa V. Patel, Lauren R. Teras, Victoria L. Stevens, Eric J. Jacobs, and Susan M. Gapstur. 2019. "Social Isolation and Mortality in US Black and White Men and Women." *American Journal of Epidemiology* 188 (1): 102–9.
7. Gavin, Kara. n.d. "Loneliness Doubled for Older Adults in First Months of COVID-19." Accessed December 10, 2024. https://www.michiganmedicine.org/health-lab/loneliness-doubled-older-adults-first-months-covid-19.
8. Hwang, Tzung-Jeng, Kiran Rabheru, Carmelle Peisah, William Reichman, and Manabu Ikeda. 2020. "Loneliness and Social Isolation during the COVID-19 Pandemic." *International Psychogeriatrics* 32 (10): 1217–20.
9. "COVID-19 Pandemic Triggers 25% Increase in Prevalence of Anxiety and Depression Worldwide." n.d. Accessed December 6, 2024. https://www.who.int/news/item/02–03–2022-covid-19-pandemic-triggers-25-increase-in-prevalence-of-anxiety-and-depression-worldwide.
10. Ferwana, Ibtihal, and Lav R. Varshney. 2024. "The Impact of COVID-19 Lockdowns on Mental Health Patient Populations in the United States." *Scientific Reports* 14 (1): 5689.
11. Czeisler, Mark É., Rashon I. Lane, Emiko Petrosky, Joshua F. Wiley, Aleta Christensen, Rashid Njai, Matthew D. Weaver, et al. 2020. "Mental Health, Substance Use, and Suicidal Ideation during the COVID-19 Pandemic - United States, June 24-30, 2020." *Morbidity and Mortality Weekly Report* 69 (32): 1049–57. https://www.cdc.gov/mmwr/volumes/69/wr/mm6932a1.htm?s_cid=mm6932a1_w.
12. Panchal, Nirmita, Heather Saunders, Robin Rudowitz, and Cynthia Cox. "The Implications of COVID-19 for Mental Health and Substance Use." KFF. March 20, 2023. https://www.kff.org/mental-health/issue-brief/the-implications-of-covid-19-for-mental-health-and-substance-use.
13. "Have Young Adults Mentally Recovered from COVID-19?" n.d. Accessed December 10, 2024. https://news.northwestern.edu/stories/2023/11/young

-adults-show-more-mental-health-distress-during-the-covid-19-pandemic-than-older-adults-study-finds.

14. DeAngelis, Tori. "Antidepressant Use among Teen Girls and Young Women Has Skyrocketed." July 1, 2024. *The American Psychological Association*. Accessed December 6, 2024. https://www.apa.org/monitor/2024/07/antidepressant-use-girls-women-covid-pandemic.
15. Palacio-Delgado, Angelica M., Miguel B. Cervera-Sánchez, Anna C. Selvas-Cortinas, Samuel A. Romo-Márquez, and Judith M. Dueñas-Jiménez. 2023. "The Psychoneuroendocrine Response of Aggression Due to COVID-19 Social Isolation." *Revista Mexicana de Neurociencia* 24 (3): 86–92.
16. Check, James V. P., Daniel Perlman, and Neil M. Malamuth. 1985. "Loneliness and Aggressive Behaviour." *Journal of Social and Personal Relationships* 2 (3): 243–52.
17. "Elliot Rodger: How misogynist killer became 'incel hero.'" BBC. April 25, 2018. https://www.bbc.com/news/world-us-canada-43892189.
18. Batey, Eve. "San Franciscans Brawl Over Social Distance at Local Grocery Store." Eater, San Francisco. March 17, 2020. https://sf.eater.com/2020/3/17/21183946/safeway-brawl-coronavirus-san-francisco.
19. Jasper, Simone. "Angry shopper leans under Plexiglass to spit on grocery worker, Pennsylvania cops say." Centre Daily. April 20, 2020. https://www.centredaily.com/news/coronavirus/article242053616.html.
20. Leon, Daniela. "Fight erupts after social distancing argument at a Colorado Springs Walmart." Fox 21 News. August 5, 2020. https://www.fox21news.com/top-stories/fight-erupts-after-social-distancing-argument-at-a-colorado-springs-walmart.
21. Scribner, Herb. "These American Airlines passengers brawled on a flight because of new face mask policy." *Deseret News*. August 21, 2020. https://www.deseret.com/u-s-world/2020/8/21/21377126/coronavirus-american-airlines-brawl-video-face-masks-policy.
22. "Teachers, Other School Personnel, Experience Violence, Threats, Harassment during Pandemic." American Psychological Association. March 17, 2022. https://www.apa.org/news/press/releases/2022/03/school-staff-violence-pandemic.
23. DesOrmeau, Taylor. "Protesters pack into Capitol, chant 'let us in' when blocked from House proceedings." MLive. April 30, 2020. https://www.mlive.com/public-interest/2020/04/protesters-pack-into-capitol-chant-let-us-in-when-blocked-from-house-proceedings.html.
24. MacFarquar, Neil. "With Homicides Rising, Cities Brace for a Violent Summer." *The New York Times*. June 1, 2021. https://www.nytimes.com/2021/06/01/us/shootings-in-us.html.
25. Diaz, Jaclyn. "4th Of July Shootings Across The Country Killed More Than 180 People." NPR. July 6, 2021. https://www.npr.org/2021/07/06/1013251202/fourth-of-july-shootings-across-the-country-kill-more-than-180-this-year.
26. Lopetrone, Erika, and Francesco N. Biondi. 2023. "On the Effect of COVID-19 on Drivers' Behavior: A Survey Study." *Transportation Research Record* 2677 (4): 742–50.
27. Brosnan, Sarah F., and Frans B. M. de Waal. 2014. "Evolution of Responses to (Un)Fairness." *Science (New York, NY)* 346 (6207): 1251776. https://pmc.ncbi.nlm.nih.gov/articles/PMC4451566.

28. Barrett, Ted. "Pelosi's office acknowledges indoor hair appointment, violating San Francisco Covid-19 restrictions." CNN. September 2, 2020. https://www.cnn.com/2020/09/02/politics/nancy-pelosi-hair-salon/index.html.
29. Mallory, Simon. 2020. "Over 1,000 health professionals sign a letter saying, Don't shut down protests using coronavirus concerns as an excuse." CNN. December 15, 2024. https://www.cnn.com/2020/06/05/health/health-care-open-letter-protests-coronavirus-trnd/index.html.
30. Cho, Hichang, Pengxiang Li, Annabel Ngien, Marion Grace Tan, Anfan Chen, and Elmie Nekmat. 2023. "The Bright and Dark Sides of Social Media Use during COVID-19 Lockdown: Contrasting Social Media Effects through Social Liability vs. Social Support." *Computers in Human Behavior* 146 (107795): 107795. https://pmc.ncbi.nlm.nih.gov/articles/PMC10123536.
31. Cheng, Cecilia, and Yan-Ching Lau. 2022. "Social Media Addiction during COVID-19-Mandated Physical Distancing: Relatedness Needs as Motives." *International Journal of Environmental Research and Public Health* 19 (8): 4621. https://pmc.ncbi.nlm.nih.gov/articles/PMC9032915.
32. "1 in 4 Remote Workers Report Declining Social Skills, Struggling With Eye Contact and Conversing." Resume Builder. December 7, 2024. https://www.resumebuilder.com/1-in-4-remote-workers-report-declining-social-skills-struggling-with-eye-contact-and-conversing.
33. Lo, Justin, Matthew Rae, Krutika Amin, Cynthia Cox, Nirmita Panchal, and Benjamin F. Miller. "Telehealth Has Played an Outsized Role Meeting Mental Health Needs During the COVID-19 Pandemic." KFF. March 15, 2022. https://www.kff.org/mental-health/issue-brief/telehealth-has-played-an-outsized-role-meeting-mental-health-needs-during-the-covid-19-pandemic.

CHAPTER FIVE

1. Panchal, Nirmita, Matthew Rae, Heather Saunders, Cynthia Cox, and Robin Rudowitz. "How Does Use of Mental Health Care Vary by Demographics and Health Insurance Coverage?" KFF. March 24, 2022. https://www.kff.org/mental-health/issue-brief/how-does-use-of-mental-health-care-vary-by-demographics-and-health-insurance-coverage.
2. Andersson, Gerhard, and Pim Cuijpers. 2009. "Internet-Based and Other Computerized Psychological Treatments for Adult Depression: A Meta-Analysis." *Cognitive Behaviour Therapy* 38 (4): 196–205.
3. Barak, Azy, Liat Hen, Meyran Boniel-Nissim, and Na'ama Shapira. 2008. "A Comprehensive Review and a Meta-Analysis of the Effectiveness of Internet-Based Psychotherapeutic Interventions." *Journal of Technology in Human Services* 26 (2–4): 109–60.
4. Wampold, Bruce E., Takuya Minami, Thomas W. Baskin, and Sandra Callen Tierney. 2002. "A Meta-(Re)Analysis of the Effects of Cognitive Therapy versus 'other Therapies' for Depression." *Journal of Affective Disorders* 68 (2–3): 159–65.
5. The Brussels Times. n.d. "Belgian Man Dies by Suicide Following Exchanges with Chatbot." Accessed December 18, 2024. https://www.brusselstimes

.com/430098/belgian-man-commits-suicide-following-exchanges-with-chatgpt.

6. Zhang, Yimeng, Xu Li, Junfeng Zhu, Zhongzhen Sheng, and Tony Rousmaniere. 2025. "'What Happens, What Helps, What Hurts:' A Qualitative Analysis of User Experiences with Large Language Models for Mental Health Support." *PsyArXiv*. https://doi.org/10.31234/osf.io/2prtn_v1.
7. Reynolds, D'arcy J., Jr., William B. Stiles, A. John Bailer, and Michael R. Hughes. 2013. "Impact of Exchanges and Client-Therapist Alliance in Online-Text Psychotherapy." *Cyberpsychology, Behavior and Social Networking* 16 (5): 370–77.
8. Wagner, Birgit, Christine Knaevelsrud, and Andreas Maercker. 2006. "Internet-Based Cognitive-Behavioral Therapy for Complicated Grief: A Randomized Controlled Trial." *Death Studies* 30 (5): 429–53.
9. Areán, Patricia A., Michael D. Pullmann, Isabell R. Griffith Fillipo, Jerilyn Wu, Brittany A. Mosser, Shiyu Chen, Patrick J. Heagerty, and Thomas D. Hull. 2024. "Randomized Trial of the Effectiveness of Videoconferencing-Based versus Message-Based Psychotherapy on Depression." *Psychiatric Services (Washington, D.C.)* 75 (12): 1184–91.
10. Winkler, Rolfe. "The Failed Promise of Online Mental-Health Treatment." *The Wall Street Journal*. December 18, 2022. https://www.wsj.com/articles/the-failed-promise-of-online-mental-health-treatment-11671390353.
11. Lardieri, Alexa. "Therapists on BetterHelp accused of inappropriate behavior and dishing out advice so bad patients quit therapy altogether." *Daily Mail*, July 29, 2024. https://www.dailymail.co.uk/health/article-13639815/BetterHelp-accused-therapy-patients-unprofessional.html.
12. Ducharme, Jamie. "The Online Therapy Bubble Is Bursting." *Time*. November 1, 2022. https://time.com/6225361/telehealth-startups-cerebral-done-ahead.
13. Hilt, Lori M., and Seth D. Pollak. 2012. "Getting out of Rumination: Comparison of Three Brief Interventions in a Sample of Youth." *Journal of Abnormal Child Psychology* 40 (7): 1157–65.
14. Mamat, Zulkayda, and Michael C. Anderson. 2023. "Improving Mental Health by Training the Suppression of Unwanted Thoughts." *Science Advances* 9 (38): eadh5292. https://www.science.org/doi/10.1126/sciadv.adh5292.
15. "How Long Will It Take for Treatment to Work?" American Psychological Association. July 31, 2017. https://www.apa.org/ptsd-guideline/patients-and-families/length-treatment.
16. Barkham, Michael, Janice Connell, William B. Stiles, Jeremy N. V. Miles, Frank Margison, Chris Evans, and John Mellor-Clark. 2006. "Dose-Effect Relations and Responsive Regulation of Treatment Duration: The Good Enough Level." *Journal of Consulting and Clinical Psychology* 74 (1): 160–67.
17. King, Michael. 2015. "Duration of Psychotherapy Has Little Association with Outcome." *The British Journal of Psychiatry: The Journal of Mental Science* 207 (2): 93–94.
18. Juul, Sophie, Janus Christian Jakobsen, Caroline Kamp Jørgensen, Stig Poulsen, Per Sørensen, and Sebastian Simonsen. 2023. "The Difference between Shorter-versus Longer-Term Psychotherapy for Adult Mental Health Disorders: A Systematic Review with Meta-Analysis." *BMC Psychiatry* 23 (1): 438.

ENDNOTES

CHAPTER SIX

1. Redding, Richard E., and Sally Satel. "Social justice in psychotherapy and beyond." *Ideological and Political Bias in Psychology*: 19 (513–33). 2023. https://link.springer.com/chapter/10.1007/978-3-031-29148-7_19.
2. "Historical Addendum to APA's Apology to Black, Indigenous and People of Color for Its Support of Structural Racism in Psychiatry." n.d. Accessed December 20, 2024. https://www.psychiatry.org:443/news-room/historical-addendum-to-apa-apology.
3. Hall, Gordon C. Nagayama, Alicia Yee Ibaraki, Ellen R. Huang, C. Nathan Marti, and Eric Stice. 2016. "A Meta-Analysis of Cultural Adaptations of Psychological Interventions." *Behavior Therapy* 47 (6): 993–1014.
4. Ratts, Manivong J., Anneliese A. Singh, Sylvia Nassar-McMillan, S. Kent Butler, and Julian Rafferty McCullough. "Multicultural and Social Justice Counseling Competencies: Practical applications in counseling." *Counseling Today*. American Counseling Association. January 2016. https://www.counseling.org/publications/counseling-today-magazine/article-archive/article/legacy/multicultural-and-social-justice-counseling-competencies-practical-applications-in-counseling.
5. ibid.
6. Ratts, Singh, Nassar-McMillan, Butler, and McCullough. "Multicultural," 8.
7. Ratts, Singh, Nassar-McMillan, Butler, and McCullough. "Multicultural," 11.
8. ibid.
9. Ratts, Singh, Nassar-McMillan, Butler, and McCullough. "Multicultural," 13.
10. ibid.
11. ibid.
12. Counseling M.S. Accessed January 2, 2025. https://www.uvm.edu/cess/chdf/program/counseling-ms.
13. The University of Vermont Master of Science in Counseling Student Handbook 2024 / 2025 Academic Year (p. 31). Accessed April 2, 2025. https://www.uvm.edu/d10-files/documents/2024-08/Counseling-MS-Student-Handbook-AY2024-2025.pdf.
14. Vanderbilt University Human Development Counseling (M.Ed.). Accessed January 2, 2025. https://peabody.vanderbilt.edu/academics/masters-programs/human-development-counseling-med/#h2-program-overview.
15. Master of Clinical Mental Health Counseling. Accessed May 2, 2025. https://www.rollins.edu/clinical-mental-health-counseling-masters.
16. Teachers College Columbia University. Accessed May 2, 2025. https://www.tc.columbia.edu/about.
17. The Wright Institute. Accessed May 2, 2025. https://www.wi.edu/masters-program.
18. About. Accessed May 2, 2025. https://www.antioch.edu/about.
19. MA in Clinical Mental Health Counseling. Accessed May 2, 2025. https://www.antioch.edu/academics/counseling-therapy/clinical-mental-health-counseling-ma.
20. Brennan R. Student Files $4.32M Civil Rights Lawsuit Against Antioch University for Retaliation Against DEI Policy Criticism. Law.com. 2024. Accessed

May 2, 2025. https://www.law.com/2024/04/18/student-files-4–32m-civil-rights-lawsuit-against-antioch-university-for-retaliation-against-dei-policy-criticism.

21. Blevins E. "Must an Antioch student bow down to 'social justice' dogma to graduate?" *The Hill*. February 6, 2023. Accessed May 2, 2025. https://thehill.com/opinion/education/3844048-must-an-antioch-student-bow-down-to-social-justice-dogma-to-graduate.
22. the radical center. Antioch University Counseling Whistleblower. YouTube. 2022. Accessed May 2, 2025. https://www.youtube.com/watch?v=gcfxiASvLbI.
23. Free the People. "Universities Are Sterilizing Language | Whistleblower Leslie Elliott | Ep 23." YouTube. 2023. Accessed May 2, 2025. https://www.youtube.com/watch?v=Rw7BKPnDjvk.
24. Stephanie Winn (Some Kind of Therapist). "Livestream with Leslie Elliott: My Therapy License is Under Attack (Again)." YouTube. 2023. Accessed May 2, 2025. https://www.youtube.com/watch?v=5hV2m2VcxWg.
25. "Internal Family Systems (IFS) Anti-Racism Group for White People - January 17 - May 23, 2025." https://www.tamaralebak.com/antiracistifs.
26. Jorge, Eloiza. "Course Description." 2025. https://eloizajorge.com/offerings/getting-free-from-whiteness.
27. Jorge, Eloiza. "About." 2025. https://eloizajorge.com/about.
28. Winters, Mary Frances, and Rohini Ahand. "A retrospective view of corporate diversity training from 1964 to the present." Academy of Management Learning & Education. 2008. 7 (3): 356–72.
29. Maurer R. "New DE&I Roles Spike After Racial Justice Protests." 2023. Accessed December 17, 2024. https://www.shrm.org/topics-tools/news/talent-acquisition/new-dei-roles-spike-racial-justice-protests.
30. Rynes, Sara, and Benson Rosen. 1995. "A Field Survey of Factors Affecting the Adoption and Perceived Success of Diversity Training." *Personnel Psychology* 48 (2): 247–70.
31. Forscher, Patrick S., Calvin K. Lai, Jordan R. Axt, Charles R. Ebersole, Michelle Herman, Patricia G. Devine, and Brian A. Nosek. 2019. "A Meta-Analysis of Procedures to Change Implicit Measures." *Journal of Personality and Social Psychology* 117 (3): 522–59.
32. Devine, Patricia G., and Tory L. Ash. 2022. "Diversity Training Goals, Limitations, and Promise: A Review of the Multidisciplinary Literature." *Annual Review of Psychology* 73 (1): 403–29.
33. Kalev, Alexandra, Frank Dobbin, and Erin Kelly. 2006. "Best Practices or Best Guesses? Assessing the Efficacy of Corporate Affirmative Action and Diversity Policies." *American Sociological Review* 71 (4): 589–617.
34. Levy Paluck, Elizabeth, and Donald P. Green. "Prejudice Reduction: What Works? A Review and Assessment of Research and Practice." *Annual Review of Psychology* (2009); 60: 339–67. doi: 10.1146/annurev.psych.60.110707.163607.
35. Kennedy, Brendan. "Former principal who sued TDSB over alleged bullying during anti-racism training dies by suicide." *The Toronto Star*. July 21, 2023. https://www.thestar.com/news/gta/former-principal-who-sued-tdsb-over-alleged-bullying

-during-anti-racism-training-dies-by-suicide/article_4b9f98a9-7394-5517-909b-c69eb581aec9.html.

36. Chang, Edward H., Katherine L. Milkman, Dena M. Gromet, Robert W. Rebele, Cade Massey, Angela L. Duckworth, and Adam M. Grant. 2019. "The Mixed Effects of Online Diversity Training." *Proceedings of the National Academy of Sciences of the United States of America* 116 (16): 7778–83.
37. Chang, Edward, Katherine L. Milkman, Laura J. Zarrow, Kasandra Brabaw, Dena M. Gromet, Reb Rebele, Cade Massey, Angela L. Duckworth, and Adam Grant. 2019. "Does Diversity Training Work the Way It's Supposed To?" *Harvard Business Review*. July 9, 2019. https://hbr.org/2019/07/does-diversity-training-work-the-way-its-supposed-to.

CHAPTER SEVEN

1. *The Wall Street Journal*. "Bestselling Books Week Ended May 28," June 2, 2022. https://www.wsj.com/articles/bestselling-books-week-ended-may-28-11654192983.
2. Kettler, Sara. "The Story of Gypsy-Rose Blanchard and Her Mother." Biography. April 4, 2019. https://www.biography.com/crime/gypsy-rose-blanchard-mother-dee-dee-murder.
3. "Munchausen Syndrome By Proxy." *PM&R KnowledgeNow* (blog). APM&R. June 8, 2021. https://now.aapmr.org/munchausen-syndrome-by-proxy.
4. Bound, Fay. 2006. "Hypochondria." *Lancet* 367 (9505): 105.
5. French, Jennifer H., and Sajid Hameed. 2025. "Illness Anxiety Disorder." In *StatPearls*. Treasure Island (FL): StatPearls Publishing.
6. Kikas, Katarina, Aliza Werner-Seidler, Emily Upton, and Jill Newby. 2024. "Illness Anxiety Disorder: A Review of the Current Research and Future Directions." *Current Psychiatry Reports* 26 (7): 331–39.
7. Redshaw, Written By: Liana. n.d. "Is Self-Diagnosis on Social Media Helping or Hurting People's Health?" Accessed January 3, 2025. https://www.tebra.com/theintake/medical-deep-dives/tips-and-trends/is-self-diagnosis-on-social-media-helping-or-hurting-peoples-health.
8. Berle, David. 2015. "Cyberchondria." In *Mental Health in the Digital Age*, ed. Vladan Starcevic, 106–17. Oxford University Press.
9. Foster, Alma, and Natasha Ellis. 2024. "TikTok-Inspired Self-Diagnosis and Its Implications for Educational Psychology Practice." *Educational Psychology in Practice* 40 (4): 491–508.
10. Cinelli, Matteo, Walter Quattrociocchi, Alessandro Galeazzi, Carlo Michele Valensise, Emanuele Brugnoli, Ana Lucia Schmidt, Paola Zola, Fabiana Zollo, and Antonio Scala. 2020. "The COVID-19 Social Media Infodemic." *Scientific Reports* 10 (1): 16598. https://www.nature.com/articles/s41598-020-73510-5.
11. Varma, Rahul, Sreeja Das, and Tushar Singh. 2021. "Cyberchondria amidst COVID-19 Pandemic: Challenges and Management Strategies." *Frontiers in Psychiatry* 12 (April): 618508. https://pmc.ncbi.nlm.nih.gov/articles/PMC8121143.

12. Forer, B. R. 1949. "The Fallacy of Personal Validation; a Classroom Demonstration of Gullibility." *Journal of Abnormal Psychology* 44 (1): 118–23.
13. *The Oxford Handbook of Analytical Sociology*, ed. Peter Bearman and Peter Hedström, Oxford: Oxford University Press, 2009, pp. 294–314.
14. Robertson, Deirdre A., George M. Savva, Bellinda L. King-Kallimanis, and Rose Anne Kenny. 2015. "Negative Perceptions of Aging and Decline in Walking Speed: A Self-Fulfilling Prophecy." *PloS One* 10 (4): e0123260. https://journals.plos.org/plosone/article?id=10.1371/journal.pone.0123260.
15. "What Is ADHD?" Accessed January 15, 2025. https://www.psychiatry.org:443/patients-families/adhd/what-is-adhd.

CHAPTER EIGHT

1. Altimari, Dave. "10 Years after Sandy Hook, the Police Who Were There Still Struggle to Forget." *The Connecticut Mirror.* December 14, 2022. http://ctmirror.org/2022/12/14/ct-sandy-hook-newtown-shooting-police-responders.
2. "What Is Posttraumatic Stress Disorder (PTSD)?" n.d. Accessed January 3, 2025. https://www.psychiatry.org:443/patients-families/ptsd/what-is-ptsd.
3. "Psychologists Who Treat the Trauma of Infertility." n.d. Accessed January 7, 2025. https://www.apa.org/monitor/2017/07–08/trauma-infertility.
4. Kirby, Elizabeth D., Sandra E. Muroy, Wayne G. Sun, David Covarrubias, Megan J. Leong, Laurel A. Barchas, and Daniela Kaufer. 2013. "Acute Stress Enhances Adult Rat Hippocampal Neurogenesis and Activation of Newborn Neurons via Secreted Astrocytic FGF2." *eLife* 2 (April): e00362. https://pmc.ncbi.nlm.nih.gov/articles/PMC3628086.
5. Oshri, Assaf, Zehua Cui, Max M. Owens, Cory A. Carvalho, and Lawrence Sweet. 2022. "Low-to-Moderate Level of Perceived Stress Strengthens Working Memory: Testing the Hormesis Hypothesis through Neural Activation." *Neuropsychologia* 176 (108354): 108354.
6. Charles, Susan T., Jacqueline Mogle, Hye Won Chai, and David M. Almeida. 2021. "The Mixed Benefits of a Stressor-Free Life." *Emotion* 21 (5): 962–71.
7. Suo, Lin, Liyan Zhao, Jijian Si, Jianfeng Liu, Weili Zhu, Baisheng Chai, Yan Zhang, et al. 2013. "Predictable Chronic Mild Stress in Adolescence Increases Resilience in Adulthood." *Neuropsychopharmacology: Official Publication of the American College of Neuropsychopharmacology* 38 (8): 1387–1400.
8. Wu, Xiaoli, Atipatsa C. Kaminga, Wenjie Dai, Jing Deng, Zhipeng Wang, Xiongfeng Pan, and Aizhong Liu. 2019. "The Prevalence of Moderate-to-High Posttraumatic Growth: A Systematic Review and Meta-Analysis." *Journal of Affective Disorders* 243 (January): 408–15.
9. Forna, Aminatta. n.d. "Who Owns Your Story?" *The Yale Review.* Accessed January 7, 2025. https://yalereview.org/article/aminatta-forma-trauma-overuse.
10. Greene, Roberta R. 2002. "Holocaust Survivors: A Study in Resilience." *Journal of Gerontological Social Work* 37 (1): 3–18.
11. Wu, Xiaoli, Atipatsa C. Kaminga, Wenjie Dai, Jing Deng, Zhipeng Wang, Xiongfeng Pan, and Aizhong Liu. 2019. "The Prevalence of Moderate-to-High

Posttraumatic Growth: A Systematic Review and Meta-Analysis." *Journal of Affective Disorders* 243 (January): 408–15.

12. Crum, Alia J, et al. 2013. "Rethinking Stress: The Role of Mindsets in Determining the Stress Response. The Journal of Personality and Social Psychology." 104 (4): 716–33.
13. Crum, Alia J., Modupe Akinola, Ashley Martin, and Sean Fath. 2017. "The Role of Stress Mindset in Shaping Cognitive, Emotional, and Physiological Responses to Challenging and Threatening Stress." *Anxiety, Stress, and Coping* 30 (4): 379–95.
14. Goyer, J. Parker, Modupe Akinola, Rebecca Grunberg, and Alia J. Crum. 2022. "Thriving under Pressure: The Effects of Stress-Related Wise Interventions on Affect, Sleep, and Exam Performance for College Students from Disadvantaged Backgrounds." *Emotion (Washington, D.C.)* 22 (8): 1755–72.

CHAPTER NINE

1. Duckworth, Angela L., Christopher Peterson, Michael D. Matthews, and Dennis R. Kelly. 2007. "Grit: Perseverance and Passion for Long-Term Goals." *Journal of Personality and Social Psychology* 92 (6): 1087–1101.
2. Benton, Tami D., Rhonda C. Boyd, and Wanjiku F. M. Njoroge. 2021. "Addressing the Global Crisis of Child and Adolescent Mental Health." *JAMA Pediatrics* 175 (11): 1108–10.
3. Weeks, Gillian A., Elcin Sakmar, Taylar A. Clark, Anastasia M. Rose, Wendy K. Silverman, and Eli R. Lebowitz. 2023. "Family Accommodation and Separation Anxiety: The Moderating Role of Child Attachment." *Research Square*, November, rs.3.rs-3621755.
4. Lebowitz, Eli R., Carla Marin, Alyssa Martino, Yaara Shimshoni, and Wendy K. Silverman. 2020. "Parent-Based Treatment as Efficacious as Cognitive-Behavioral Therapy for Childhood Anxiety: A Randomized Noninferiority Study of Supportive Parenting for Anxious Childhood Emotions." *Journal of the American Academy of Child and Adolescent Psychiatry* 59 (3): 362–72.
5. Chua, Kao-Ping, Anna Volerman, Jason Zhang, Joanna Hua, and Rena M. Conti. 2024. "Antidepressant Dispensing to US Adolescents and Young Adults: 2016–2022." *Pediatrics* 153 (3): e2023064245.
6. "The Age of Anxiety: A History of America's Turbulent Affair with Tranquilizers." 2009. *The Age of Anxiety: A History of America's Turbulent Affair with Tranquilizers*. https://psycnet.apa.org/record/2008–08039–000.
7. "Medical Complications: Common Alcohol-Related Concerns." n.d. Accessed January 28, 2025. https://www.niaaa.nih.gov/health-professionals-communities/core-resource-on-alcohol/medical-complications-common-alcohol-related-concerns.
8. Ghasemiesfe, Mehrnaz, Brooke Barrow, Samuel Leonard, Salomeh Keyhani, and Deborah Korenstein. 2019. "Association between Marijuana Use and Risk of Cancer: A Systematic Review and Meta-Analysis: A Systematic Review and Meta-Analysis." *JAMA Network Open* 2 (11): e1916318.

9. Gross, James J., and Robert W. Levenson. 1993. "Emotional Suppression: Physiology, Self-Report, and Expressive Behavior." *Journal of Personality and Social Psychology* 64 (6): 970–86.
10. Richards, Jane M., and James J. Gross. 2000. "Emotion Regulation and Memory: The Cognitive Costs of Keeping One's Cool." *Journal of Personality and Social Psychology* 79 (3): 410–24.
11. Vohs, Kathleen D., Brian D. Glass, W. Todd Maddox, and Arthur B. Markman. 2011. "Ego Depletion Is Not Just Fatigue: Evidence from a Total Sleep Deprivation Experiment." *Social Psychological and Personality Science* 2 (2): 166–73.
12. Quartana, Phillip J., and John W. Burns. 2010. "Emotion Suppression Affects Cardiovascular Responses to Initial and Subsequent Laboratory Stressors." *British Journal of Health Psychology* 15 (Pt 3): 511–28.
13. Grossarth-Maticek, R., J. Bastiaans, and D. T. Kanazir. 1985. "Psychosocial Factors as Strong Predictors of Mortality from Cancer, Ischaemic Heart Disease and Stroke: The Yugoslav Prospective Study." *Journal of Psychosomatic Research* 29 (2): 167–76.
14. Bushman, Brad J. 2002. "Does Venting Anger Feed or Extinguish the Flame? Catharsis, Rumination, Distraction, Anger, and Aggressive Responding." *Personality & Social Psychology Bulletin* 28 (6): 724–31.
15. Geen, Russell G., David Stonner, and Gary L. Shope. 1975. "The Facilitation of Aggression by Aggression: Evidence against the Catharsis Hypothesis." *Journal of Personality and Social Psychology* 31 (4): 721–26.
16. Hornberger, R. H. 1957. *The Differential Reduction of Aggressive Responses as a Function of Interpolated Activities*. Iowa.
17. Rimé, Bernard, Pierre Bouchat, Louise Paquot, and Laura Giglio. 2020. "Intrapersonal, Interpersonal, and Social Outcomes of the Social Sharing of Emotion." *Current Opinion in Psychology* 31 (February): 127–34.
18. Liverant, Gabrielle I., Stefan G. Hofmann, and Brett T. Litz. 2004. "Coping and Anxiety in College Students after the September 11th Terrorist Attacks." *Anxiety, Stress, and Coping* 17 (2): 127–39.
19. Martin, Ryan C., Kelsey Ryan Coyier, Leah M. VanSistine, and Kelly L. Schroeder. 2013. "Anger on the Internet: The Perceived Value of Rant-Sites." *Cyberpsychology, Behavior and Social Networking* 16 (2): 119–22.

CHAPTER TEN

1. Gaydos, Ryan. "Indiana Youth Basketball Game Descends into Chaos as Parent, Ref Brawl." Fox News. May 23, 2023. https://www.foxnews.com/sports/indiana-youth-basketball-game-descends-chaos-parent-ref-brawl.
2. WRTV Staff. "Viral Video Shows Fight Between Parent and Referee at Fort Wayne Basketball Game." *WRTV Indianapolis*. May 22, 2023. https://www.wrtv.com/news/local-news/viral-video-shows-fight-between-parent-ref-at-fort-wayne-basketball-game.

3. Golub, Matthew. "Fan Attacks Referee in Crazy Indiana Youth Basketball Fight." *New York Post*. May 22, 2023. https://nypost.com/2023/05/22/fan-attacks-referee-in-crazy-indiana-youth-basketball-fight.
4. Fox 11, Los Angeles. "Teens, Parents Attacked in Brawl after Irvine Soccer Game." YouTube. October 22, 2023. https://www.youtube.com/watch?v=gh47giRbi4k.
5. Philadelphia, 6ABC. Feb. 21 2024. "Police investigating after parents caught on video fighting at youth hockey game." Yahoo News. February 21, 2024. https://www.youtube.com/watch?v=q6kCAR6ok9Q.
6. Albom, Mitch, and Detroit Free Press. 2019. "Opinion: Youth Baseball Brawl Latest Example of Parents Being Babies." *USA TODAY High School Sports Wire*. June 23, 2019. https://www.usatodayhss.com/story/sports/high-school/2019/06/23/opinion-youth-baseball-brawl-example-parents-being-babies/76275272007.
7. Campbell, Andy. "Timothy Forbes Bit Off Part Of Basketball Coach's Ear At Son's Game In Massachusetts, Cops Say." HuffPost. March 13, 2012. https://www.huffpost.com/entry/parent-bit-off-coach-ear_n_1341380.
8. "Man Who Shot and Killed Lancaster Youth Football Coach Formally Sentenced." NBC 5, Dallas-Fort Worth. August 7, 2023. https://www.nbcdfw.com/news/local/man-who-shot-and-killed-lancaster-youth-football-coach-formally-sentenced/3311518.
9. Heubeck, Elizabeth. "Parents' Bad Behavior at School Sports Events Has Gotten Extreme." *Education Week*, February 3, 2023. https://www.edweek.org/leadership/parents-bad-behavior-at-school-sports-events-has-gotten-extreme/2023/02.
10. Borelli, Stephen. "Sports Parents Are out of Control and Officials Don't Feel Safe. Here's What's at Risk." *USA TODAY*. October 15, 2023. https://www.usatoday.com/story/sports/2023/10/15/parent-behavior-in-youth-sports-is-abusive-officials-dont-feel-safe/71194511007.
11. Weiler, Betty, Anna M. Gstaettner, and Pascal Scherrer. 2021. "Selfies to Die for: A Review of Research on Self-Photography Associated with Injury/Death in Tourism and Recreation." *Tourism Management Perspectives* 37 (100778): 100778.
12. Martin, Michel. "Growing List of Public and Private People Are Being Targeted by Swatting Attempts." *NPR*, February 2, 2024. https://www.npr.org/2024/02/02/1228541386/growing-list-of-public-and-private-people-are-being-targeted-by-swatting-attempt.
13. Cooper, Christian. "Opinion." *The New York Times*. May 26, 2023. https://www.nytimes.com/2023/05/26/opinion/birds-freedom.html.
14. Ok, Ekin, Yi Qian, Brendan Strejcek, and Karl Aquino. 2021. "Signaling Virtuous Victimhood as Indicators of Dark Triad Personalities." *Journal of Personality and Social Psychology* 120 (6): 1634–61.
15. Sizoo, Bram, Derek Strijbos, and Gerrit Glas. 2022. "Grievance-Fueled Violence Can Be Better Understood Using an Enactive Approach." *Frontiers in Psychology* 13 (October): 997121.
16. Burman, Theo. "Luigi Mangione Manifesto: Read Reported Document in Full." Newsweek. December 11, 2024. https://www.newsweek.com/luigi-mangione-manifesto-full-document-1998945.

17. Parker, Terri. "Corporations Increase Executives' Security Following Threats, and Online Sympathy for Luigi Mangione." WPBF. December 12, 2024. https://www.wpbf.com/article/corporations-increase-executives-security-threats-sympathy-luigi-mangione-florida-ceo-thompson/63175418.
18. Spechler, Diana. "The Rise of Donald Trump Demands We Embrace a Harder Kind of Self-Care." Quartz. November 11, 2016. https://qz.com/834607/the-rise-of-donald-trump-demands-a-new-kind-of-self-care.
19. O'Keeffe, Kevin. "A Self-Care Guide of TV to Watch to Forget about Donald Trump's Rise." Mic. November 11, 2016. https://www.mic.com/articles/159165/a-self-care-guide-of-tv-to-watch-to-forget-about-donald-trump-s-rise.

CHAPTER ELEVEN

1. "How Accurate Is Mental Health Advice on TikTok?" PlushCare. January 8, 2025. https://plushcare.com/blog/tiktok-mental-health.
2. O'Malley, Katie. "Gwyneth Paltrow opens up about 'conscious uncoupling' backlash after divorce from Chris Martin." *The Independent*. March 20, 2019. https://www.independent.co.uk/life-style/dating/gwyneth-paltrow-conscious-uncoupling-chirs-martin-divorce-explanation-statement-a8830031.html.
3. Wharton, Amy S. 2009. "The Sociology of Emotional Labor." *Annual Review of Sociology* 35 (1): 147–65.
4. Beck, Julie. 2018. "The Concept Creep of 'Emotional Labor.'" *The Atlantic*. November 26, 2018. https://www.theatlantic.com/family/archive/2018/11/arlie-hochschild-housework-isnt-emotional-labor/576637.
5. Benesch, Sarah, and Matthew T. Prior. 2023. "Rescuing 'Emotion Labor' from (and for) Language Teacher Emotion Research." *System* 113 (102995): 102995.
6. Mitra, Paroma, Tyler J. Torrico, and Dimy Fluyau. 2025. "Narcissistic Personality Disorder." In *StatPearls*. Treasure Island (FL): StatPearls Publishing.

CHAPTER TWELVE

1. Maat, Saskia de, Frans de Jonghe, Robert Schoevers, and Jack Dekker. 2009. "The Effectiveness of Long-Term Psychoanalytic Therapy: A Systematic Review of Empirical Studies." *Harvard Review of Psychiatry* 17 (1): 1–23.
2. Bachrach, H. M., R. Galatzer-Levy, A. Skolnikoff, and S. Waldron Jr. 1991. "On the Efficacy of Psychoanalysis." *Journal of the American Psychoanalytic Association* 39 (4): 871–916.
3. Briggs, Stephen, Gopalakrishnan Netuveli, Nick Gould, Antigone Gkaravella, Nicole S. Gluckman, Patricia Kangogyere, Ruby Farr, Mark J. Goldblatt, and Reinhard Lindner. 2019. "The Effectiveness of Psychoanalytic/Psychodynamic Psychotherapy for Reducing Suicide Attempts and Self-Harm: Systematic Review and Meta-Analysis." *The British Journal of Psychiatry: The Journal of Mental Science* 214 (6): 320–28.
4. Shepherd, Caroline, and Nigel Beail. 2017. "A Systematic Review of the Effectiveness of Psychoanalysis, Psychoanalytic and Psychodynamic Psychother-

apy with Adults with Intellectual and Developmental Disabilities: Progress and Challenges." *Psychoanalytic Psychotherapy* 31 (1): 94–117.

5. Paris, Joel. 2017. "Is Psychoanalysis Still Relevant to Psychiatry?" *Canadian Journal of Psychiatry. Revue Canadienne de Psychiatrie* 62 (5): 308–12.
6. "Searching for Meaning." n.d. https://www.apa.org. Accessed March 6, 2025. https://www.apa.org/monitor/2011/11/meaning.
7. *Psychology Today*. n.d. "Find an Open Relationships Non-Monogamy Therapist." Accessed March 7, 2025. https://www.psychologytoday.com/us/therapists?category=open-relationships-non-monogamy.
8. Loree, Kate. 2022. *Open Deeply: A Guide to Building Conscious, Compassionate Open Relationships*. Berkeley, CA: She Writes Press.
9. Orion, Rhea. 2018. *A Therapist's Guide to Consensual Nonmonogamy: Polyamory, Swinging, and Open Marriage*. London, England: Routledge.
10. Haldeman, Douglas C. 2022. "Introduction: A History of Conversion Therapy, from Accepted Practice to Condemnation." In *The Case against Conversion "Therapy": Evidence, Ethics, and Alternatives*, 3–16. Washington: American Psychological Association.
11. Vider, Stephen, and David S. Byers. "A Half-Century of Conflict Over Attempts to 'Cure' Gay People." *Time*. February 12, 2015. https://time.com/3705745/history-therapy-hadden.
12. Topping, Alexandra. "'Countless Lives Damaged': UK's Dark History of Gay Conversion Practices." *The Guardian*. October 3, 2022. https://www.theguardian.com/world/2022/oct/03/countless-lives-damaged-new-book-details-uk-dark-history-gay-conversion-practices.
13. Stack, Liam. "Mike Pence and 'Conversion Therapy': A History." *The New York Times*. November 30, 2016. https://www.nytimes.com/2016/11/30/us/politics/mike-pence-and-conversion-therapy-a-history.html.
14. Chijioke, Lawrence. "My Family Forced Me to Endure Violent Conversion Therapy. So I Left Home & Never Looked Back." LGBTQ Nation. December 4, 2023. https://www.lgbtqnation.com/2023/12/my-family-forced-me-to-endure-violent-conversion-therapy-so-i-left-home-never-looked-back.
15. Reynolds, Emily. "The Cruel, Dangerous Reality of Gay Conversion Therapy." WIRED. July 7, 2018. https://www.wired.com/story/what-is-gay-conversion-therapy.
16. Spitzer, Robert L. 2003. "Can Some Gay Men and Lesbians Change Their Sexual Orientation? 200 Participants Reporting a Change from Homosexual to Heterosexual Orientation." *Archives of Sexual Behavior* 32 (5): 403–17; discussion 419–72.
17. Spitzer, Robert L. 2012. "Spitzer Reassesses His 2003 Study of Reparative Therapy of Homosexuality." *Archives of Sexual Behavior* 41 (4): 757.
18. Drescher, Jack, Alan Schwartz, Flávio Casoy, Christopher A. McIntosh, Brian Hurley, Kenneth Ashley, Mary Barber, et al. 2016. "The Growing Regulation of Conversion Therapy." *Journal of Medical Regulation* 102 (2): 7–12.
19. Beckstead, A. Lee, and Susan L. Morrow. 2004. "Mormon Clients' Experiences of Conversion Therapy: The Need for a New Treatment Approach." *The Counseling Psychologist* 32 (5): 651–90.

20. Haldeman, Douglas C. 2002. "Therapeutic Antidotes: Helping Gay and Bisexual Men Recover from Conversion Therapies." *Journal of Gay & Lesbian Psychotherapy*, April. https://doi.org/10.1300/J236v05n03_08.
21. Shidlo, Ariel, and Michael Schroeder. 2002. "Changing Sexual Orientation: A Consumers' Report." *Professional Psychology, Research and Practice* 33 (3): 249–59.
22. Haldeman, Douglas C. 2022. "Introduction: A History of Conversion Therapy, from Accepted Practice to Condemnation." In *The Case against Conversion "Therapy": Evidence, Ethics, and Alternatives*, 3–16. Washington: American Psychological Association.
23. Loyal. "Conversion Therapy and LGBT Youth." The Williams Institute at UCLA School of Law. June 16, 2019. https://williamsinstitute.law.ucla.edu/publications/conversion-therapy-and-lgbt-youth.
24. Trevor News. "New Report Reveals Alarming Prevalence of Conversion Therapy, With Over 1,300 Active Practitioners Across the U.S." The Trevor Project. December 12, 2023. https://www.thetrevorproject.org/blog/new-report-reveals-alarming-prevalence-of-conversion-therapy-with-over-1300-active-practitioners-across-the-u-s.

CHAPTER THIRTEEN

1. Chand, Suma P., Daniel P. Kuckel, and Martin R. Huecker. 2025. "Cognitive Behavior Therapy." In *StatPearls*. Treasure Island (FL): StatPearls Publishing.
2. "What Is Cognitive Behavioral Therapy?" 2017. American Psychological Association. July 31, 2017. https://www.apa.org/ptsd-guideline/patients-and-families/cognitive-behavioral.
3. Hollon, Steven D., Robert J. DeRubeis, Paul W. Andrews, and J. Anderson Thomson Jr. 2021. "Cognitive Therapy in the Treatment and Prevention of Depression: A Fifty-Year Retrospective with an Evolutionary Coda." *Cognitive Therapy and Research* 45 (3): 402–17.
4. Rizvi, Shireen L., Alma M. Bitran, Linda A. Oshin, Qingqing Yin, and Allison K. Ruork. 2024. "The State of the Science: Dialectical Behavior Therapy." *Behavior Therapy* 55 (6): 1233–48.
5. Kothgassner, Oswald D., Andreas Goreis, Kealagh Robinson, Mercedes M. Huscsava, Christian Schmahl, and Paul L. Plener. 2021. "Efficacy of Dialectical Behavior Therapy for Adolescent Self-Harm and Suicidal Ideation: A Systematic Review and Meta-Analysis." *Psychological Medicine* 51 (7): 1057–67.
6. Ciesinski, Nicole K., Kristen M. Sorgi-Wilson, Joey C. Cheung, Eunice Y. Chen, and Michael S. McCloskey. 2022. "The Effect of Dialectical Behavior Therapy on Anger and Aggressive Behavior: A Systematic Review with Meta-Analysis." *Behaviour Research and Therapy* 154 (104122): 104122.
7. Goldstein, Tina R., John Merranko, Noelle Rode, Raeanne Sylvester, Nina Hotkowski, Rachael Fersch-Podrat, Danella M. Hafeman, et al. 2024. "Dialectical Behavior Therapy for Adolescents with Bipolar Disorder: A Randomized Clinical Trial." *JAMA Psychiatry (Chicago, IL)* 81 (1): 15–24.

8. Vogel, Emily N., Simar Singh, and Erin C. Accurso. 2021. "A Systematic Review of Cognitive Behavior Therapy and Dialectical Behavior Therapy for Adolescent Eating Disorders." *Journal of Eating Disorders* 9 (1): 131.
9. Adler-Tapia, Robbie, and Carolyn Settle. 2009. "Evidence of the Efficacy of EMDR with Children and Adolescents in Individual Psychotherapy: A Review of the Research Published in Peer-Reviewed Journals." *Journal of EMDR Practice and Research* 3 (4): 232–47.
10. Bisson, Jonathan I., Neil P. Roberts, Martin Andrew, Rosalind Cooper, and Catrin Lewis. 2013. "Psychological Therapies for Chronic Post-Traumatic Stress Disorder (PTSD) in Adults." *Cochrane Database of Systematic Reviews* 2013 (12): CD003388.
11. Chen, Ying-Ren, Kuo-Wei Hung, Jui-Chen Tsai, Hsin Chu, Min-Huey Chung, Su-Ru Chen, Yuan-Mei Liao, Keng-Liang Ou, Yue-Cune Chang, and Kuei-Ru Chou. 2014. "Efficacy of Eye-Movement Desensitization and Reprocessing for Patients with Posttraumatic-Stress Disorder: A Meta-Analysis of Randomized Controlled Trials." *PloS One* 9 (8): e103676.

CHAPTER FOURTEEN

1. Oliver Conroy, J. "An Apocalyptic Cult, 900 Dead: Remembering the Jonestown Massacre, 40 Years On." *The Guardian*. November 17, 2018. https://www.theguardian.com/world/2018/nov/17/an-apocalyptic-cult-900-dead-remembering-the-jonestown-massacre-40-years-on.
2. Weinraub, Claire, Christina Ng, Acacia Nunes, and Haley Yamada. "Heaven's Gate Survivor Reflects on the Cult's Mass Suicide 25 Years Ago." ABC News. March 11, 2022. https://abcnews.go.com/US/heavens-gate-survivor-reflects-cults-mass-suicide-25/story?id=83213680.
3. Kreps, Daniel. "'Love Has Won' Leader Amy Carlson's Cause of Death Released." *Rolling Stone*. December 3, 2021. http://www.rollingstone.com/culture/culture-news/love-has-won-leader-amy-carlsons-cause-of-death-released-1266385.
4. Hermann, Nellie. "The Upper West Side Therapy Cult That Broke All the Rules." The New Republic. August 17, 2023. https://newrepublic.com/article/173520/upper-west-side-therapy-cult-broke-rules-stille-sullivanians-review.
5. Winter, Jessica. "The Upper West Side Cult That Hid in Plain Sight." *The New Yorker*. June 14, 2023. https://www.newyorker.com/books/under-review/the-upper-west-side-cult-that-hid-in-plain-sight.
6. Hitchcock, Callie. "A New York Cult That Promised the End of the Nuclear Family." The Nation. December 7, 2023. https://www.thenation.com/article/archive/sullivanians-cult-alexander-stille.
7. Hermann, Nellie. "The Upper West Side Therapy Cult That Broke All the Rules." The New Republic. August 17, 2023. https://newrepublic.com/article/173520/upper-west-side-therapy-cult-broke-rules-stille-sullivanians-review.
8. Winter, Jessica. "The Upper West Side Cult That Hid in Plain Sight." *The New Yorker*. June 14, 2023. https://www.newyorker.com/books/under-review/the-upper-west-side-cult-that-hid-in-plain-sight.

9. Hitchcock, Callie. "A New York Cult That Promised the End of the Nuclear Family." The Nation. December 7, 2023. https://www.thenation.com/article/archive/sullivanians-cult-alexander-stille.
10. Alexander Stille. *The Sullivanians: Sex, Psychotherapy, and the Wild Life of an American Commune.* New York: Picador, 2024.
11. Lewin, Tamar. "Custody Case Lifts Veil On a 'Psychotherapy Cult.'" *The New York Times.* June 3, 1988. https://www.nytimes.com/1988/06/03/nyregion/custody-case-lifts-veil-on-a-psychotherapy-cult.html.
12. Goldberg, Barbara. "Sullivanian Cult Trial Opens." UPI. April 3, 1989. https://www.upi.com/Archives/1989/04/03/Sullivanian-cult-trial-opens/1025607579200.
13. Alexander Stille. *The Sullivanians: Sex, Psychotherapy, and the Wild Life of an American Commune.* New York: Picador, 2024.
14. Steven Naifeh, Gregory White-Smith. *Jackson Pollock: An American Saga.* New York: Clarkson Potter, 1989.
15. Judy Collins. *Cravings.* New York: Nan A. Talese, 2017.
16. Qtd. in Winter, Jessica. "The Upper West Side Cult That Hid in Plain Sight." *The New Yorker.* June 14, 2023. https://www.newyorker.com/books/under-review/the-upper-west-side-cult-that-hid-in-plain-sight.
17. Timnick, Lois. "Psychologists in 'Feeling Therapy' Lose Licenses." *Los Angeles Times.* September 30, 1987. https://www.latimes.com/archives/la-xpm-1987-09-30-me-7303-story.html.
18. Samuel, Sigal. "The Biggest Unknown in Psychedelic Therapy Is Not the Psychedelics." Vox. June 19, 2024. https://www.vox.com/future-perfect/355687/fda-mdma-therapy-maps-lykos-cult.
19. MacBride, Katie. "'Aharon Said It Was Healing:' How Psychedelic Therapy Was Undermined by Abuse." Inverse. November 16, 2021. https://www.inverse.com/mind-body/grossbard-bourzat-psychedelic-assisted-therapy-abuse.
20. "Psychotherapy Cults." Cult Recovery 101. March 17, 2018. https://cultrecovery101.com/cult-recovery-readings/psychotherapy-cults.
21. Singer, Margaret Thaler. 1996. "Therapy, Thought Reform, and Cults." *Transactional Analysis Journal* 26 (1): 15–22.